The
Wild Side Guide
to Vancouver Island's Pacific Rim

Long Beach
Tofino
Ucluelet
Port Alberni
Nitinat
Bamfield

Jacqueline Windh

Harbour Publishing

N O O T K A   S O U N D

Sydney River

COUGAR ANNIE'S

Megin R.

Megin Lake

Moyeha River

Bedwell River

HESQUIAT
HARBOUR

ESTEVAN POINT

HOT SPRINGS COVE

Atleo River

Herbert Inlet

Bedwell Sound

FLORES ISLAND

AHOUSAT

Fortune Channel

C L A Y O Q U O T   S O U N D

Vargas I.

Meares I.

Opitsat

Tofino Inlet

Tofino

Pacific Rim Highway

Esowista

L O N G   B E A C H

W I C K A N I N N I S H   B A Y

0 km   Scale in kilometres   25 km

F L O R E N C I A   B A Y

Port Hardy

Vancouver

Port Alberni

Nanaimo

Tofino

Ucluelet

Bamfield

Victoria

USA

See pages 50–51 for
tribal, provincial and
national parks.

Buttle Lake
Comox Lake
Denman Island
Hornby Island
Fanny Bay
Inland Island Highway
Island Highway
Elsie Lake
NCOUVER ISLAND
Horne Lake
Great Central Lake
Beaver Creek Rd
Cameron Lake
Pacific Rim Highway 4
Sproat Lake
Port Alberni
Kennedy River
Pacific Rim Highway 4
Nahmint Lake
Franklin River Rd
Henderson Lake
Alberni Inlet
Nahmint
Kennedy Lake
Toquart Bay Rd
t Main
Kildonan
Toquart Bay
Toquart Lake
South Main
Port Albion Rd
Salmon Beach
Mussel Beach
Ucluelet
Broken Group Islands
Deer Group Islands
Sarita
Bamfield Road
Poett Nook
Barkley Sound
Nitinat
Bamfield
Pachena Bay
Nitinat Lake
West Coast Trail

Surfers often stay in the water right until dark at Chesterman Beach, Tofino.

Quick Contents

A comprehensive table of contents appears on pages 33–36.

The protected waters of Kennedy Lake make it a great swimming spot for the whole family.

Please note:

The tourism industry in the Pacific Rim is dynamic. All effort has been made to make company information complete and accurate as of the time of printing. However, since businesses come and go, confirm information on company websites or through the local tourism info centres.

All phone numbers listed are area code 250 unless otherwise noted. All currencies are in Canadian dollars unless otherwise noted.

Prices quoted are current as of the writing of this book, but are subject to change. Please confirm prices with individual businesses when you make your bookings.

For further information, or to comment or provide feedback, visit http://wildsideguide.wordpress.com.

The Pacific Rim

SWEEPING SURF-WASHED BEACHES, DARK AND MYSTERIOUS RAINFOREST and lofty glacier-capped mountain peaks define the region known as Vancouver Island's Pacific Rim. A few short decades ago, the Pacific Rim was all but inaccessible except to the most determined travellers. Now it is one of Canada's most visited tourist destinations!

UNIQUELY PACIFIC RIM: WHAT TO DO
- Watch whales swimming wild and free.
- Get out on the water in a tour boat or a kayak.
- Experience the ancient rainforest, slowly and quietly. Sit under a tree that is hundreds, or maybe thousands, of years old.
- Go for a beach walk alongside crashing surf on a sunny day. Or in a storm. Or on a moonless night.
- Watch giant salmon work their way up a tiny rainforest creek in autumn.
- Fish for salmon or halibut on the open ocean, or cast for steelhead or trout on the rivers and lakes. Year-round!
- Go surfing or take a lesson.
- Stay out on the water at a remote wilderness lodge.
- Hang out on a dock and watch the boats go by.
- Sample our fine cuisine, fresh-caught seafood and homegrown Vancouver Island produce, at a small locally owned restaurant.

Until 1959, all travellers arrived to Vancouver Island's west coast by boat. Even today, the villages of Bamfield, Tofino and Ucluelet retain their maritime flavour. Fishing is still a part of the local economies, but many other ocean experiences await visitors too, both on and in the water, such as whale-watching, kayaking and surfing. More than half of British Columbia's sand beaches are found along this stretch of coast, and no visit would really be complete without at least one mellow beach walk alongside the roaring surf.

But the activities don't stop at the ocean's edge. Some of the world's largest stretches of intact coastal temperate rainforest lie here on the

Pacific Rim, and there are numerous opportunities to explore this ancient ecosystem, from short boardwalk trails to serious backpacking expeditions. The pristine and undisturbed habitat is also home to abundant wildlife, and one of the few accessible places where animals such as bears and wolves may be observed in the wild.

With paved roads, improved access has brought more visitors and generated more facilities. Now, even while participating in the nature and wilderness activities the region is famous for, visitors don't have to rough it. Luxury resorts, museums and galleries, world-class spas and fine international cuisine are also part of today's Pacific Rim experience.

The Pacific Rim is my home. We now receive more than one million visitors every year, but I have met many who came here and missed some of the key experiences. With this guidebook, I give you an inside look at the

A pair of paddlers heads out at sunset. Pacific Rim—a bit of background and history to enrich your visit, as well as some of my own hints about favourite places, where to go and what to see. Have a great trip!

The main attraction for visitors to the Pacific Rim has traditionally been the wilderness activities. Now, the towns themselves also boast a number of attractions: restaurants with world-class chefs serving local and fresh Vancouver Island produce and seafood, art galleries, award-winning spas, museums and cultural displays.

Bear mask by Tla-o-qui-aht carver Buddy George.

Below: Tofino wildlife artist Mark Hobson paints in his floating wilderness studio.

The wild west coast is a congregating ground for artistic types—painters, weavers, sculptors and more. Tofino and Ucluelet are both known for their galleries, ranging from traditional art galleries to trendy design houses with cappuccino bars, and Bamfield has several galleries operated by the artists themselves. Port Alberni's thriving arts community surprises many who expect only a logging town; here you will find art galleries, as well as events ranging from craft sales to literary festivals and live theatre.

Hesquiaht carver Mark Mickey's carvings can be found in museums and private collections around the world.

Children at Ahousat village.

The original occupants of Vancouver Island's west coast are the Nuu-chah-nulth. Traditionally, they pursued a maritime culture, carving giant dugout canoes out of cedar logs, and depending on the sea for both food and transportation. Today, the Nuu-chah-nulth Tribal Council consists of 13 tribes. Nuu-chah-nulth arts—massive carved cedar poles that support the roofs of their longhouses, elaborate carved and painted masks and headdresses, and fine weavings of cedar bark—come from traditions handed down through many generations.

This totem pole, at the village of Opitsat, depicts the crests of the Tla-o-qui-aht Martin family.

Long Beach. The extreme wave action on the coast has created some of Canada's biggest and most spectacular beaches. Long Beach, a chain of long wave-washed beaches separated by rocky headlands and extending along over 20 km/12.4 mi of coastline in Pacific Rim National Park Reserve between Tofino and Ucluelet, tops the list.

Big Tree Trail on Meares Island.

There are few places on this planet where you can stand under groves of ancient, moss-festooned trees that are centuries or even millennia old. For many visitors, the first rainforest glimpse is of the towering Douglas firs in Cathedral Grove (MacMillan Provincial Park), on the highway on the way to Port Alberni. There are several rainforest walking trails in the Port Alberni area (page 66), a few near the villages of Bamfield (page 94), Ucluelet (page 118) and Tofino (page 163), and many well-maintained short trails around Long Beach, in Pacific Rim National Park Reserve (page 144).

Highway 4 winds through Cathedral Grove, just east of Port Alberni.

Cycling is a great way to explore the Pacific Rim—at least over the less rainy summer months. Around Port Alberni there are numerous cycling day trips to do and many logging roads to travel. Tofino and Ucluelet both have good bike paths that extend for several kilometres out of town, and you can ride for a long way along the sand on Long Beach.

Cyclists enjoy a ride off-road on Long Beach.

Approach the shoreline with caution when a big swell is running.

The storms that pound the west coast over winter are dynamic displays of Nature's power. Going "storm-watching" and experiencing the fury of real west coast winds with all of your senses is a far more memorable experience than simply watching it through glass. For the best chance of witnessing a winter storm, time your visit for between November and March.

A stormy beach walk from the Wickaninnish Inn, Tofino.

19

Opposite: The clear water and tiny islets of the Broken Group make for beautiful paddling in Barkley Sound.

The Pacific Rim is one of the great sea kayaking destinations on the planet, with nearly endless possibilities for day trips. Those with their own kayaks can launch from many relatively sheltered sites on ocean inlets. Guided day trips and rentals are also available from most regions. Protected areas to paddle include Bamfield Inlet, parts of the Broken Group, Ucluelet Harbour and some of the inlets in Clayoquot Sound. Some of the world's most spectacular paddling is on the more exposed coast: the Deer Group, the outer part of the Broken Group, and the outer beaches of Clayoquot Sound. The more sheltered waters inside Clayoquot Sound and Barkley Sound provide miles of paddling, laden with magnificent scenery and opportunities to view wildlife, for paddlers of all skill levels.

Although open canoes are used less on Vancouver Island than kayaks today, large and stable dugout canoes designed for the open ocean were the main means of transport for local communities here for millenia. You can go on paddling adventures, in genuine handmade canoes, with the Tla-o-qui-aht tribe out of Tofino (page 170). Those with their own canoes can launch on most of the larger lakes—but beware of the winds. Rentals are available on Great Central Lake and Sproat Lake (page 68), both near Port Alberni.

Tlaook Cultural Adventures offers tours of Clayoquot Sound in traditional handmade dugout canoes.

Above:
The MV Frances
Barkley.

Right: For many
people, the Pacific Rim
offers them their first
opportunity to see
whales in the wild.

Tufted puffins are
one of the many
unusual bird species
that can be observed in
the Pacific Rim.

For those who really want a mellow experience in a larger boat, there are a number of scenic cruises. The 200-passenger MV *Frances Barkley* runs the length of Alberni Inlet, from Port Alberni to Kildonan and Bamfield, year-round, and makes stops including Ucluelet and the Broken Group over the summer. This day trip is an absolutely great way to do some sightseeing while getting a feel for the maritime flavour of our small coastal communities. Many companies offer scenic cruises, ranging from two-hour trips to view wildlife, to sunset or dinner cruises, to custom overnight wilderness charters.

Thousands of grey whales pass by the coast on their northward spring migration in March and April. Chances are very good of seeing both grey whales and humpbacks on any commercial tour through the summer months. Most whale-watching tours also offer opportunities to see seals, sea lions, porpoises, sea otters, bald eagles and many seabirds including, if you are lucky, tufted puffins!

Once hunted to excess, humpback whales are common along Vancouver Island's west coast again.

Photo by Kathy Johnson

Although there are two main seasons for viewing bears, it is possible to see bears year-round. Since they don't fully hibernate in our temperate climate, always keep your eyes peeled when driving along any of the roads south or west of Port Alberni. From May to August bears feed along the shorelines of sheltered inlets, turning over rocks to look for crabs and fish at low tide, and it is common to see mothers teaching their cubs to forage here. You can often get close to them by boat.

Throughout spring and early summer, mother bears and cubs forage along the shorelines at low tide.

During the annual salmon spawn, huge fish return to the streams of their birth after spending years in the ocean. Battling predators such as bears, seals, wolves and eagles, and often incurring injuries, they ascend the streams and rivers to lay their eggs and ensure the survival of the race. Seven native species of salmon make their home in West Coast waters: sockeye, coho, chinook (also called king or spring), pink, chum, steelhead and cutthroat trout (now considered a salmon).

In late fall and early winter, chum salmon ascend tiny rainforest streams to lay their eggs.

The fishing is great in Port Alberni, the self-proclaimed "Salmon Capital of the World."

Photo courtesy of Salmon Eye Charters

Vancouver Island's west coast is a mecca for birdwatchers. The many distinct environments, from mountaintop alpine to rainforest to shorelines to open ocean, as well as the fact that it is on the Pacific Flyway route for birds migrating between the Arctic and the tropics, mean that a huge variety of species can be seen here. Bald eagles, great blue herons and loons are commonplace, and serious birders usually manage to check off something new: tufted puffins, rhinocerous auklets, marbled godwits or red-necked phalaropes, to name a few.

In April and May, western sandpipers gather by the thousands to feed on Tofino's mudflats.

The Pacific Rim offers some of the greatest variety of fishing to be found anywhere. The offshore waters provide exciting fishing for salmon, halibut and rockfish for most of the year. In summer, several species of salmon can be caught both offshore and near shore, and you can go saltwater fly fishing for sea-run cutthroat trout and coho salmon in Clayoquot Sound's more sheltered inlets.

Vancouver Island is considered to be one of the best cold-water diving destinations in the world. It is renowned for its exceptional visibility, which can be up to 46 m (150'). Around the Broken Group, in Barkley Sound, there are several shipwrecks to dive at, but the real attraction here and in Clayoquot Sound is the abundant marine life (see page 101).

The innumerable lakes and inlets of the Pacific Rim provide endless opportunities for people who own their own boats. There are many public boat launches that recreational boaters can use to access both freshwater lakes and the ocean. You can also rent houseboats by the week on Sproat Lake—no boating experience required, all necessary instruction provided (page 86). If you like the feel of salt wind in your hair, you can go sailing on the ocean, on a 33' Viking on Barkley Sound out of Bamfield (page 99).

Opposite: The clear waters off Vancouver Island make it one of the best cold-water dive destinations in the world.

Photo courtesy of Rutger Geerling

Tofino's Fourth Street dock is the main tie-up for fishing boats.

Vancouver Island's west coast is the locus of Canada's surf culture, with Tofino at the core. Although the surf scene erupted here at the same time as in California, during the 1960s and '70s, local surfers managed to keep it secret. But in 2009, Tofino played host to Canada's first ever pro surf competition, and local boy Pete Devries took the win, putting Vancouver Island firmly on the world surf map. The region is also favoured by windsurfers and kiteboarders for its strong and (reasonably) predictable winds. Nitinat Lake is the prime windsurfing/kiteboarding spot on Vancouver Island. Other popular sites include Cameron Lake, Sproat Lake and Kennedy Lake.

Vancouver Island is a great place to plan a car-camping trip, with numerous campgrounds, many of them on waterfront, with both tent and RV sites. There are a number of well-maintained BC parks and private campgrounds in the area, and many more remote, generally unserviced campgrounds and recreational sites accessible throughout the region along rough logging roads.

Tofino's Pete Devries in competition at Chesterman Beach. To really experience the Pacific Rim, you need to get out on the water. Aside from the many cruises, whale-watching tours and kayak trips, there are many places where you can actually stay out on the water—remote lodges accessible only by boat or float plane. Some are oriented toward specific activities such as fishing or diving, while others are simply remote wilderness getaways.

*Left: Rendezvous Adventures'
secluded lodge at Rainy Bay,
Barkley Sound.*
Photo courtesy of Rendezvous Dive
Adventures

*Below: You don't have to rough
it—many scenic campsites are
accessible by car.*

Above: Float plane is the fastest way to access some of the more remote outposts.

The Pacific Rim region is true wilderness. For serious adventurers with backcountry experience, possibilities for expeditions by foot abound! The West Coast Trail, which heads southward from Bamfield, was created as an escape route for shipwrecked sailors and is now a world-famous hiking trail. There is also a network of hiking trails in the alpine country of Strathcona Provincial Park.

Above: A fine summer day's hiking in the high country of Strathcona Provincial Park.

Right: Backcountry travellers are likely to encounter wildlife such as wolves, bears or cougars.

Contents

PORT ALBERNI — 59

BAMFIELD AND NITINAT — 88

TOFINO AND CLAYOQUOT SOUND 150

RESOURCES 198

Background Information

Geography

GEOLOGY

The process of plate tectonics is responsible for both the complex geology and the stunning geography of North America's west coast. One hundred million years ago, an island chain that geologists call "Wrangellia" collided with western North America. The mostly volcanic rocks of Wrangellia make up the bulk of what today is Vancouver Island.

Glacial striations on the rockwalls above Highway 4 are testimony to the ice that flowed down this valley during the Ice Age.

VOLCANO OR EROSION?

Many people look at the pointy mountains of Vancouver Island, such as Tofino's misleadingly named "Lone Cone," and assume that they are extinct volcanoes. Although a lot of the rock is indeed volcanic, the shapes of these mountains are actually formed by erosion. Pressure from the forces of plate tectonics has uplifted the land and erosion by both glacial action and by wind and rain has sculpted the lofty peaks we see today.

A later tectonic collision added a little bit more rock to Vancouver Island's west coast. Fifty-five million years ago, layers of black mudstone and sandstone from the ancient sea floor were thrust up onto Wrangellia. These rocks are called the "Pacific Rim Terrane," and form a narrow strip of black and twisted outcrops extending along the coast from Ucluelet to Tofino and up the western side of Vargas Island.

Many of the landforms that we see today are a result of glacial action. The last Ice Age peaked 17,000 years ago, and most of the ice had retreated from the coast by 11,000 years ago. For the first few thousands of years following the retreat of the ice sheets, sea level on the outer coast oscillated. It was much lower than present levels at the peak of the Ice Age, as the water was tied up in the great ice sheets, and then much higher as the meltwater flooded into the sea—eventually stabilizing at the present level.

In some places, you can still see evidence of higher sea levels as beach berms (small cliffs in the sand), several hundred metres inland from the present shoreline. Much of the sand on the outer beaches has formed from glacial till that has been cleaned and sorted by wave action, and boulders left by the glaciers can be seen resting on top of many coastal outcrops.

These flat rock shelves were eroded by wave action, Flores Island.

TSUNAMIS AND EARTHQUAKES

The Pacific Rim lies on an active tectonic margin, and that puts us at risk for both earthquakes and tsunamis.

A very large earthquake on the coast is likely to generate a tsunami within a few minutes to one hour of the quake. We are also at risk of being hit by a tsunami generated by an earthquake many thousands of kilometres away. If you experience a large earthquake —one that is strong enough to start knocking things off shelves or lasts for more than one minute—or if you receive a tsunami warning, proceed immediately to high ground. In Port Alberni, loudspeaker announcements will warn you to get to the landward side of the railway tracks or Fifth Avenue; in both Tofino and Ucluelet, the local schools (both near the downtown cores) are the emergency mustering stations, and they are high enough to be out of range of a tsunami wave. Do not put yourself at risk by crossing low coastal areas, for example driving along roads adjacent to beaches, to escape.

If you feel an earthquake, if possible get out of buildings and away from anything such as trees or poles that may fall on you. If you cannot get out of a building in time, stand in a structurally secure area, such as a doorway, and away from any windows that may shatter.

CLIMATE

The climate of the Pacific Rim is influenced by two main factors: the Pacific Ocean and the high mountain ranges. The ocean moderates the climate, so that temperatures are never very extreme. The mountain ranges influence where the damp Pacific air masses dump their precipitation, forming areas of high rainfall as well as drier and sunnier rain shadow regions.

The sunniest days are generally throughout the summer, May through September—though balmy sunny days appear throughout the winter without warning. On the outermost coast, August is infamous for its fog (and known to locals as "Foggust"). The beaches and outer islands may be fogged in for weeks on end, while only a few hundred metres inland the sun is blazing away.

The climate in Port Alberni is quite contrary to that of the outer coast, since it is not affected so much by the open ocean. Summertime temperatures here can hit 40° C (104° F) or more, whereas a hot day on the coast would rarely exceed 25° C (77° F). The fog pattern is also reversed—when coastal residents get tired of Foggust's chill, they often head to Port Alberni for some summer sunshine. But over the winter months, the Alberni Valley may be fogged in for days or even weeks, while the coastal beaches glisten under crisp blue skies. Port Alberni receives significant snowfall over winter, too, which may temporarily shut down the roads, whereas most of the precipitation on the outer coast falls as rain.

The Pacific Rim is famous for its winter storms, now the basis of the relatively new tourism activity of storm-watching. Powerful winds drive the rain horizontally, and huge storm waves batter the coast. At sea level the

	Tofino/Ucluelet/ Bamfield	Port Alberni
Summer mean maximum temperature	17.5°C (63.5°F)	23°C (73.4°F)
Summer mean minimum temperature	13.5°C (56.3°F)	10°C (50°F)
Winter mean maximum temperature	8°C (46.4°F)	5°C (41°F)
Winter mean minimum temperature	1.5°C (34.7°F)	0°C (32°F)
Annual rainfall	3.5 m (11.4 ft)	2 m (6.5 ft)

precipitation nearly always falls as rain, and snow is very rare. However, only 100 m (328') up this rain may turn to blizzard conditions and severely affect driving conditions at the two passes: Port Alberni Summit (375 m/1,230') between Nanaimo and Port Alberni, and Sutton Pass (175 m/574') between Port Alberni and the outer west coast of Vancouver Island.

The wettest place in all of continental North America is Henderson Lake, located about 25 km (15.5 mi) northeast of Ucluelet but inaccessible by road; it receives 6.65 m (22') of rain each year. Although most of the precipitation does fall through

The Rainforest Trail in Pacific Rim National Park Reserve is one of many places where you can walk through ancient old-growth rainforest.

WHAT IS "TEMPERATE RAINFOREST"?
Some defining characteristics of "temperate rainforest" are:
• high rainfall spread throughout the year, which promotes lush growing conditions
• moderate temperatures, which distinguish it from warmer "tropical" rainforests
• layered nature of the forest, with trees of many ages growing together
• a diversity of other plants such as ferns and shrubs and epiphytes (plants that live on other plants, such as ferns, mosses and lichens)

the winter months, a few days of solid hard pelting rain can hit at any time of year. Locals know not to go too far from home without their rain gear.

ECOSYSTEMS

Ecologically, most of this region is considered to be "coastal temperate rainforest." The rainforest developed very slowly after the retreat of the giant glaciers 11,000 years ago. Bedrock and glacial deposits of clay and till were slowly colonized by mosses, sedges and grasses. When sufficient soil had

PACIFIC RIM NATIONAL PARK RESERVE

On May 4, 1971, Pacific Rim National Park Reserve was dedicated at Long Beach in the presence of Princess Anne and then-Minister of Northern Affairs Jean Chrétien. Throughout the '70s and '80s, deals were struck between the government and private landowners, as well as the logging companies who had been granted timber rights to some of the lands, to acquire the lands for the new park. The Pacific Rim lies entirely within the traditional territory of the Nuu-chah-nulth people. Until land claims have been resolved, Pacific Rim is a National Park "Reserve."

Pacific Rim National Park Reserve extends for 120 km (75 mi) along Vancouver Island's west coast, and consists of three units. The southernmost and largest section is the **West Coast Trail unit**, at 256 sq km (98.8 sq mi). This world-famous 75 km (46.6 mi) hiking trail, a rugged wilderness route suitable only for fit and experienced hikers, extends from Bamfield to Port Renfrew. For more information, see pages 95–96.

The Broken Group Islands make up the central section of the park. It is 106 sq km (41 sq mi) in size—only 13.5 sq km (5.2 sq mi) of which are over land. This cluster of small islands, located at the broad mouth of Barkley Sound between Ucluelet and Bamfield, is water-accessible only, and a popular kayaking destination. There are companies offering boat service to the Broken Group—both scenic boat tours as well as water taxis capable of transporting kayaks—based in Port Alberni, Bamfield and Ucluelet. For more information, see pages 68, 98, 113 and 121–123.

The northernmost unit of the park is **Long Beach**, 137 sq km (52.9 sq mi) in size, accessible by paved road (the segment of Highway 4 between Tofino and Ucluelet). There are eight short and well-maintained walking trails, road access to Grice Bay (and a boat launch here), and an interpretive centre and campground (open over summer only). For more information about the Long Beach area, see page 140.

The park's official operating season is from mid-March to mid-October, although you can access Long Beach and the Broken Group throughout the year. The West Coast Trail is closed from October through April. Check the park's website for current fees and information. Pacific Rim National Park Reserve was included within the Canada National Parks Act in 2001.

For more information, contact:
Pacific Rim National Park Reserve, 726-7721, fax: 726-4720, pacrim.info@pc.gc.ca
www.pc.gc.ca/pn-np/bc/pacificrim/
National Park information line 1-888-773-8888
For camping reservations: 1-877-737-3783, www.pccamping.ca

built up, a forest of pine and spruce and later Douglas fir started to grow. This forest had only reached sufficient development, with enough soil, shade and shelter that baby cedar trees could begin to grow in any number, by about 4,000 years ago.

The wet climate makes forest fires very rare, allowing the trees to reach great age and size. Some of the oldest and widest trees known in North America are the western red cedars from this region, which can be up to 2,000 years old. Sitka spruces and Douglas firs can achieve heights of up to 80 m (262') or more.

Other ecosystems within the Pacific Rim region include coastal bog, broad sand beaches, intertidal and shallow offshore marine areas, and alpine regions.

FLORA AND FAUNA

The main trees in the coastal forest are evergreens such as western red cedar, western hemlock, Pacific yew and Sitka spruce. At higher levels yellow cedar, mountain hemlock, Douglas fir and amabilis fir appear. Deciduous trees such as Pacific dogwood, arbutus and bigleaf maple are common on the drier side of Sutton Pass and around Port Alberni. The forest understory consists mainly of berry bushes (abundant salal, as well as red huckleberry, tree blueberry, evergreen huckleberry and salmonberry), ferns, a few herbaceous plants and mosses and liverworts.

Vancouver Island's rainforest is home to a variety of wildlife, and the Pacific Rim area is one of the few regions where many of these animals can be seen in the wild (see page 55). Large mammals include the black bear, cougar, grey (timber) wolf, Pacific black-tailed deer and Roosevelt elk. There are no grizzly bears on Vancouver Island. Smaller mammals include the raccoon,

Black bears are common along shorelines and riverbanks.

WILDERNESS ETIQUETTE

Much of the Pacific Rim region is genuine wilderness. It is important that campers travel knowledgeably and respectfully, in order not to damage sensitive wildlife habitat or endanger themselves or the wildlife.

Camping. Do not damage vegetation in order to create tent sites. Wherever possible, camp on beaches or in natural clearings.

Campfires. Fires are permitted in most places, but they are damaging to the environment and are discouraged. Use stoves for cooking. Fires on sand beaches do not need stone rings. If you make a fire ring, be sure to dismantle it when you leave. If you are camping on a beach, make the fire below the high-tide line and use only driftwood. Some years there are fire restrictions; inquire before you head out.

Food. All of this country is bear and wolf habitat—even the smallest of islands. All of the animals can and do swim! Avoid taking smelly or oily foods such as tinned fish. Cook below the high-tide line, so that smells are washed away. Carry long ropes and food bags, and cache food high up trees. (Bears can reach significantly higher than we can!)

Drinking water. Pack your own water, or boil or treat water for drinking.

Ablutions and human waste. Some of the remote provincial parks have outhouses—find out where they are before you go (page 188). When camping on the coast, use the intertidal zone for elimination of human waste and for brushing teeth. Choose areas that are not heavily used by other campers, and that have high wave action. If there are other groups camping on the same beach, it is courteous to discuss with them the area to be used. Larger groups should bring portable toilets along. If you are hiking in the backcountry away from the coast, wander into the forest far away from trails, streams and lakes for elimination of human waste. All toilet paper must be packed out or burnt.

Garbage. This should not need to be said—pack out everything you bring in. Do not bury garbage—not even toilet paper.

Dogs. It is not recommended to take dogs into the wilderness. They may frighten or chase smaller wildlife, and in recent years many have been killed by wolves. If you do travel with a dog, keep it with you and on a leash at all times.

pine marten, mink and red squirrel. Marine mammals that frequent the nearby waters of the Pacific include the grey whale, humpback whale, orca, California sea lion, Steller sea lion, fur seal, harbour seal, harbour porpoise, sea otter and river otter (which can be found both in the sea and in rivers and lakes).

The Pacific Rim is home to many birds that nest here—some migrating south for the winter and others that remain year-round—and it is a stop for a diversity of birds migrating between the Arctic and the tropics. The varied environments—open ocean, shorelines, forest and mountain—make this a top birdwatching region.

Pacific salmon are keystone species on the West Coast—the whole ecosystem depends upon their survival. They start their lives in creeks and rivers deep within the rainforest, spend most of their lives in the open marine environment, then return to the rainforest to spawn and die. The returning salmon are an important food source for bears, seals and many other mammals and birds, and their decaying carcasses provide a natural fish fertilizer that nourishes the forest.

History

NATIVE PEOPLE

Sparse archeological evidence shows that people were living along BC's northern coast as many as 11,000 years ago, just as the giant ice sheets were retreating. The fluctuating sea levels following the Ice Age have washed away evidence of any early coastal settlements on Vancouver Island.

The people who lived on Vancouver Island's outer coast at the time of European contact now call themselves Nuu-chah-nulth. Archeological evidence from carbon dating undertaken in Barkley Sound firmly supports their ancestors having been here up to 5,000 years ago, but they probably arrived even earlier than that.

The Nuu-chah-nulth were first known to Europeans as the "Nootka," a name mistakenly given them by Captain Cook. At that time they consisted of dozens of very small tribes that occupied the outer coast from Kyuquot Sound southward to what is now Neah Bay, Washington state. Linked by common cultural traditions, family relationships and language, these small tribes all had names. Although distinct from the people who lived on the northern and eastern parts of Vancouver Island, they had no specific name for their own cultural group, calling themselves qu-us, which means "the people."

Cedar bark is used by Nuu-chah-nulth people to twist into ropes or to weave into hats, capes and baskets.

Contact with Europeans caused population loss of native tribes across the Americas, mainly as a result of introduced diseases. The Nuu-chah-nulth population before contact is estimated at between 10,000 and 31,000. By 1939 less than 2,000 Nuu-chah-nulth people remained. Population loss made some tribes extinct, and forced other small tribes to amalgamate.

In 1979, these related tribes formally united and took the name Nuu-chah-nulth, meaning "all along the mountains and sea." Today, the Nuu-chah-nulth group consists of about 13 recognized tribes: Huu-ay-aht, Hupacasath, Tseshaht, Uchucklesaht, Ahousaht, Hesquiaht, Tla-o-qui-aht, Toquaht, Ucluelet, Ehattesaht, Kyuquot/Cheklesahht, Mowachat/Muchalaht and Nuchatlaht. The Ditidaht are a closely related tribe from the Nitinat region. Each of these tribes maintains their principal village site ("reserve"). Some are road accessible, and some are only accessible by water. Only a few have services for visitors. For more information, see www.nuuchahnulth.org or www.ditidaht.ca or inquire at one of the tourist information centres listed throughout this book.

THE FIRST EUROPEANS

Vancouver Island was one of the last parts of North America to be visited by Europeans. Nearly 350 years after Jacques Cartier landed on what was to become the city of Montreal, the first European ship, the Spanish frigate *Santiago,* sailed northward up the continent's west coast. In August 1774, the *Santiago* anchored at a small cove within the territory of the Hesquiaht people, on the outer coast between Nootka and Clayoquot Sounds. The Natives paddled out to the ship and some goods were traded, but the Spaniards sailed away without ever having set foot on shore.

Four years later, Captain James Cook sailed northward and into the territory of the Mowachaht, the next tribe north of the Hesquiaht. Cook befriended Chief Maquinna and the British stayed for a month, trading with the Mowachaht while replenishing food stores and undertaking ship repairs at the village of Yuquot (later renamed Friendly Cove by Cook).

Some of the items traded included sea otter skins. Many months later, when Cook's ships arrived in China (Cook himself had been killed en route in Hawaii), it was realized that these skins could be traded for great profit overseas.

Over the following decades numerous ships—mainly British and American—arrived to trade flour, sugar and glass beads for the valuable skins. Meanwhile, Britain and Spain came to the brink of war about who "owned" this valuable coast; the Spaniards had arrived here first, but the

DRAKE'S SECRET VOYAGE?

Two centuries before either the Spaniards or Captain Cook had made it to Vancouver Island's outer coast, the English explorer Sir Francis Drake set out on a great voyage of discovery: the westward circumnavigation of the globe.

Drake is known to have stopped in what is now northern California and southern Oregon. However, there is some evidence that Drake may have ventured much farther northward—possibly as far as Vancouver Island's mid-coast! This theory, put forth by Samuel Bawlf in *The Secret Voyage of Sir Francis Drake 1577–1580* (Douglas & McIntyre, 2004), claims that Queen Elizabeth I suppressed information about Drake's voyage in order to keep the Spanish from finding out about England's new discoveries.

Much of the evidence is circumstantial, relying on reinterpretations of Drake's maps, and the entire theory is disputed by many scholars. However, Hesquiaht Natives have long said that white men in ships visited their people many generations before the arrival of Captain Cook.

British had been first to actually set foot on it. The Spaniards set up a fort at Yuquot. The dispute was finally settled by negotiation overseas with the "Nootka Accord," and in 1795 the Spaniards retreated from the coast.

Chief Maquinna.
BC Archives,
A-02678

By the beginning of the 1800s the sea otters were all but gone, hunted to near-extinction. Relations between the Natives and the visitors—especially the Americans—were not always friendly. In 1803 Chief Maquinna attacked the American ship *Boston*, killing most of the crew and keeping two survivors captive for nearly two years. (One of the captives, John Jewitt, went on to publish his memoirs—a book that is not only a story of high adventure, but also a rare and valuable early record of Native life around the time of European contact). In 1811, in the vicinity of what is now Tofino, in retaliation for a previous American attack which had destroyed their village, the Tla-o-qui-aht tribe attacked the American ship *Tonquin*, killing the entire crew save for one half-Native interpreter who eventually found his way back to America.

With the sea otter trade finished and white–Native relations souring, most Euro-American ships avoided the coast for nearly half a century. By the 1860s, traders started to return—this time looking for quick profits from whaling and fur seals and timber. Trading posts were established at Barkley Sound's southern entrance, and in Spring Cove, at its northern entrance, as well as on an island in Clayoquot Sound. These trading posts were the seed communities of what eventually became the villages of Bamfield, Ucluelet and Tofino. Two sawmills were founded: one at Port Albion, just across the harbour from present-day Ucluelet, and one at what would become the major logging town of Port Alberni.

SETTLERS

By the late 1800s, the non-Native arrivals to the west coast of Vancouver Island were not only traders passing through, they were settlers looking to make their lives here. Some established sawmills or worked as loggers; some became commercial fishermen; some saw the glimmer of gold in small river deposits that quickly ran out; and many tried their luck at farming. Trying to attract homesteaders to the Coast, the government established a pre-emption system. Would-be farmers could work toward ownership of a plot of land by settling, clearing and undertaking improvements, all duly inspected and verified by the government. Carving a farm from the rainforest was not an easy job, and most of these farms soon failed, but these old pre-emptions (now subdivided) form the basis of much of the private land ownership in the region today.

BUSINESS, SMALL-TOWN STYLE

The locals joke that business in the villages of Bamfield, Ucluelet and Tofino are "whether-dependent: whether the owners feel like opening or not." Although it is said in jest, it is also true. Many of us have chosen to live out here, at the end of the road, for life values: small and safe communities, fresh clean air and alternative or flexible lifestyles. Over winter, and occasionally at other times as well, some businesses shut right down so that the owners can go on vacation or tend to other aspects of their lives. (You'd be surprised at how many of us used to be stressed-out career people!)

The trading posts at Bamfield, Spring Cove and Clayoquot became commercial centres for the spread-out, water-based communities of the Pacific Rim. There were no roads into these areas, so travel was by boat—often in traditional Native dugout canoes fitted out with oars, and in later years with motors. Many immigrants came from Great Britain, the United States and Scandinavia. Two waves of Chinese immigrants came and left, trying their luck at placer mining for gold in the late 1800s and again in the 1930s. Japanese fishermen arrived in the 1920s, and for a few decades there were more Japanese than white settlers on the stretch of coast from Tofino to Bamfield. However, during World War II the Japanese were forcibly removed to internment camps in the BC interior by the Canadian government. After the war, only a few Japanese families returned to the coast.

COMMUNITIES TODAY

These coastal towns still have core communities made up of descendents of the settlers who arrived here only a couple of generations back. Today, Port Alberni (population 17,500) is the largest town on the island's west coast. South and west of Port Alberni are smaller coastal villages: Bamfield (pop. 300), Ucluelet (pop. 1,300) and Tofino (pop. 1,500). All of these towns, with economies formerly based firmly in fishing and logging, are now changing and expanding rapidly to meet the demands of the new boom industry, tourism. Port Alberni has most of the facilities to be expected in a modern town. The smaller villages have all the basic services and facilities such as grocery stores and banks, but locals still have to cross the island for many of their needs, like specialist medical appointments, buying household items and clothing or watching a movie.

There are also a number of small Nuu-chah-nulth tribal villages around the region; only some are accessible to visitors. Nitinat (page 104), Esowista, or Long Beach (page 141), Ahousaht on Flores Island (page 194) and Hot Springs Cove north of Tofino (page 195) all have facilities for visitors; the remainder of the Nuu-chah-nulth villages are private communites and should not be visited without prior permission. For the most part, other than around the Alberni Valley, the area between the towns and villages is unpopulated forestland.

Getting Here and Around

GETTING TO VANCOUVER ISLAND'S PACIFIC RIM IS MUCH EASIER NOW than it was in the old days. Highway 4, terminating in Tofino, is Canada's only paved roadway to the open Pacific. Unless you're already on Vancouver Island, you'll need to take a ferry to get here. The majority of travellers arrive here by a combination of ferryboat and car, though bus and plane are also options.

FINALLY, A ROAD!
The road from Port Alberni to the west coast was finally completed in 1959: a private logging road with a locked gate at Sproat Lake limiting public access to evenings and night. That August, 74 vehicles from Tofino and Ucluelet, accompanied by logging trucks, made the first-ever road trip across Sutton Pass to the town of Port Alberni. Clayoquot Sound resident Neil Buckle, who lived on Long Beach at the time, recalls being a part of that "cavalcade" in his '54 Ford pickup. Neil recalls that day, "There was a spot where, for low-slung cars, they had to pull them through with a bulldozer. But we just rammed on through! As soon as we got to pavement, everyone started racing and passing one another. We went all the way to Victoria!"

Until 1959, all travellers arrived to Vancouver Island's west coast by boat. Even today, the villages of Bamfield, Tofino and Ucluelet retain their maritime flavour. Fishing is still a part of the local economies, but many other ocean experiences await visitors too, both on and in the water, such as whale-watching, kayaking and surfing. More than half of British Columbia's sand beaches are found along this stretch of coast, and no visit would really be complete without at least one mellow beach walk alongside the roaring surf.

But the activities don't stop at the ocean's edge. Some of the world's largest stretches of intact coastal temperate rainforest lie here on the

BORDER CROSSING
Ferries between Washington state and Vancouver Island cross an international border. Make sure that all travellers have valid passports or Enhanced Drivers Licenses, regardless of their nationality.

Travelling by ferry is part of the whole Vancouver Island experience —both for visitors and locals.

Pacific Rim, and there are numerous opportunities to explore this ancient ecosystem, from short boardwalk trails to serious backpacking expeditions. The pristine and undisturbed habitat is also home to abundant wildlife, and one of the few accessible places where animals such as bears and wolves may be observed in the wild.

With paved roads, improved access has brought more visitors and generated more facilities. Now, even while participating in the nature and wilderness activities the region is famous for, visitors don't have to rough it. Luxury resorts, museums and galleries, world-class spas and fine international cuisine are also part of today's Pacific Rim experience.

The Pacific Rim is my home. We now receive more than one million visitors every year, but I have met many who came here and missed some of the key experiences. With this guidebook, I give you an inside look at the Pacific Rim—a bit of background and history to enrich your visit, as well as some of my own hints about favourite places, where to go and what to see. Have a great trip!

BY BOAT—CARS, CYCLISTS AND FOOT PASSENGERS

You can get to Vancouver Island by ferry from the BC mainland (Vancouver) and from Washington state. Although reservations are not required, they are recommended for the summer months and when travelling on weekends.

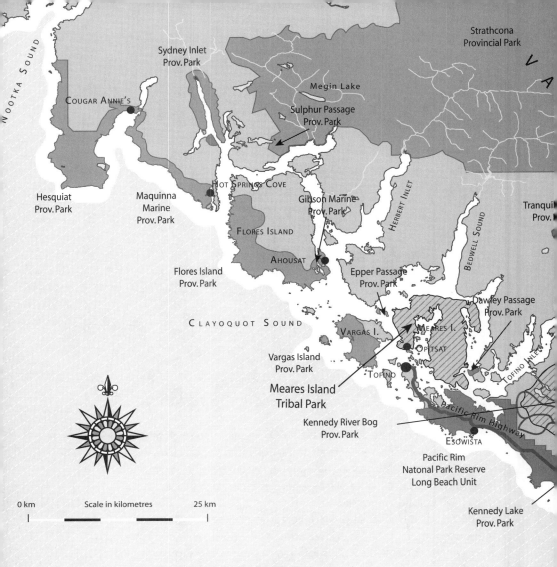

Nootka Sound

Cougar Annie's

Sydney Inlet
Prov. Park

Strathcona
Provincial Park

Megin Lake

Sulphur Passage
Prov. Park

Hesquiat
Prov. Park

Maquinna
Marine
Prov. Park

Hot Springs Cove

Gibson Marine
Prov. Park

Herbert Inlet

Tranquil
Prov.

Flores Island

Flores Island
Prov. Park

Ahousat

Bedwell Sound

Clayoquot Sound

Epper Passage
Prov. Park

Dawley Passage
Prov. Park

Vargas I.

Meares I.

Vargas Island
Prov. Park

Opitsat

Meares Island
Tribal Park

Tofino

Tofino Inlet

Kennedy River Bog
Prov. Park

Pacific Rim Highway

Esowista

Pacific Rim
National Park Reserve
Long Beach Unit

Kennedy Lake
Prov. Park

Central Vancouver
Island Parks

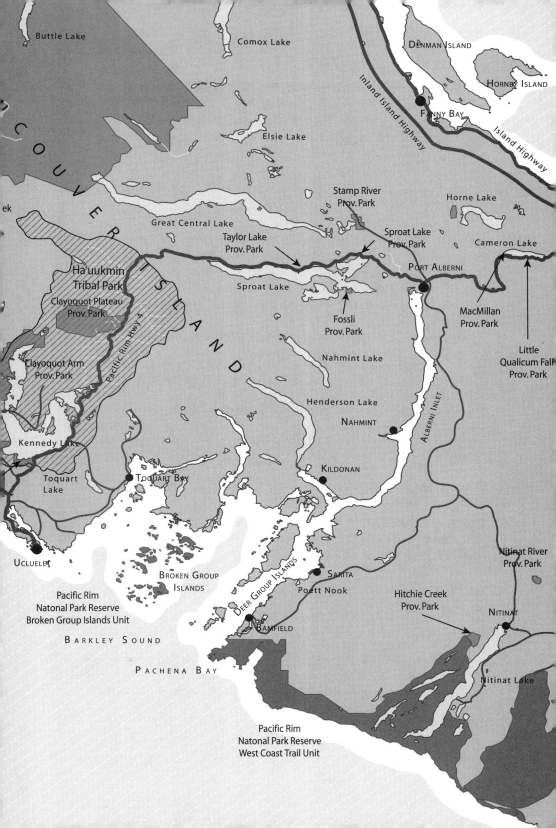

Buttle Lake

Comox Lake

Denman Island

Hornby Island

Inland Island Highway

Island Highway

Fanny Bay

Elsie Lake

VANCOUVER ISLAND

Great Central Lake

Stamp River
Prov. Park

Horne Lake

Taylor Lake
Prov. Park

Sproat Lake
Prov. Park

Cameron Lake

Ha'uukmin
Tribal Park

Sproat Lake

Port Alberni

Clayoquot Plateau
Prov. Park

Fossli
Prov. Park

MacMillan
Prov. Park

Pacific Rim Hwy 4

Nahmint Lake

Little
Qualicum Fall
Prov. Park

Clayoquot Arm
Prov. Park

Henderson Lake

Nahmint

Alberni Inlet

Kennedy Lake

Kildonan

Toquart
Lake

Toquart Bay

Ucluelet

Broken Group
Islands

Deer Group Islands

Sarita

Poett Nook

Nitinat River
Prov. Park

Pacific Rim
National Park Reserve
Broken Group Islands Unit

Hitchie Creek
Prov. Park

Nitinat

Bamfield

Barkley Sound

Pachena Bay

Nitinat Lake

Pacific Rim
National Park Reserve
West Coast Trail Unit

FROM WASHINGTON:

Anacortes to Swartz Bay/Sidney, BC (just outside Victoria) on **Washington State Ferries**. Daily departures, crossing time 2 to 3 hours. Fares US$8-17 foot passengers, $36+ vehicles. From Washington state call 1-800-808-7977, from Seattle and out-of-state 206-464-6400, www.wsdot.wa.gov/ferries.

Port Angeles to Victoria on the **MV Coho**. Daily departures, crossing time 90 minutes. Fares US$15 foot passengers ($7 children), $53+ vehicles. From USA call 360-457-4491, from Canada 386-2202, www.cohoferry.com.

FROM BC MAINLAND ON BC FERRIES:

Fares $7-15 foot passengers, $58+ vehicles one-way. For information and reservations contact 1-888-223-3779, www.bcferries.com.

Vancouver (Tsawwassen terminal) to Swartz Bay/Sidney (just outside of Victoria), eight or more departures daily, crossing time 95 minutes.

Vancouver (Tsawwassen terminal) to Duke Point/Nanaimo, 8 or more departures daily, crossing time 2 hours.

Vancouver (Horseshoe Bay terminal) to Departure Bay/Nanaimo, 8 or more departures daily, crossing time 95 minutes.

KILOMETRES VS. MILES
The metric system is used in Canada. One kilometre is 0.6 of one mile.
Approximate speed conversions:
50 km/h = 30 mph • 60 km/h = 40 mph • 80 km/h = 50 mph • 100 km/h = 60 mph

---

BY BOAT—FOOT PASSENGERS AND CYCLISTS

DOWNTOWN SEATTLE, WA TO DOWNTOWN VICTORIA, BC:

The Victoria Clipper operates once daily over winter and 2 to 3 times daily for the rest of the year, crossing time is about 3 hours. Return fares range from $73 to $155 per adult (advance purchases cheapest). From Seattle call 206-448-5000, from Victoria 382-8100, 1-800-888-2535, www.victoriaclipper.com.

BELLINGHAM, WA TO DOWNTOWN VICTORIA:

Victoria San Juan Cruises offer a narrated scenic cruise once daily early May to September only, crossing time 3 hours. One-way fares include dinner, US$40 to $60. Call 360-738-8099, 1-800-443-4552, www.whales.com.

PORT ANGELES, WA TO DOWNTOWN VICTORIA:

The Victoria Express operates 1 to 3 times daily late May to mid-September only, crossing time 1 hour. Fare is US$12.50 with possible fuel surcharges. From US call 360-452-8088, from Canada 361-9144, www.victoriaexpress.com.

BY CAR

Many drivers underestimate travelling times en route to the Pacific Rim. The views from Highway 4 are breathtaking, as the road turns and twists along steep rock faces, hanging above river valleys and looking out to the mountains. But it is narrow and winding, and there are few places to pass slow RVs or logging trucks. Don't pressure yourself by planning a tight travel schedule. Every year there are many serious accidents on this road. Check weather conditions if you are travelling in winter; rain at sea level can become snow higher up, and may block the passes at Port Alberni Summit between Nanaimo and Port Alberni and Sutton Pass between Port Alberni and the west coast. For road conditions call 1-800-550-4997 or visit www.drivebc.ca and search for the Highway 4 webcam or info.

BY BUS

The Tofino Bus has taken over Greyhound's routes and provides service from Victoria and Nanaimo to Port Alberni and Tofino/Ucluelet. It can carry bikes with advance reservations, and surfboards up to 8' in length. Return fares to Tofino/Ucluelet from Victoria are $130, and from Nanaimo $84. The bus runs daily year-round, with more frequent departures between March and November and around the Christmas season. Some trips are timed to meet BC Ferries service from Vancouver; check for updated schedule information at 725-2871, 1-866-986-3466, www.tofinobus.com.

The West Coast Trail Express provides shuttle bus service May 1 to September 30 from Victoria, Nanaimo and Port Alberni to Nitinat, Bamfield and Pachena Bay, and to Port Renfrew, serving both trailheads of the West Coast Trail. They also provide charter service to anywhere on Vancouver Island. Contact 477-8700, 1-888-999-2288 or www.trailbus.com, reservations recommended.

The Pachena Bay Express operates a charter bus service May to October out of Bamfield, with taxi-like service on request to anywhere on Vancouver Island, including transporting hikers the 7 km/4.4 mi from Bamfield to the West Coast Trail trailhead. Contact 728-1290, 877-728-1290 or http://pachenabayexpress.pachena.ca.

BY BIKE

You can get to the Pacific Rim by bike, but it is hard work. From Nanaimo to Port Alberni, riding on the highway is permitted and there is adequate shoulder space. From Port Alberni to Nitinat or Bamfield the ride is on gravel logging roads. Travel with care, get out of the way of logging trucks and make sure you are equipped with appropriate tires and repair kits.

DRIVING DISTANCES AND APPROXIMATE TIMES

Sidney (Swartz Bay ferry terminal) to Victoria	28 km/17 miles on good highway	30 minutes
Victoria to Nanaimo	113 km/70 miles on good highway	1¼ to 1½ hours
Nanaimo to Port Alberni	80 km/50 miles, part good highway and part narrow, winding highway	1 to 1½ hours
Port Alberni to Bamfield	80 km/50 miles on gravel logging road	1½ to 2 hours
Port Alberni to Nitinat	80 km/50 miles on gravel logging road	1¼ to 1½ hours
Port Alberni to Tofino–Ucluelet junction	90 km/56 miles on very narrow and winding highway. Between the spectacular scenery and the lack of opportunities to pass slower vehicles this is usually a very slow stretch of road.	1½ to 2 hours
junction to Ucluelet	8 km/5 miles on narrow winding highway	10 minutes
junction to Tofino	33 km/20 miles on narrow winding highway	30 minutes
Tofino to Ucluelet	41 km/25 miles on narrow winding highway	40 minutes
Victoria to Nitinat (backroads route via Lake Cowichan and Youbou)	77 km/47 miles on paved highways to Lake Cowichan, then 40 km/24.8 mi on gravel logging roads	3 hours
Nitinat to Bamfield	57 km/35 miles on gravel logging roads	1¼ hours

The highway between Port Alberni and Tofino/Ucluelet is absolutely not recommended to cyclists. The road is barely wide enough for motor vehicles. There is no shoulder for long stretches, and no room for error as the road is edged by rock faces and steep drops down to the river. You can get yourself and your bike to Tofino or Ucluelet on the Tofino Bus, or from Port Alberni to Bamfield or Ucluelet by boat through Lady Rose Marine Services. There are plans to create a bike path linking Tofino and Ucluelet, but at the moment only 15 km/9.3 mi has been completed, and the central 25 km/15.5 mi are on the narrow highway.

BY PLANE

There is scheduled service on small **commuter planes** and **float planes** between Vancouver and Tofino/Ucluelet. Stormy or foggy weather can cause flight delays or cancellations, particularly between October and March, so it is not wise to plan any tight travel connections around these flights during these months.

The flight from either Vancouver or Victoria is about 45 minutes each way. Fares range from $320–$400 return. Orca Airways flies into the **Tofino/ Ucluelet airport**, at the golf course at Long Beach, about 15 km (9.3 mi) from Tofino and 25 km (15.5 mi) from Ucluelet. **Car rentals** are available at the airport through Budget (see below). If you are booked into a hotel they may come and get you, or you can call a **taxi** (Tofino Taxi 725-3333, Ucluelet Taxi 726-4415). Float planes land at the docks right in the towns.

Aside from the airport-based airlines listed below, you can also look into chartering a **float plane** for direct service from downtown Vancouver or Victoria straight to the villages or outlying areas. There are float plane companies based in both cities, as well as in Tofino (page 153) and Ucluelet (page 113). Chartering a plane for one person would be very expensive, but if your party can fill a plane (Cessna three people, Beaver six to seven people; weight restrictions may apply) the per-person cost is quite reasonable. Charters generally start at about $550/hr.

Harbour Air, out of Vancouver, operates the world's largest float plane fleet, with aircraft that can seat from 3 to 14 people. Flights leave from Vancouver airport, and charter service is available to any of the Pacific Rim towns in this book. 604-274-1277, 800-665-0212, www.harbour-air.com.

Hyack Air, out of Victoria, offers float planes for charters from downtown Victoria, and promises scheduled service between Victoria and Tofino in the future, so contact them for current info. 384-2499, www.hyackair.com.

SHARING THE WILDERNESS

Many large predators make the wilds of the Pacific Rim their home: black bears, grey wolves and cougars. They can be dangerous to humans—but in most human-animal encounters, it is actually the animals who end up worse off. Bears and wolves have been shot after becoming habituated to human food and becoming bold and aggressive. Many animals are killed every year on the roads as well.

Please take care with your food and garbage. At public campgrounds, keep food stored in secure containers and put garbage in containers provided. *Never* feed any wildlife, *ever*. Encouraging habituated behaviour only ensures them an early death.

Heed public warnings when wolves, bears or cougars have been seen in the area. In parks and high-use areas these will be prominently posted.

Bears do not normally prey on humans, but may become aggressive if threatened. Wolves and cougars are predatory, so keep small children and dogs near you. Travel in groups and keep close together.

If you encounter a wolf or cougar, gather your group together, pick up small children, and do whatever you can to appear large and noisy. Maintain eye contact, and try to back away slowly. For more information or to report sightings, contact Parks Canada, 726-7165.

Orca Airways flies from **Vancouver airport to Tofino/Ucluelet airport**, one-way from $160, 1-888-359-6722, www.flyorcaair.com.

Tofino Air offers scheduled service, June to September only, between **Tofino and Vancouver Airport**, $188 one-way. 725-4454, 1-888-436-7776, www.tofinoair.ca.

KD Air provides several scheduled flights daily between Vancouver airport and Port Alberni (Vancouver-Qualicum Beach by air, then by road to Port Alberni; the entire trip takes 75 minutes). $167 one-way, with discounts for seniors and children. 1-800-665-4244, www.kdair.com.

CAR RENTALS

In Port Alberni:

Budget Car & Truck Rental 724-4511, 1-800-268-8900, www.budget.ca.

In Tofino/Ucluelet:

Budget Car & Truck Rental, located at the airport near Long Beach, 725-2060, 1-800-268-8900, www.budget.ca.

Getting around locally

BY BUS AND TAXI

There are not many options for scheduled public transport.

Port Alberni has **public transit** for getting around the town itself. For maps and schedule information call 723-3341, www.busonline.ca/regions/pta.

Taxis in Port Alberni, Ucluelet and Tofino are listed under the "Getting around" sections for these towns. There are also van and four-wheel drive services that operate like taxis with hourly charter rates.

AROUND TOFINO AND UCLUELET:

Between Tofino and Ucluelet the **Beach Bus** operates daily year-round, twice daily in summer, with stops at the beaches and trails in Pacific Rim National Park Reserve and at the Tofino Airport/Golf Course. Call 725-2871 or 1-866-986-3466, www.tofinobus.com.

Pacific Rim Five Star Navigators runs a taxi-type service with luxury 4WD SUVs that can transport you at your own schedule to any of the parks or beaches around Tofino or Ucluelet, as well as get you out on the back roads. 725-8393, www.pacificrimnavigators.ca.

AROUND BAMFIELD:

The **Pachena Bay Express** operates around southern Vancouver Island upon request from May to October, 728-1290, 877-728-1290 or http://pachenabayexpress.pachena.ca.

BY WATER

All of these communities were first settled by water, and boats continue to be the most convenient way to make certain journeys.

Lady Rose Marine Services travels between **Port Alberni, Bamfield, Ucluelet and the Broken Group islands**. The historic **MV _Frances Barkley_** travels year-round to and from Port Alberni and Bamfield, with a stop at Kildonan, on Tuesdays, Thursdays and Saturdays. Through the summer months there is an additional Bamfield run on Sundays, as well as service from Port Alberni to Ucluelet and the Broken Group on Mondays, Wednesdays and Fridays. The 200-passenger **Frances Barkley** can carry kayaks and bikes. Fares depend upon the route travelled, but are quite economical (Port Alberni to Bamfield one-way $33, Port Alberni to Ucluelet one-way $36). Call 723-8313 year-round, or 1-800-663-7192 April 1 through September 30, www.ladyrosemarine.com.

The **Juan de Fuca Express** runs nearly daily (dependent both upon bookings and weather) boat service between **Port Renfrew and Bamfield**—the two ends of the **West Coast Trail**—from May through October, $125 one-way, reservations well in advance are necessary, 1-888-755-6578, 1-877-332-5333, http://members.shaw.ca/berry5868/juanfuca.htm.

Empress Water Taxi based in Port Alberni runs charters in **Alberni Inlet** and **Barkley Sound** for up to 12 passengers, 724-9495, 724-4996.

Broken Island Adventures Water Taxi, based in Bamfield, is available to charter between **Bamfield and Ucluelet and around Barkley Sound**. They can transport bikes and kayaks, and will do

Float planes are an important means of transport on the West Coast.

kayak drops from Bamfield to the Broken Group and the Deer Group islands. Call 728-3500, 1-888-728-6200, www.brokenislandadventures.com.

Other **water taxis** based in Ucluelet or near Tofino service **Barkley Sound** (page 105) and **Clayoquot Sound** (page 139).

BY FLOAT PLANE

If you're a hard-core adventurer, grab a topo map and let your imagination run wild! A float plane can drop you into places that would be nearly impossible to hike to. Find yourself a secluded little lake to camp at, and arrange a pick-up for a few days later, or use the float plane to get you and your gear to the starting point of a serious wilderness expedition. Many float planes can take kayaks or canoes strapped to their floats. Float planes are a convenient way to get around, and the prices are actually not too steep if your group size is right to fill up a plane (usually three for a Cessna, and six or seven for a Beaver). Float plane companies offer charter services (starting at $550/hr), and some also have scheduled runs to certain destinations, operating out of Tofino (page 153) and Ucluelet (page 113).

If you are really serious about seeing the wilds from up high, **West Coast Wild Adventures**, based in Ucluelet, specializes in float plane tours, including a full-day tour, with several stops along the way, to visit the "seven wonders of Vancouver Island," $2,500 for up to three people. They will also organize custom multi-day float plane safaris for you. 726-7715, 726-8668, 1-877-992-9453, www.wcwild.com.

A NOTE ABOUT ACCESSIBILITY

Though accessibility to the Pacific Rim's attractions has improved greatly over the past 10 years, extra care should be taken by those with wheelchairs or strollers and those with physical challenges. Even at the area's most popular beaches, wheelchair access is inconsistent. Many of the local hotspots—such as the Pacific Rim National Park Reserve's Broken Group Islands and West Coast Trail Unit—are extremely rugged, and are considered backcountry areas. These are no "walks in the park."

The Pacific Rim National Park Reserve's Long Beach Unit does have a number of disabled access facilities. Roads and parking areas there are paved (except those at Kennedy Lake), and facilities are wheelchair-accessible. Recent improvements to Ucluelet's Wild Pacific Trail make access for wheelchairs and strollers much easier (page 109).

Even in the villages, boardwalked paths can be hazardous. If you are unsure about accessibility, check with one of the tourist information centres (listed on page 198) before you set out.

Port Alberni

Port Alberni

At the head of the longest inlet on Vancouver Island, the town of Port Alberni looks out upon west coast waters, even though it is actually closer to the island's east coast. This historic town, nestled under imposing Mt. Arrowsmith and extending from the shores of Alberni Inlet to the banks

UNIQUELY PORT ALBERNI: WHAT TO DO
- Hop on the steam train for a visit to Chase & Warren winery and the McLean Mill.
- Go fishing in the ocean, lake or river—any time of year.
- Fuel up with a Mexican breakfast at Harbour Quay before hitting the Saturday market.
- Spend a week lounging in the sun on a houseboat on Sproat Lake.
- Visit the Rollin Art Centre to see the gardens and work by local and regional artists.
- Go swimming, waterskiing, tubing, canoeing, kayaking, windsurfing or petroglyph-viewing at Sproat Lake.

THREE MAGIC MOMENTS:
1. A meal at the Water's Edge Pub and Bistro, Harbour Quay, looking out at the sun sparkling on the water.
2. A morning stroll along the riverside at Victoria Quay—wildlife viewing from town!
3. Salmon leaping up the rapids in the Stamp River in autumn.

of the Somass River, originally was two different urban centres: the city of Alberni by the river-mouth, and the actual port town of Port Alberni. Even today, the layout of the town reflects this history. Anyone driving through to the west coast will pass through the old town of "Alberni", centred on Highway 4 and Gertrude Street (3rd Street), with Victoria Quay as its main water access. This part of town is now referred to as "North Port". The centre of the old town of "Port Alberni" is to the south,

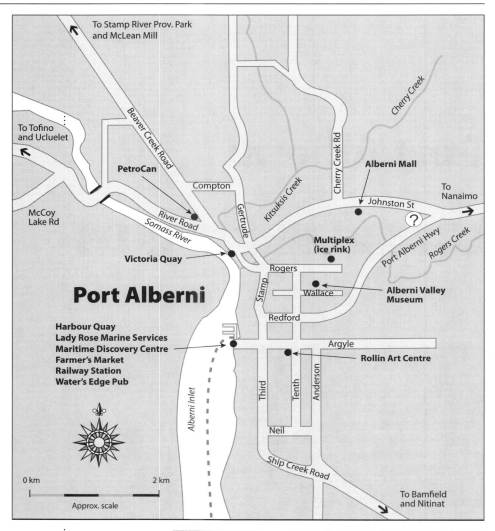

Port Alberni

To Stamp River Prov. Park
and McLean Mill

To Tofino
and Ucluelet

McCoy
Lake Rd

PetroCan

Beaver Creek Road

Compton

Gertrude

Kitsuksis Creek

Cherry Creek

Cherry Creek Rd

Alberni Mall

Johnston St

To
Nanaimo

River Road

Somass River

Victoria Quay

Multiplex
(ice rink)

Rogers

Stamp

Wallace

Redford

Port Alberni Hwy

Rogers Creek

Alberni Valley
Museum

Harbour Quay
Lady Rose Marine Services
Maritime Discovery Centre
Farmer's Market
Railway Station
Water's Edge Pub

Argyle

Rollin Art Centre

Alberni Inlet

Third

Tenth

Anderson

Neil

Ship Creek Road

0 km   2 km

Approx. scale

To Bamfield
and Nitinat

*Port Alberni is
nestled on the
banks of the
Somass River and
at the foot of Mt.
Arrowsmith.*

focussed around 3rd and Argyle, with the docks at Harbour Quay and the railway station as its main transportation centres. This division, with two distinct centres in a town of this size, has challenged the business community, and storefronts remain unoccupied in both parts of town. At present, Highway 4 up-hill from old Alberni is where you will find the malls as well as chain-stores ranging from Starbucks to Wal-Mart. Old Port Alberni, especially on and around Argyle Street, is where you will find more of the older, or owner-run, businesses, as well as the charming old Capitol Theatre.

Once merely a mill town, with the province-wide downturn in the logging industry, Port Alberni has redefined itself. The million or so tourists who used to pass straight through on their way to Tofino, Ucluelet and Long Beach can now find good reason to stop in the self-proclaimed "Salmon Capital of the World," a region that boasts 26,000 inhabitants

THE TSUNAMI OF '64

In March of 1964, a series of powerful waves generated by a magnitude-8.5 earthquake in Anchorage, Alaska, funnelled down Alberni Inlet, increasing in height and energy as the inlet narrowed. Between midnight and 7am six separate waves struck the town, the highest one reaching 3 m (9.8') above the high-tide mark. Miraculously, although 58 properties were destroyed and hundreds of buildings and cars were damaged, no one was killed. Port Alberni now has an efficient loudspeaker system to warn of impending tsunamis.

including the Cherry and Beaver Creek districts. The two waterfront areas have been fixed up and make for a pretty stroll: Harbour Quay on the inlet and Victoria Quay along the banks of the Somass River. There are several museums and historical sites with displays about local natural history and the town's logging heritage, and the range of restaurants and accommodation options is ever-increasing. Then there is the fishing. There are few places in the world where you can literally do it all from one place: cast for steelhead in the rivers, go for trout on the lakes and then get out on the ocean for some salmon.

Though the small coastal towns were once the Pacific Rim's main attractions, today many visitors prefer Port Alberni. It is less touristy, a little more down-to-earth and the prices for food and accommodation are a lot more reasonable. Far from the influence of the open Pacific Ocean, it also experiences some real summer heat and is a place to enjoy some warm summer swimming in the many lakes surrounding it. Port Alberni is a great stopping point en route to the west coast, as well as a good base for access to nearby Sproat, Cameron and Great Central Lakes and to several provincial parks.

GETTING AROUND

The easiest way to get around Port Alberni is by car. There is only one **car rental agency** in Port Alberni: **Budget Car & Truck Rental**, 724-4511, 1-800-268-8900, www.budget.ca.

The local **bus system** has four different routes that service most of the residential and commercial areas in town. For route and schedule information call 723-3341, www.busonline.ca/regions/pta. For **taxi** service, call **Alberni District Fairway Taxi**, 723-3511 or **United Cab**, 723-2121, 1-888-829-4489.

Lady Rose Marine Services offers scheduled boat service from Port Alberni to Bamfield year-round and to Ucluelet over the summer season, several times a week, 723-8313 year-round, or 1-800-663-7192 April through September, www.ladyrosemarine.com.

SERVICES

The **Port Alberni Visitor Centre** is located on the Alberni Highway on the east edge of town and is open daily year-round (restricted hours over winter), 724-6535, www.avcoc.com.

With gas stations, banks, supermarkets and specialty shops, Port Alberni is the last well-serviced stop for those continuing out to the west coast. If you are heading to Bamfield, Ucluelet or Tofino, you would be wise to stock up on groceries and goods here.

The main commercial areas are in old Port Alberni (10th Ave and 3rd Ave near Argyle) and the malls and chain stores and restaurants on Johnston (Highway 4) as you enter town from the east. It is challenging to find organic produce in Port Alberni, but you can at least buy local: local meats at **Pete's Mountain Meats** at 5104 River Road (corner of Beaver Creek Road), and fruit and veggies 1 km further along on your way out of town at **Naesgaards**, 5681 River Road, www.naesgaards.com. For health foods, natural foods and supplements, pay a visit to **Healthy Habits** at 4505 Victoria Quay, open daily. Port Alberni's quaint old 1939 **post office** on Johnston, two blocks up from Victoria Quay, is now closed, but still worth a quick visit as an historic period building; for functioning post offices, try the main office at the Pacific Rim Mall (Highway 4 and Cherry Creek Rd.) or the Shoppers Drug Mart at 10th and Redford.

There is no proper internet café in Port Alberni. You can get high-speed **internet access** at the **Visitor's Centre** on the highway, 724-6535. The following restaurants have wireless internet access for customers: **McDonalds** (Johnstone and Tebo), **Serious Coffee** (10th and Redford), and **Cup & Saucer Eatery** at Victoria Quay.

THINGS TO DO

Explore the waterfront! **Harbour Quay**, at the bottom of Argyle Street, fronts onto Alberni Inlet, and it is possible to see porpoises and seals and even the occasional whale from here. A collection of cafés, galleries and restaurants all housed in historic buildings make this an interesting place to while away a few hours, stopping for lunch or dinner at the **Waterfront Café** with its sparkling ocean view.

Victoria Quay, a few kilometres to the north, fronts onto the Somass Estuary, and has a pretty waterfront walking path that follows the riverbank. From this path you may see salmon jumping and bears foraging across the river in fall, and over winter you might glimpse a mink scooting over the rocks along the riverbank or trumpeter swans out on the water. After your stroll, pop into the **Clambucket** restaurant or the **Cup & Saucer Eatery** for a meal alongside the river.

As you explore town, be sure to keep an eye out for the **murals**—a total of 18—painted by artists Brad Piatka and Walter Collins. And down by the river at Victoria Quay, make sure you check out the giant **Nuu-chah-nulth sculptures** here: two Hupacasath welcome figures, as well as a magnificent life-size carving of a Nuu-chah-nulth whaling canoe in action.

Find out what's playing at the **Capitol Theatre**. Port Alberni's recently restored vintage movie house, 4904 Argyle, is now home to an active live theatre group that puts on several productions per year, 723-1195, www. atthecapitol.org.

If you are in town for the weekend, be sure to catch the **Farmer's Market**, which takes place every Saturday, 9am to noon at Harbour Quay, year-round (it pays to get there early). In addition to local seasonal produce, you will find homemade preserves and baked goods, as well as arts and crafts, woodworking and homemade products such as soap and fabric arts.

The Alberni Pacific Railway's restored 1929 steam-powered locomotive runs through the Alberni Valley all summer.

Photo courtesy of Vancouver Island North Film Commission

Annual festivals

For current information and dates, contact the Port Alberni Visitor Centre, 724-6535, www.avcoc.com. **Folk Fest** takes place on the Canada Day (July 1) long weekend, and includes music, dancing, foods and other live entertainment. **Forest Fest** is held on a weekend in early July at the McLean Mill; it includes a Loggers' Stomp Dance, children's concert, and visual arts, spoken word arts and theatre, all with a forest theme. **Thunder in the Valley**, with drag races out at the old Alberni Valley Airport, is on the middle weekend of August. **Salmon Festival and Derby**, with thousands of dollars in prizes, a children's bullhead fish derby, live entertainment and salmon BBQs, takes place on the Labour Day weekend. The **Fall Fair** is an annual event that has been running for 60+ years; it includes an agricultural show, home show, midway with rides, and logger sports, and takes place the weekend after Labour Day. The **Motorcycle Parade**, mid- to late September, fills the town with Harleys, starting in Little Qualicum and continuing to Harbour Quay in Port Alberni, followed by a dance. The **Robertson Creek Hatchery**, 724-6521, has its annual open house on the third Sunday of each October, at the peak of the autumn salmon spawn.

A pole in the process of being carved is testimony to living Tseshaht culture.

Museums and educational tourism

Port Alberni has many museums and cultural and historical displays that focus on the area's logging and maritime heritage as well as on First Nations culture and natural history.

Maritime Discovery Centre beside Harbour Quay, housed in an actual lighthouse, is a museum that showcases the maritime history of Vancouver Island's west coast. Alongside, the newly opened **Hutchison Gallery** focuses on Port Alberni history, with permanent displays on the 1964 tsunami, lighthouse living, and underwater research undertaken by Neptune Canada. Open daily June to September, admission by donation, 723-2181, www.alberniheritage.com.

Alberni Valley Museum has an impressive display on Nuu-chah-nulth culture, as well as exhibits on logging, fishing, farming and pioneer life. It also features rotating temporary exhibits about both local and international subjects. Open Tuesday through Saturday year-round, Thursdays until 8pm. Admission by donation, 723-2181, www.alberniheritage.com.

The **McLean Mill**, built in 1926, is the only operating steam-powered mill in Canada, and features displays and activities for both adults and children. Accessible by road, or by the historic steam train that leaves from Harbour

Quay, the mill-plus-theatre package is $15 (senior, child and family rates also available). Open daily over summer, selected dates in fall and winter, 723-1376, www.alberniheritage.com.

The **Heritage Train Station** at Harbour Quay is the old 1912 CP Railway Station, and the departure point for the Alberni Pacific Railway, a steam train that takes you on a 35-minute journey through the Alberni Valley with stops at the Chase & Warren Winery and the McLean Mill. Train ride plus mill-and-theatre package $30 (senior, child and family rates also available). Runs Thursday to Monday through the summer months. 723-1376, www.alberniheritage.com.

Amusements

The **Port Alberni Healthy Living Guide** is oriented towards residents, but in it you'll find the most up-to-date info on what rereational activities are going on in the valley, including many programs for children. It is published three to four times a year; pick up a copy in the Echo Recreation Centre (Wallace and Tenth) or download it: www.portalberni.ca/parks-and-rec.

There is a deep-tank **indoor pool** (plus a shallow end, a tots' pool, hot tub and sauna, and gym), at the **Echo Aquatic and Fitness Centre**, 4255 Wallace at Tenth, open daily till 10pm (closed 3 weeks in August–September), adults $8.30, families $17, $3.25 for shower only, 720-2514. You can go **ice skating** at the **Alberni Valley Multiplex**, 3737 Rogers near Tenth, open daily September to March (call for free-skate schedule), adults $8.30, families $16.80, skate rentals available, 720-2518.

FRESH WILD SEAFOOD

For the best fish you will ever find, look for fresh wild sockeye salmon, at a fraction of supermarket prices, sold along Highway 4 on the Tseshaht reserve on the west side of town, from June to August. The salmon are captured as they head up-river—summer catches are more like ocean fish, while later in the season the fish have lost much of their fat and are a bit more like trout.

You can usually get a whole sockeye for $10–15. If you know how to fillet it, barbecue the whole fillet *skin-side-up* (so the fat dribbles into the flesh, keeping it moist), not too hot, for 15 minutes or so, then carefully flip it and give it only a few minutes on the other side – just long enough that the flesh separates when you poke it with a knife. If you cut it into steaks, grill (or fry) it just long enough that the flesh starts to separate. Then, salt and pepper . . . don't add fancy sauces that will disguise the exquisite flavour.

You can also find fresh local seafood—fresh finfish and shellfish as well as canned or smoked products—at the Cod-Father at Harbour Quay, in season but usually open mornings through summer, 723-7114, and St. Jean's Cannery and Smokehouse, 3653 3rd Ave. 723-7744, 1-866-754-3191, www.stjeans.com, with their fresh seafood as well as canned and locally smoked products (and also a processing depot and smoking available for fishers), open February through Christmas.

Impact Bowling, 3752 Fourth Ave., has 5-pin bowling lanes, open 12-4 and 6-10 over winter, more restricted hours over summer, phone for info, 723-5522, www.impactbowling.ca. The **Alberni Golf Club** is right in town at 6449 Cherry Creek Rd., and has an 18-hole course, pro shop and restaurant. Open daily 7am to dusk, $40-55 for 18 holes. Clubhouse 723-7111, Pro Shop 723-5422, www.albernigolf.com.

Nightlife

Arlington Pub at the Arlington Hotel, 5022 Johnston Rd., 723-5661.
Westwind Pub, 4940 Cherry Creek Rd., 724-1324.

Galleries

Ahtsik Native Art Gallery, 7133 Pacific Rim Highway (on the way westward out of town), a newly opened authentic native art gallery run by reknowned Tseshaht carver Gordon Dick, featuring his own work as well as that of other west-coast native artists, open year-round Thursday through Monday, 723-3425, 877-324-8745, www.gordondick.ca.

Clock Tower Gallery, 5440 Argyle at Harbour Quay, local sculpture, pottery, silver jewellery and First Nations arts and crafts, open daily year-round, 724-5999.

Rollin Art Centre, 3061 Eighth Ave., both fine art gallery and Japanese gardens and childrens garden, gift shop on site, building was a gift from Port Alberni's sister city, Abashiri, Japan. Admission is free, open Tuesday through Saturday 11am–4pm year-round, 724-3412.

Waterfront Gallery, Harbour Quay, painting, etchings and jewellery by artist **Janice Sheehan**, restricted hours over winter, 724-3243, www.janicesheehan.com.

Books

For some local reading material, check out Port Alberni's independently owned bookstores, **Curious Coho Books** two blocks up from Victoria Quay at 4841 Johnston, open daily year-round (until late on Thursdays and Fridays), or **Literati Books** downtown at Third and Argyle, specializing in pre-owned, literature, history, open Monday to Saturday year-round, 730-2980.

Walks and day hikes

Several walks and hikes can be done right from Port Alberni town. Visit the Port Alberni Visitor Centre to look at a copy of the very useful *Alberni Valley Trail Guide*, updated and republished in 2006. This booklet lists walking trails within the town limits as well as longer hikes, and is available at the Visitor's Centre. Tim Leadam's *Hiking the West Coast of Vancouver Island* (Greystone, 2005) also lists hikes for this region.

Kitsuksis Dyke Walking Path is an easy 1.5 km (0.9 mi) loop along Kitsuksis Creek, within town. You can park near the end of Margaret Street, north of Highway 4/Johnston Rd. and access the creekside trail from the street. Several bridges cross the creek to make your loop. If you continue a few hundred metres northeastward from the bridge at Spencer Park you will come to a waterfall by the railway trestle; you may see coho salmon jumping here in the fall.

Log Train Trail, Northern Section is a 20 km (12.4 mi) route that follows the old logging railroad. You can follow this trail on foot, bike or horseback. Trail access and parking is at the end of Maebelle Rd., west of Highway 4 and just south of the Visitor Centre, or at the McLean Mill. It is 7.5 km (4.6 mi) from Maebelle Rd. to the mill, and another 12.5 km (7.7 mi) to the north end of the trail at Somers Rd.

Log Train Trail, Southern Section has been extended. The first 3 km (1.9 mi) section departs from the south side of Highway 4, opposite Maebelle Rd., passes through the Alberni Demonstration Forest, and crosses Rogers Creek via a footbridge before climbing up through the forest to Burde St. From Burde St., a newly constructed section continues another 5 or so km south. This new section of trail is not shown in the Alberni Valley Trail Guide, but maps are available at the Echo Recreation Centre.

Rogers Creek Nature Trail is an easy 3 km (1.9 mi) walk (each way) along a forested path. Park on the east side of the Alberni Highway (1.4 km/0.9 mi south of the Visitor Centre) on the south side of Rogers Creek, and follow the path eastward along the creek. You will pass the intersection with the Log Train Trail, then walk through some nice sections of forest, past a giant Douglas fir tree and alongside quiet pools in the creek. There are numerous other bush trails coming off this trail, suitable for exploration by experienced navigators.

Cycling

There is a lot of good off-road biking around Port Alberni. Bikes are permitted along the 20 km (12.4 mi) **Log Train Trail**, and there are many gravel logging roads in the area—check the *Backroad Mapbook & Recreational Atlas, Vancouver Island* (www.backroadmapbooks.com).

For technical mountain biking, there is a whole network of trails just outside town, including steep sections of single-track, log hops, rock drops and more. For trail information, inquire at the Visitor Centre, or at **Ozzie's Cycle**, Tenth and Roger, 724-6556. The trails depart from the Old Nanaimo Highway, 1 km (0.6 mi) east of the Visitor Centre; park behind Coombs Country Candy.

Unfortunately, there are no longer any companies offering bike rentals in Port Alberni.

Kayaking and canoeing

Experienced paddlers can rent kayaks to paddle around **Alberni Inlet**, **Sproat Lake** or **Great Central Lake**. or you can sign up for a guided trip. Self-contained and experienced groups can also head out from here via **Lady Rose Marine Services** for multi-day trips to the **Broken Group** or the **Deer Group** (loading boats and gear onto the MV *Frances Barkley*) for a drop-off in Bamfield to access the Deer Group, or to Sechart to access the Broken Group. Lady Rose Marine Services also has kayaks available to rent. 723-8313 year-round, or 1-800-663-7192 April through September, www.ladyrosemarine.com.

Alberni Outpost offers hourly and daily kayak rentals (singles $15-35 for 3 hrs or from $25/day; doubles $25-50 for 3 hrs or from $30/day), inquire about custom guided day-trips, 723-2212, 1-800-325-3921, www.albernioutpost.com. **Batstar Adventure Tours** offer all-inclusive guided multi-day trips to both the Broken Group and the Deer Group from $1,600. 724-2098, 1-877-449-1230, www.batstar.com.

Nature tours and wildlife viewing

The "Salmon Capital of the World" is a great base from which to head out to witness the miracle of the salmon spawn. You can find creeks with spawning salmon from August through to December, within an hour's drive of town.

Taylor River—stop at the rest area on the east side of Sutton Pass (39

KAYAKING ON THE OCEAN

Yes, it *is* ocean—even though on some mornings, looking out from the docks in town, the harbour may appear a glassy lake. Conditions can change abruptly: every six hours with the tide, and less predictably with the wind. Many areas are exposed to *swell*, big ocean waves that have travelled from afar and form surf when they hit shore, or to complicated rough water formed by the interaction of wind, waves and current.

There are some relatively sheltered paddling routes suitable for beginner paddlers, but I want to make clear my use of that word. *By "beginner" I mean paddlers who have done at least some basic training*—at very least in the fundamentals of kayak strokes, navigation and rescues. If you have no kayaking experience at all, to ensure your safety you should paddle with a guide (or a friend who has the equivalent experience of a guide). The water here is cold, all year round, and attempting to swim to shore is not likely to save your life in the case of a capsize.

Practise your rescues, and practise them in the conditions that you are likely to encounter on your trips: in the cold water, in rough water, in loaded boats. Pools are great for *learning* your rescues, but if you have not practised them in the types of conditions that might capsize you, you cannot be confident that you can actually save yourself when it really matters.

Travel with proper nautical charts. Other maps do not show the important ocean features that kayakers need to know about. Find out where boat channels are, and avoid them. Do not land on private land or on areas marked on the chart as "Indian Reserve." Ask around before you depart to get those crucial little tidbits of "local knowledge."

km/24.2 mi west of Port Alberni, 51 km/31.7 mi east of the Tofino–Ucluelet junction) to see salmon ascending the river. Best viewing is with lower water levels. Both coho and sockeye spawn here in November and December. **Stamp River Provincial Park** has a viewing area to watch returning salmon—an early sockeye run in mid-June, and the main run of sockeye and chinook from late August to early October.

Sea kayaking is a way to experience the west coast with all of your senses.

   Winers Creek, 14 km/8.7 mi west of Port Alberni, has salmon runs in April to May and again in October. You can stay right beside the creek mouth at the West Bay Hotel, and also enjoy the bird sanctuary and the local family of beavers here. **Somass River** has runs of chinook, coho and sockeye. You

CANOEING THE BIG LAKES

You can plan your own trip on any of the big lakes in the Pacific Rim: **Cameron Lake, Nitinat Lake, Sproat Lake, Great Central Lake** and **Kennedy Lake**. Just remember that there is a reason that these lakes are all popular windsurfing spots, and plan your trip accordingly. Typical conditions in summer are calm mornings, with strong westerly winds coming up around mid-morning or early afternoon—but really, strong winds can blow from any direction at any time. Plan your trip carefully, looking at the weather at the time, and routes that offer shelter and safe landing sites in case conditions change. Travel with appropriate maps and equipment, and respect private property and Indian Reserves. In general, most of the Pacific Rim's rivers are not easily navigable by canoe. Some can be explored in summer by a combination of paddling and dragging the canoe up- or downstream, but inquire locally about the river you are interested in first—you could be disturbing sensitive salmon spawning beds. In winter, water levels are too high for canoeing.

cannot see the actual spawn, but from the river mouth at Victoria Key in downtown Port Alberni you can see active jumping salmon in late summer and early fall, and you may also see bears strolling along the opposite shore around low tide.

Robertson Creek Hatchery, a 15-minute drive south of Port Alberni along Highway 4, is a great place to see returning coho, chinook and steelhead in early and mid-September. **Rainbird Excursions** offers daylong adventures led by a local naturalist to some of the outlying areas—either to Ucluelet, returning up Alberni Inlet on the Frances Barkley, $75, or out to Bamfield for a hike to Tapaltos Beach. Half-day trips from $50, full-day $100-155, 1-866-723-7102, www.rainbirdexcursions.com.

Birdwatching

Some of Port Alberni's best birdwatching can be found along sheltered shorelines. There are good viewing spots of the **Somass River estuary** from downtown Port Alberni, at Victoria Quay as well as across from it. The estuary is a favoured feeding spot for migratory birds using the Pacific Flyway, and 155 species have been recorded here. You may be lucky enough to see trumpeter swans during winter. To access the quieter area across from town (formerly known as the J. V. Clyne Bird Sanctuary), drive northwestward out of town along River Road and turn left as soon as you cross the metal girder bridge, at the Tseshaht Reserve. Follow this road for a kilometer or two along the shoreline; the gate might be locked, so be prepared to walk part of the way.

The West Bay Hotel on Sproat Lake 20 km/12.4 mi west of Port Alberni is perched on the edge of a bird sanctuary where you can watch great blue herons feeding at the water's edge, as well as many other birds and the local family of beavers. **Rainbird Excursions**, based in Port Alberni, offers birdwatching tours in the forests and mountains around Port Alberni as well as along the outer coast, from $50, 1-866-723-7102, www.rainbirdexcursions.com.

Scenic cruises

The MV **Lady Rose**, the historic supply ship that service the villages of Bamfield, Ucluelet and Kildonan from Port Alberni for decades, has been retired from service. But her parent company, Lady Rose Marine Services, still operates the 200-passenger MV **Frances Barkley** up and down the inlet. This is a working ship, providing supplies and mail to the remote coastal communities; you can use it for transport, but you can also treat it as a pleasant day-cruise and hop on the ship for the return trip down and back up Alberni Inlet. Departures 8am Tuesday, Thursday and Saturday year-round and daily over summer, $50–74 round trip. 723-8313 year-round, or 1-800-663-7192 April through September, www.ladyrosemarine.com.

Fishing

In Port Alberni, you can buy fishing licences at the Government Agent Office, 4711 Elizabeth St., 724-9200; Alberni Seafood & Tackle, 2970 Alberni Highway, 723-9333; Gone Fishin', 5069 Johnston Rd., 723-1172; Canadian Tire, 3550 Johnston Rd., 720-0085; and Lakeshore Service & Marina, 10412 Lakeshore Rd., 723-3033.

SALTWATER FISHING

Saltwater fishing from the self-proclaimed world's salmon capital is mainly for salmon and halibut, either up **Alberni Inlet**, in the **Broken Group** or offshore from **Bamfield** (one hour from Port Alberni by boat). Chinook, coho and some halibut are pretty consistent in Barkley Sound and around the Broken Group from June through September. Salmon moving up the inlet toward spawning streams can be targeted from Port Alberni over the summer months: sockeye from mid-June through to mid-August, chinook from mid-August until the first big rains in late September, and coho from August through early October.

Hummingbird Charters run half- and full-day trips in their 26' cruiser for $500-$800, 2+ day fishing/accommodation packages from $900, 720-2111, 1-888-720-2114, www.hummingbirdcharters.com. **Last Cast Guiding** offers half- and full-day trips in their 24' cruiser, in the inlet, the Broken Group and offshore, from $400-1000, 954-8060, 1-866-968-4665, www.lastcastguiding.com. **Murphy's Sport Fishing** offers 6- and 8-hour ocean charters in boats ranging from 20–28', from $420 for 2–3 people, accommodation packages available, 1-877-218-6600, www.murphysportfishing.com. **Native Sea Safari**, 22' half-top aluminum boat, 6-, 8- and 10-hour trips in Alberni Inlet and offshore with experienced guide, from $450 for up to 3 people, 723-0336, 720-9979, www.nativeseasafari.ca. **Slivers Charters** offers 5- to 10-hour ocean fishing packages in 21–28' boats, $425-850, accommodation packages available, 724-2502, 1-877-314-6800, www.catchsalmon-ca.net.

RIVER FISHING

You can also fish for coho and chinook salmon in the **Stamp River** in September and October, fly fishing when the water level is low or using regular gear when it is a bit higher. Steelhead are in the rivers almost year-round, with the best fishing from October to April. Serious fishers should check out **Murphy's Riverside Lodge** on the Stamp River, a short walk away from the river fishing and a five-minute drive to the boat docks for saltwater fishing. River fishing trips start at $420 for 2 people, fishing/accommodation packages and ocean trips also available. 1-877-218-6600, www.murphysportfishing.com.

In most other areas the steelhead fishery is catch-and-release only; check

A happy fisherman shows off the day's catch.
Photo courtesy of Salmon Eye Charters

PACIFIC SALMON

There are seven species of Pacific salmon. Steelhead and cutthroat trout used to be classified as trout, but scientists have decided that they actually have more in common with the Pacific salmon genus. Unlike Atlantic salmon, most Pacific salmon return to the streams of their birth only once, dying after they have spawned. Salmon populations in different river systems have different characteristics; even though they are the same species, each population is unique and it is hard to introduce salmon from one system into another. Many rivers contain several salmon species, and some even have distinct runs of the same species.

Chinook—Can be over 50 kg (100 lbs). Complex spawning patterns. Usually spawn in the fall, but some populations from larger rivers spawn in the spring or summer.

Pink—Smallest of salmon; spawn when they are only two years old.

Sockeye—Have the darkest and oiliest flesh. Spawn between late summer and early winter, usually at four years of age. Although some fry migrate to the sea soon after hatching, most spend a period of time in lakes before descending to the sea. "Kokanee" salmon spend their entire life cycle in fresh water.

Chum—Most widespread Pacific salmon, occurring from northern California to the Beaufort Sea. Spawn in the fall, often in very tiny coastal streams, between two and six years old.

Coho—Widespread in BC and a favourite of anglers. The young spend between one and three years in streams, or occasionally larger rivers or lakes, before they descend to the ocean. Do not migrate as far out to sea as do other salmon species; usually spawn in late summer or fall.

Steelhead—A sea-going type of rainbow trout. Unlike other Pacific salmon species, about 20 percent survive spawning, and return to spawn in a subsequent year. Can live up to nine years. There are both "summer-run" and "winter-run" steelhead; fish move up the rivers nearly all year round, but actual spawn is between January and May for both runs. The young spend between one and three years in the rivers before moving to the ocean.

Sea-run cutthroat—There are both sea-run and landlocked types. Spawn at between three and four years of age, and are capable of returning to spawn in subsequent years. They spawn over winter, and the young remain in the rivers for one to two years.

current fishing regulations. Sea-run cutthroat trout are in many rivers and estuaries year-round, but are especially active in the spring. **China Creek**, on the east side of Alberni Inlet, has a good cutthroat run from January to March. Rainbow trout are fished in many rivers from spring through to fall. Freshwater fishing is best done with local guides, as they will know precisely when the fishing is best in specific lakes and rivers.

LAKE FISHING

There are three large lakes close to Port Alberni, as well as numerous small lakes accessible by logging road or by float plane. The Backroad Mapbook has 20 pages of information about the many lakes of Vancouver Island, including access information, fish species present, and best season to fish—even for the tiny and hard-to-get-to lakes. The three larger lakes are all accessible by paved road.

FISHING LICENCES

Fishing is not permitted anywhere in the Pacific Rim without an appropriate licence. With your licence you will receive current information about daily catch limits.

Freshwater fishing (non-tidal licence) is regulated by the provincial government. One-year licences are valid from April 1 to March 31 of a given year, and cost $36 for BC residents, $55 for other Canadian residents, and $80 for foreigners, plus $6 for a salmon stamp to keep any salmon that are caught. One- and eight-day licences are also available. Children under 16 do not need a licence. For more information, look up www.fishing.gov.bc.ca, call 1-800-663-7867, or contact one of the vendors listed in each region's section.

Saltwater fishing (tidal licence) is regulated by the federal government. One-year licences, valid April 1 to March 31, cost $22 for Canadian residents and $106 for non-residents, plus $6 for a salmon stamp. One-, three- and five-day licences are also available, and licences for children under 16 are free. These licences are also valid for collecting shellfish such as clams, scallops or crabs. You can get a licence online from http://www.pac.dfo-mpo.gc.ca/recfish/, call 604-666-0566, or contact one of the vendors listed in each section.

Cameron Lake, 20 km/12.4 mi east of Port Alberni, has brown trout, rainbow trout and cutthroat trout year-round. There is a boat launch at the east end of the lake, on the highway. **Great Central Lake** is stocked with steelhead, and also has rainbow trout, cutthroat trout, Dolly Varden char and sockeye salmon. The best fishing is from April to June and in September and October, with good rainbow trout in April and May and cutthroat in June. To get here, turn north on Great Central Lake Rd. 10 km/6.2 mi west of Port Alberni, and follow it about 8 km/4.9 mi to **The Ark Resort**, where there is a public boat launch as well as canoe rentals. If you want to stay where the action is, settle down here for a few days at **Rosy's Lodge on Logs**, a floating lodge at the Ark Resort, 723-2657, www.arkresort.com.

Sproat Lake has rainbow trout, cutthroat trout, coho salmon and kokanee salmon (a landlocked sockeye). The fishing is good from February through to October, with steelhead fishing in April and May, cutthroat trout in June, and rainbow trout from June through September. The public boat launch is in **Sproat Lake Provincial Park**, 10 km/6.2 mi west of Port Alberni, but the lake extends another 20 km/12.4 mi west from here. There are several campgrounds, cottages, cabins and B&Bs on Sproat Lake, as well as the **West Bay Hotel** right on the highway, and many of them offer boat moorage; see pages 85–87.

Boating

There are public boat launches at:

Sproat Lake Provincial Park, 10 km/6.2 mi west of town.

Great Central Lake. Public access, for a fee, at the Ark Resort at the east end of the lake only.

Port Alberni town. Two boat launches, both for a fee, in downtown Port Alberni. At the Harbour Quay Marina, 723-1413, you launch into the inlet near the Somass River mouth, and at the nearby Clutesi Haven Marina River Rd. (near Victoria Quay) you can launch directly into the river, 724-6837.

Alberni Inlet. On the east side of Alberni Inlet, for a fee at China Creek Regional Park (12 km/7.5 mi from Port Alberni along the Bamfield gravel road), and on the west side of Alberni Inlet there is a small launch for kayaks and cartop boats at Arden Creek Recreation Site (20 km/12.4 mi from Port Alberni; head out via McCoy Lake Rd).

Diving

There are no longer any sports diving shops in Port Alberni.

Rendezvous Dive Adventures, out on Barkley Sound, offers diving courses and overnight tour packages from $130 per night at their secluded private lodge in Rainy Bay, and can provide tank refills (air/nitrox) on site in Rainy Bay, 735-5050, 1-877-777-9994, www.rendezvousdiving.com.

WHERE TO STAY

A great range of accommodation is available here. For up-to-date information check out the Port Alberni Chamber of Commerce site at 724-6535, www.avcoc.com, or listings in www.portalbernilodging.worldweb.com. The listings that follow are right in town. There are also many rural and beachfront accommodation options (and even houseboats!) within about 15 km/9.3 mi of town; see pages 85–87. All rates quoted are for double occupancy unless otherwise stated.

Campgrounds

Redford Motor Inn, 3723 Redford, full hookup RV sites $18, tent sites $10, free showers, coin laundromat, open year-round, 724-0121.

Somass Motel and RV Campground, 5279 River Rd. across the road from the river, RV sites with partial hookup, coin laundry, outdoor pool, pets welcome, $21, open May to October, 724-3236, 1-800-927-2217, www.somass-motel.ca.

Timberlodge & RV Campground, on Highway 4 as you enter Port Alberni from Nanaimo, sauna, indoor pool, laundry, small pets welcome, tent sites $25, full hookup RV sites $20–45, open year-round, 723-9415, www.timberlodgerv.ca.

Hostels

Fat Salmon Backpackers, 3250 Third Ave., a large international hostel with communal kitchen, laundry available, $21-25 for dorm beds, open year-round, 723-6924. www.fatsalmonbackpackers.com.

Tsunami Backpackers Guesthouse, 5779 River Rd. on the riverbank, a small quiet home-turned-hostel, kitchen, internet, laundry service, BBQs, cheap bike and canoe rentals, dorm beds $20, private rooms $32-72, open year-round, 724-9936, www.tsunamibackpackers.hostel.com.

Bed and breakfasts

Alberni Dew Drop Inn Bed and Breakfast, 547 Maebelle Rd., rural property on the edge of town near Log Train Trail, room or suite, children and dogs welcome, open year-round, $50–80, 724-9608, www.albernidewdrop.com.

Cedar Wood Lodge, 5895 River Rd., 4-star rooms with private bathrooms, gas fireplaces, common games area, buffet breakfast, $95–135, open year-round, 724-6800, 1-877-314-6800, www.cedarwood.bc.ca.

Edelweiss B&B, 2610 Twelfth Ave., suites with private bathrooms, "honeymoon suite" with jacuzzi, $55–90, open year-round, 723-5940, 1-877-723-5940, www.edelweissbb.ca.

Hummingbird Guesthouse & Charters, 5679 River Rd., luxury suites with patios, BBQs, outdoor hot tub, mountain views and riverfront dock, $125–160, fishing/accommodation packages also available, 720-2111, 1-888-720-2114, www.hummingbirdguesthouse.com.

Inntorestin B&B, 3590 Estevan Dr., valley views from residential neighbourhood, children welcome, $80, April to September only, 724-3156, www.inntorestin.ca.

Merlot House, 3095 Seventh Ave., downtown location with harbour view, shared bath, children welcome, $80, open year-round, 723-3700, www.merlothouse.com.

UpTown Place Hikers Rest B&B, 3034 Eighth Ave., downtown close to Harbour Quay and across from Rollin Arts Centre, shared or private bath, $55–75, open May to October, 724-5886, fbknoll@telus.net.

Motels

Bluebird Motel, 3755 Third Ave., sleeping and housekeeping unit, located near Lady Rose Marine Services dock, $55-70, 723-1153, 1-888-591-3888, www.bluebirdalberni.ca.

Esta Villa Motel, 4014 Johnston near the eastern entrance to town, sleeping and housekeeping units, pets welcome, $70-120, 724-1261, 1-800-724-0844, www.alberni.net/estavilla/.

Redford Motor Inn, 1723/3723 Redford St., rooms with kitchenettes, family units, $55–70, 724-0121, redfordinn@hotmail.com.

Riverside Motel, 5065 Roger St., rooms with full kitchens, BBQs, small pets on approval, $70-100, 724-9916, 1-800-636-9916, www.bctravel.com/ci/riverside.html.

Somass Motel and RV Campground, 5279 River Rd. across the road from the river, rooms and suites with kitchenettes, coin laundry, outdoor pool, pets welcome, $60-130, 724-3236, 1-800-927-2217, www.somass-motel.ca.

Timberlodge & RV Campground, on Highway 4 as you enter Port Alberni from Nanaimo, sauna, indoor pool, laundry, $65-105, open year-round, 723-9415, www.timberlodgerv.ca.

Tyee Village Motel, 4155 Redford at 11th, some units with kitchen, pets on approval, outdoor pool, Dugout Café alongside, $65-85, open year-round, 723-8133, 1-800-663-6676, www.tyeemotel.com.

Hotels

Best Western Barclay Hotel, 4277 Stamp Ave., don't expect friendly service or information at the front desk, call for rates and information, 724-7171, 1-800-563-6590, www.bestwesternbarclay.com.

Hospitality Inn, 3835 Redford, rooms and units with microwaves and fridges, pets welcome, also pub and restaurant, $85–145, 723-8111, 1-877-723-8111, www.hospitalityinnportalberni.com.

Howard Johnson, 4850 Beaver Creek Rd. 1 km/0.6 mi from Highway 4, rooms with TV, also pub and restaurant, pets welcome, planning to have pool and gym for 2010, $80–100, 724-2900, 1-800-446-4656, www.greenporthotel.com.

WHERE TO EAT

You will have no problem finding all the familiar fast food here, with most of the mainstream franchises. Port Alberni restaurants have such standardized offerings that it seems the menus are regulated! With few variations, most places offer a broad but pretty much identical selection of clam chowder, salads, burgers and seafood. The noteable exceptions to this standard "town fare" are Aroma and Little Bavaria. For a quick meal that includes a trip down memory lane (or perhaps pre-memory lane for some), there is even an authentic drive-in.

Locals' top choices are marked with ☉.

✪ **All Mex'd Up**, on Harbour Quay, 723-8226. A little taco shop with a lot of flavour: burritos, tacos, enchiladas and more—look out for fish tacos on weekends and the Saturday breakfast, $3-11, open daily 11-5 May to September and 9:30am on Saturdays.

✪ **Aroma**, 4624 Tenth Ave. (at Roger), 723-3331. A delightful new addition to the local restaurant scene, innovative cuisine by Chef Jamie Janzen with both European and Asian influences. Broad and interesting menu, mains $12-18, small space so reservations are recommended.

✪ **Batstar Bistro and Coffee Bar**, sadly, has closed.

✪ **Blue Door Cafe**, 5415 Argyle (Harbour Quay), 723-8811. Unique and friendly, open early, famous for its all-day hearty "fisherman's breakfasts," seafood sandwiches, homemade soups, freshcut fries, and "big logger burger." Breakfast $7–10, sandwiches and burgers $6–12. Open daily year-round, 6am–3:30pm.

Chances Rim Rock Gaming Centre, 4890 Cherry Creek Rd., 724-7625, www.chances.ca. Restaurant and brew pub with casino atmosphere at the gaming centre. Soups, variety of salads, and mains, lunch $9-14, dinner $10-24. Open daily year-round for lunch and dinner.

✪ **Clambucket Restaurant**, 4479 Victoria Quay, 723-1315. Views across Somass Estuary, standard fare plus seafood, including clams, shrimp, oysters, mussels and scallops, and fish and oyster burgers, as well as "bucket-size" cocktails. Takeout menu. Most mains $10–15. Open daily year-round for lunch and dinner.

Cod-Father Seafood Market, Harbour Quay, 723-7114. More of a fresh fish market, but often open over summer and occasionally in winter for fresh fish and chips, $8.

✪ **Cup & Saucer Eatery**. 4505 Victoria Quay, 723-9449. A lunch favourite with its simple home-style cooking, soup, salad, sandwiches. Breakfasts $4-9, lunch $5-10, open to 6pm daily.

Dolce Vita Bar & Grill, 4885 Southgate (at Gertrude), 724-5050. In addition to the standard "town menu" offers some Greek and Mexican items, stir-fries, pizza, and main dishes of seafood and steaks. Takeout and delivery. Salads, burgers and sandwiches $9-11, mains $12-26. Open daily year-round 11am to late.

✪ **Dugout Cafe**, at the Tyee Village Motel, 11th and Redford, 723, 1882. Standard hearty small-town diner meals, with Chef Larry claiming to make the best fish and chips in town, also burgers, pasta and Chinese food, famous for its breakfasts from $2-12, mains $9-14, open 7 to 7 daily year-round.

Eagles Nest (at Alberni Golf Club), 6449 Cherry Creek Rd., 723-7111. Salads, wraps, sandwiches, fish and chips, and daily specials, $7–12. Open for lunch year-round, and for dinner spring through fall.

✪ **Golden Dragon Restaurant**, 5027 Johnston Rd. (one block up from Victoria Quay), 723-8641 or 724-4032. Standard Chinese fare, à la carte and buffet, as well as "Canadian" food—steaks, fish and chips, roast turkey and pork chops. Mains $6–17. Takeout and free delivery. Open daily year-round 11am to late.

The Harvest Restaurant at Hospitality Inn, 3835 Redford St., 723-8111, 1-877-723-8111. Offers stir-fries, pasta, seafood and steak mains. Nightly dinner specials. Breakfast $10, dinner $10–20. Open daily year-round for breakfast, lunch and dinner.

J&L Drive-in, 4422 Gertrude (at Pemberton), 723-6331. Burgers, hot dogs, fish and chips, $3–$7. Open daily year-round for lunch and dinner.

○ **Little Bavaria**, 3035 Fourth Ave. (just east of Argyle), 724-4242. A refreshing change from the standard "town menu." Authentic German recipes; menu highlights include an interesting soup selection ($5-7), liver dumplings, cabbage rolls and schnitzels, $15–20. Open daily year-round for dinner, lunch weekdays only.

Mountain View Bakery & Deli & Espresso Bar, 4561 Gertrude, 724-1813. Sweets, baked goods, sandwiches, $4-6. Monday to Saturday 7:30-6, to 9pm in summer.

○ **Pescadores**, 5093 Johnston at Victoria Quay, 736-1100. Chef Bev Zarantello cooks up mains ranging from Mexican, to seafood and steak, to Asian rice and noodle bowls. Breakfast $8-12, lunch and dinner $13-24. Open Monday to Saturday year-round.

○ **Sehmi Japanese Restaurant**, 2404 Timberlane Rd. (at the Timberlodge on Highway 4), 723-9415, www.timberlodgerv.ca. Sushi, bento boxes, teriyaki , eat-in or take-out $5-30. Open daily year-round.

Solda's Family Restaurant, on Beaver Creek Road at River Road, 723-2474. A Port Alberni family-run tradition since 1969, burgers, wraps, pasta and pizza, light portion option available, mains $9-15. Open daily year-round for breakfast, lunch and dinner, also Sunday smorgasbord.

○ **Stamps Café** in the Best Western Barclay Hotel, 4277 Stamp Ave., 724-7171. Open early with a good-value hearty breakfast special. Sandwiches; chicken, salmon and halibut burgers; pasta; rice bowls; good variety of mains. Sandwiches and burgers $7–13, mains $10–17. Open daily year-round for breakfast, lunch and dinner.

Swale Rock Café, 5328 Argyle (Harbour Quay), 723-0777, www.swalerock.ca. Located in the historic Carmore Building across from the heritage Train Station, offers standard fare plus rice bowls, seafood specialties, curries, and deep-fried "fisherman's bread." Lunches $9-12, dinner mains $12-30, seafood platter for two $75. Open daily year-round for breakfast, lunch and dinner (closed Monday evenings in winter).

Turtle Island Fish and Chips, Harbour Quay, 723-4227 fish and chips and clam chowder, $9-14, open 11-7 daily April to October.

Venice Pizza, 4885 Southgate, 723-2611, pizza pick-up and deliveries, also will delivery any meals from Dolce Vita Restaurant next door. Open daily year-round.

○ **Water's Edge Pub & Bistro**, 5440 Argyle (Harbour Quay), 723-8862. Standard menu in pub atmosphere, weekly seafood specials. The big attraction here is the view, with the possibility of seeing porpoises and seals while you dine. Salads and wraps $8–10, pasta and mains $13–20, seafood platter for two $42. Buffet and Sunday brunch. Open daily year-round.

○ **Westwind Pub Bar & Grill**, 4940 Cherry Creek Rd. (east side of Johnston), 724-1324. A local favourite for its warm and casual atmosphere and good eats. Greek, Mexican, Indian and Thai variations, Asian stir-fries. Takeout menu. Burgers, sandwiches, salads and wraps $10-13, mains $12-17. Open daily year-round for lunch and dinner.

Around Port Alberni

The region surrounding Port Alberni, still for the most part off the beaten tourist track (beelining directly to the coast), deserves to be explored. To the north lies the rolling farmland of the Alberni Valley, to the south are the saltwaters of Alberni Inlet, and to the west are large freshwater bodies: Sproat Lake and Great Central Lake (see page 51).

THINGS TO DO
In the Alberni Valley

Wineries are well established on the southern part of Vancouver Island, but are new to the Pacific Rim. The Alberni Valley's sole winery, **Chase & Warren**, planted in 1996, released its first wines in 2003. It is located at Beaver Creek, 15 km/9.3 mi north of Port Alberni. Only a few of the grapes are actually grown in the region, although there are plans to expand the acreage under cultivation over the coming years. There is a $5 charge for tastings. Open afternoons, daily year-round. The winery is also a scheduled stop on the steam train that runs from Port Alberni over summer. For information contact 724-4909, www.chaseandwarren.ca.

Take a day-tour of the Alberni Valley with a local naturalist, visiting five waterfalls and a suspension bridge, or head to the high country to look for the endangered Vancouver Island marmot, with **Rainbird Excursions**, $116-132, 1-866-723-7102, www.rainbirdexcursions.com.

Ready to pick—Chase & Warren specializes in white wines.

Photo courtesy of Chase & Warren

There are no longer any companies offering bicycle rentals, but if you have bikes that you can bring with you to the valley, the paved country roads and the **Log Train Trail** can provide you with many days of exploration. Head up **Beaver Creek Road** and pay visits to the winery, the **McLean Mill**, and **Stamp Falls Provincial Park** along the way, or follow the shorelines of **Sproat Lake** by doing a circuit along **Faber Road, Stirling Arm Drive,** and **McCoy Lake Road**. You'd want mountain bikes rather than road bikes for the **Log Train Trail**, but the route is not technical. The forest is lovely, and you stand a good chance to see wildlife ranging from owls to bears, so travel quietly and keep your eyes peeled.

Around Alberni Inlet

Port Alberni was settled by boat, and even up to the end of the 1950s the only way to get to Ucluelet or Bamfield from here was by water or on foot. Today, the best way to really see the inlet—to take in the best views as well as to get a sense of the region's maritime heritage—is by boat. A number of companies based in Port Alberni offer day cruises up Alberni Inlet (page 64), the most notable of them being the **Lady Rose Marine Services** which has been serving tiny outposts up and down Alberni Inlet with the now-retired MV *Lady Rose*, and the 200-passenger MV *Frances Barkley*, since 1960.

If you insist on travelling by road, and if your car has decent clearance and suspension, you can explore up the inlet along the gravel logging roads. First, get your hands on the *Backroad Mapbook* so you can navigate the web of logging roads. Second, travel with caution: many of these rough and narrow roads are still active with heavy (speeding) logging trucks. Finally, make sure you are well equipped and self-contained; it is advisable to have more than just one spare tire with you, along with extra food supplies and water in case you unexpectedly have to stay out for a night.

You can follow the Bamfield road out of town to explore **China Creek** and the east side of the inlet, or turn off on McCoy Lake Rd., 3 km/1.9 mi west of town along Highway 4, to access **Stirling Arm Main Line** and the roads down the west side of the inlet, toward Arden Creek and Macktush Creek.

Around Sproat Lake

There are many places to stay around Sproat Lake, many of which are right on the waterfront; see below for a selection of campgrounds, cottages, B&Bs and even houseboats! If you have your own boat, you can launch it at **Sproat Lake Provincial Park**.

From the Provincial Park, look out to the water for the two **Martin Mars water bombers**. If they are not out working at putting out forest fires, these giant float planes may be anchored here over the summer months. When not in service, the *Philippine Mars* may be onshore and open for tours.

The *Hawaii Mars* has been recently upgraded, and is often on active duty fighting fires in various parts of the USA and in Canada. These planes are the largest water bombers in the world, and can scoop up to 27 tons of water in one swoop. They are taken off the water for the stormy season, but you may still see them in their hangars on shore at the bomber base, just west of the Provincial Park, from fall through spring. For info and schedules, 723-8100, www.martinmars.com.

Sproat Lake Provincial Park is one of a handful of sites on Vancouver Island where ancient **petroglyphs** are easily accessible. A short walk along the lakeshore from the parking lot takes you to these ancient stone pictures—images of killer whales and mythical sea monsters carved into stone centuries ago, long before the first Europeans set foot here.

The shoreline around the West Bay Hotel, 15 km/9.3 mi west of Port Alberni, is designated as a **bird sanctuary**. You can rent canoes here to explore the shoreline, from $15 for 3 hours, 723-2722, www.westbayhotel.ca. Experienced kayakers can rent kayaks from **Alberni Outpost** (singles $15-35 for 3 hrs or from $25/day; doubles $25-50 for 3 hrs or from $30/day), or inquire about custom guided day-trips, 723-2212, 1-800-325-3921, www.albernioutpost.com.

Around Great Central Lake

To watch and learn about salmon as they pass through the stages of their life cycle, visit the **Robertson Creek Hatchery**, 724-6521. Robertson Creek is a tributary to the Stamp River, draining from Great Central Lake. The hatchery project began with the construction of an artificial spawning channel in 1959, and the hatchery has been in operation since 1972. It releases eight million chinook and one million coho smolts and 180,000 steelhead smolts annually. (Baby salmon are "fry"; they are called "smolts" when they mature to the point of migrating from their freshwater hatching grounds to the sea.) It is open to the public year-round (gates are locked at 4pm), but the most interesting times to visit are in spring and fall. Through April and May you can witness the Spring Salmon Fry Rearing and Release, and from September through November you can see the returning salmon working their way up the creeks. There is an annual open house on the third Sunday in October. A forested walking trail leaves from here to Great Central Lake, about a 1½- to 2-hour return trip.

Feel like boating? The **Ark Resort**, 11000 Central Lake Rd., has a public boat launch (for a fee), moorage, and offers canoe rentals ($12/hr, $70/day). They also rent camping gear, if you feel inspired to hike up to **Della Falls**—a 2- to 4-day return trip from the west end of Great Central Lake. 723-2657, www.arkresort.com.

Provincial Parks

There are several provincial parks in the area, a number of them with campgrounds.

Englishman River Falls Provincial Park. Approximately 50 km/31 mi east of Port Alberni, this 97 ha (240 ac) park consists of both old-growth and second-growth forest of Douglas fir, cedar and bigleaf maple. Several short and easy hiking trails pass through the forest and follow the river, with spectacular views of two waterfalls and a canyon. There is a deep pool at the bottom of the lower falls which makes a good swimming spot in summer. You can also view spawning salmon here in the fall. Facilities include a large day-use area, open year-round, and a campground open April 15 to October 15.

Little Qualicum Falls Provincial Park. This large park (440 ha/1,087 ac) covers most of the southern shore of Cameron Lake, about 20 km/12.4 mi east of Port Alberni. Scenic views of the waterfalls on Little Qualicum River and mountain peaks across the lake make this one of the prettiest parks around. There are three day-use areas and one campground. There is no boat launch, but you can launch kayaks or canoes at the day-use areas. Aside from swimming and fishing, this long narrow lake is also a good windsurfing spot. The day-use areas are open year-round, and the campground open April 15 to October 15.

Sproat Lake Provincial Park. Located 13 km/8 mi west of Port Alberni, this small (43 ha/106 ac) park features a short trail along the edge of the lake that takes you to ancient petroglyphs. Walking along the water's edge you may also get views of the famous Martin Mars float planes. There is a boat launch in this park. Sproat Lake is a great place for fishing, waterskiing, canoeing, swimming and windsurfing. The two campgrounds and day-use area are open year-round, but with limited services during the off-season October 15 to March 22.

Stamp River Provincial Park. This large (327 ha/801.4 ac) park has hiking trails that meander through the rainforest and follow alongside the Stamp River. It is located 25 km/15.5 mi northwest of Port Alberni, on Beaver Creek Rd. This is a great place for watching the salmon spawn, which begins at the end of August with the arrival of the sockeye, and continues through the autumn and early winter with both coho and chinook. Fishing is sometimes restricted within the park, so check current regulations when you visit.

The campground and day-use area are open year-round, but with limited services during the off-season October 15 to April 15.

Taylor Arm Provincial Park. This 71 ha (175 ac) park is located on the highway 12 km/7.5 mi west of Port Alberni, on the northern shore of Sproat Lake. It is mainly a group camping facility. There are two day-use areas as well as beaches on the shores of the Lake. It is open for group camping from April 1 to October 15.

Fossli Provincial Park. This small, undeveloped park is located on the south side of Sproat Lake. Access is either by boat (you can launch motorboats or canoes at Sproat Lake Provincial Park), or by car along active logging roads and then walking in. For road access, turn south on McCoy Lake Rd. (approximately 6 km/3.7 mi west of Port Alberni along Highway 4); drive 3 km/1.9 mi then turn left on Sterling Arm Rd.; drive 0.9 km/0.6 mi then turn right on the Sterling Arm Mainline; drive 4 km/2.5 mi then park at the pullout just before the second bridge. A 30-minute walk along the old logging road leaving the parking area will take you to an old homestead and a pebbly beach on Sproat Lake. There is a picnic table and a pit toilet here; no camping.

MacMillan Provincial Park (Cathedral Grove). This beautiful little park (157 ha/388 ac), straddling the highway 16 km/10 mi east of Port Alberni, is a tiny fragment of original ancient and majestic Douglas fir old-growth forest surrounded by clearcuts. After losing the protection of the surrounding forest, a windstorm on New Year's Day in 1997 knocked down hundreds of the giant trees here. Even so, the many huge Douglas firs—some up to 800 years old and more than 9 m (29.5') in circumference—make this park my favourite stop on the drive across the island. There are walking trails that loop through the forest on both sides of the highway, and pit toilets; no camping.

Della Falls. Canada's highest waterfall, Della Falls, is located within **Strathcona Provincial Park** but cannot be easily reached from any of the park's main entrances. Official BC Parks info has it that the trail has

Lovely walking trails pass under majestic Douglas firs at Cathedral Grove, MacMillan Provincial Park.

WILDERNESS EXPEDITIONS

Most of Vancouver Island's west coast is true wilderness, and the very best way to get to know it is slowly, on foot or in a kayak. There are boundless possibilities for overnight adventures by land or by water, year-round. Experienced outdoorspeople will have no trouble seeking out their own adventures in this wild country.

Most of the Pacific Rim is extremely remote—out of cellphone range, and for the most part out of marine VHF radio range unless a boat happens to be passing by, and you happen to know what frequency they are monitoring. (Although boats are supposed to monitor emergency channel 16, the reality out here is that most of them don't.) If you are travelling without a guide, you absolutely *must* be sure that you have the appropriate experience and gear for the trip that you are undertaking. There are coast guard stations in the towns, but the possibility of contacting anyone for help from most remote areas is actually quite slim.

Responsible, local guides not only help to ensure that you have a safe trip, they also enrich your wilderness experience: they generally know the easiest and most convenient routes to travel, they often know when and where to expect to see wildlife, and they provide you with a deeper understanding of the area's natural history and culture. Please think carefully about your decision of whether to travel with or without a guide.

been closed for several years now due to bridges that are out—but experienced back-country hikers who are prepared to wade rivers and scramble over logs have been able to get through. This is not an easy trail, but it is passable to people experienced in self-sufficient wilderness travel. Access is by a hiking trail from the west end of Great Central Lake. The trail has snow on it for most of the year, and is generally passable only from late June through September; the waterfalls are less impressive in late summer, however. The trail from the lake to the base of the falls is 16 km/9.9 mi each way; from here another steep 5 km/3 mi hike takes you up to Love Lake and to spectacular scenic views of the falls. Minimum recommended time to do this hike is three days, two nights. The trailhead is accessible only by boat. If you are making your own way there, head to the west end of the lake and look out for a dock on the south side, just before the dead trees. Or, hire transport: the **Ark Resort** takes full advantage of its monopoly on motorized lake transport by charging $130 per person for return transport to the trailhead (regardless of group size, but minimum of two); they also offer canoe rentals for trail access (as well as camping equipment rentals), see page 81. To do this trip in a completely supported fashion with an experienced guide, as well as all transport, meals, accommodation and even hiking gear taken care of, $1150 per person, contact **Batstar Adventure Tours** in Port Alberni, 724-2098, 1-877-449-1230, www.batstar.com.

WHERE TO STAY
Campgrounds

Aside from the provincial park campgrounds listed above, there are a number of private campgrounds in the area. There are also Recreation Sites where camping is permitted, but with few or no facilities, accessible via the logging roads that head out of Port Alberni: along the south side of Sproat Lake, and along the west side of the inlet and around Nahmint Lake. You need both a solid vehicle and a good map to access these sites; look up the *Backroad Mapbook* for more information.

Ark Resort, 11000 Central Lake Rd. 14 km/8.7 mi west of Port Alberni along Highway 4 on Great Central Lake, full hookup RV sites $37, tent sites $25, free showers, coin laundromat, canoe and motorboat rentals, and access by boat from here to Della Falls trailhead (see Strathcona Provincial Park, above), 723-2657, www.arkresort.com.

Arrowvale Campground & Cottages, 5955 Hector Rd. 6 km/3.7 mi west of Port Alberni, grassy campsites on a working farm by the Somass River, flush toilets, laundromat and free showers, access to 2 km/1.2 mi of hiking trails along the river, summer fishing and swimming, RV sites with partial hookup $29, tent sites $22-25, open year-round, 723-7948, www.arrowvale.ca.

China Creek Park Marina, China Creek Rd. 15 km/9.3 mi south of Port Alberni, tent and RV sites, flush toilets, showers, marina and coffee shop, open May to October, 723-9812.

Lakeshore Campgrounds and Cottages, 9752 Lakeshore on Sproat Lake, full RV hookup, flush toilets, showers, boat, kayak, canoe and pedal boat rentals, boat launch and moorage, pets on approval, open year-round, tent sites $32, RV sites $45-49, cottages for four $150, 723-2030, www.lakeshorecampgroundandcottage.com.

Bed and breakfasts

Cedar Hill B&B, 8320 Faber Rd., adult-oriented with views of Sproat Lake, $100, open year-round, 724-6777, www.cedarhillbb.com.

Lakewoods B&B, 9778 Stirling Arm Cres., on the beach at Sproat Lake, adult-oriented, private baths, $75–90, open year-round, 723-2310, www.bbexpo.com/bc/lakewoods.htm.

Riverside Lodge B&B, 6150 Ferguson Rd. on the Stamp River, log home with fireplace, private bath and deck, $140 with full breakfast, open year-round, 723-3474, www.stampriverlodge.com.

The Roses B&B, 5570 Kitsuksis St., country setting with hot tub and fireplace, rooms with shared bath $70, suite with private bath $80, open year-round, 723-3507, www.therosesbb.com.

The Sheridan–Sproat Lake, 8945 Faber Rd. on the beach at Sproat Lake, patios and hot tub, private baths, full breakfast, $90–110, open year-round, 723-1617, www.thesheridan.ca.

The Stirling Fern Bed and Breakfast, 10189 Stirling Arm Cres., private forested setting, spacious rooms with private bath, $100–110, open year-round, 724-5846, www.thestirlingfernbedandbreakfast.com.

Water's Edge B&B, 9606 Stirling Arm Cres. on Sproat Lake, private beach and dock, open year-round, $70, 724-5354, www.alberni.net/watersedge.

Cabins and cottages

Arrowvale Campground & Cottages, 5955 Hector Rd. 6 km/3.7 mi west of Port Alberni, grassy campsites on a working farm by the Somass River, flush toilets, laundromat and free showers, access to 2 km/1.2 mi of hiking trails along the river, summer fishing and swimming, cottages sleep 4 $120–150, open year-round, 723-7948, www.arrowvale.ca.

Bear Wattsh Inn, 5201 Hecter Rd.. barely out of town but it feels like the wilderness. Two cabins run by the Watts family on the Tseshaht River on the banks of the Somass River, a great wildlife viewing spot for birds, and, in late summer and fall, for spawning salmon and bears. From $100/night, 724-2603, 731-5795, www.bearwattshinn.com.

Stirling Shores Vacation Rentals, 9094 Stirling Arm Dr. on Sproat Lake, 2-br house with sundeck sleeps 4, $300; private adjoining suite with patio, kitchen, sleeps up to 4, $100; dock for swimming accessible to both units, 724-2092, www.stirlingshores.com.

Hotels

West Bay Hotel Resort, 10695 Lakeshore Rd. 15 km/9.3 mi west of Port Alberni on Sproat Lake, rooms with lake or mountain view, also restaurant, bar and convenience store, liquor store, canoe rentals, moorage available, $50–100, 723-2722, www.westbayhotel.ca.

Houseboats

You can rent houseboats on Sproat Lake, but they are generally booked well ahead of time. The houseboats are like trailers set upon pontoons, up to 60' long and sleeping up to 14 people. Some even have hot tubs or fireplaces. You can cruise around the lake by day, then nose them up to a beach for the night. No previous boating experience is necessary; the operators will spend an hour or two instructing you on use before you set out. Season is April to October. **Fish and Duck Houseboats** has 8 houseboats of varying sizes, rates start at $250/night or $1500/week, 724-4462, 1-877-364-3280, www.fishandduckhouseboats.com.

Remote lodges

Eagle Nook Ocean Wilderness Lodge, located on Vernon Bay 10 km/6.2 mi north of Bamfield, accessible only by float plane or boat. A four-star remote lodge with regular water taxi service from Ucluelet. Charter water taxi service from Bamfield and Port Alberni is also available, and direct float plane service can be organized from nearly any base, including Seattle. All rates include meals of fine West Coast cuisine. Accommodation/meal package prices vary with season and length of stay, but start at $500/night, with fly-in packages also available. Open mid-May to late September. 728-2370 (when open) or 1-800-760-2777 year-round, www.eaglenook.com.

Murphy's Riverside Lodge on the Stamp River, rooms with private entrance and bath and goosedown quilts, in a solid wooden lodge with a huge stone fireplace, 10 km/6.2 mi by road from Port Alberni, a fishermen's favourite, $120–140, open year-round. 1-877-218-6600, www.murphysportfishing.com.

Rendezvous Dive Adventures offers overnight tour packages to a secluded private wilderness lodge in Rainy Bay, Barkley Sound, kayaks on site and dive instruction available, all-inclusive packages $153 per person, group rates also available. 735-5050, 1-877-777-9994, www.rendezvousdiving.com.

Rosy's Lodge on Logs, at the Ark Resort on Great Central Lake, 11000 Central Lake Rd. 14 km/8.7 mi west of Port Alberni. Canoe rentals, fishing and swimming in the lake and Stamp River, 2-hour (return) hike to Robertson Fish hatchery. Access by boat to Della Falls trailhead (see Strathcona Provincial Park, page 83). Accommodates groups of up to 9 people, $65 each per night includes breakfast. Dinner and packed lunches also available. 723-2657, www.arkresort.com.

Sechart Whaling Station Lodge, 5425 Argyle, 723-8313, the site of an old whaling station in operation from 1905 to 1917 and a great base from which to explore the Broken Group by kayak, accessible from Port Alberni via Lady Rose Marine Services, $215-225 double including meals, open year-round, 723-8313, 1-800-663-7192 (toll-free line April through September only), www.ladyrosemarine.com.

WHERE TO EAT

Fish and Duck Pub 8551 Bothwell Rd. (just off Faber), pub-style lunch and dinner, open daily year-round, 724-4331, 1-866-364-3280.

West Bay Hotel Resort, 10695 Lakeshore Rd. 15 km/9.3 mi west of Port Alberni on Sproat Lake, has a restaurant with casual fare such as burgers and wraps, $5–12 and "home-made" mains $9-14, 723-2722, www.westbayhotel.ca.

Bamfield and Nitinat

Bamfield

Bamfield and neighbouring Anacla (Pachena Bay) are the bases for many wilderness activities on land and especially out on the water. Bamfield is perhaps best known as the northern trailhead of the world-renowned West Coast Trail, a rugged 75 km/46.6 mi hike south to Port Renfrew. Thousands of experienced hikers make this trek every year.

Bamfield, population around 250, is an incredibly unique village. It has no police, no bylaws, and no mayor. The Chamber of Commerce is run by local volunteers. A few years ago, when deciding on a slogan to promote tourism

UNIQUELY BAMFIELD: WHAT TO DO
- Stroll along the boardwalk in West Bamfield.
- Visit the Bamfield Marine Sciences Centre to explore the local marine biology.
- Spend a week hiking the length of the rugged, 75 km (46.6 mi) West Coast Trail—or just do the first 10 km (6.2 mi).
- Hike out to historic Cape Beale Lighthouse.
- Fish for salmon, halibut and cod in the inshore waters of Barkley Sound.
- Experience international high-calibre live classical musical performances in a scallop-shell auditorium overlooking the ocean at Music by the Sea.
- Get out on the water and try out a windsurfer, kite board or stand-up paddleboard on Nitinat Lake.

THREE MAGIC MOMENTS:
1. Brady's Beach at sunset.
2. Pachena Lighthouse on a windy afternoon.
3. Paddling the Nitinat River with bears and spawning salmon.

in their town, residents nearly chose "Bamfield is not for everyone." Although in the end "Superb, spectacular" was selected, Bamfield definitely is not for everyone. It's quiet and slow, and there is not much to do. Tourists have complained there are not enough places here to spend their money. Business hours may be irregular. Snack bars, galleries and B&Bs may shut down for weeks or months at a time. It pays to call in advance—especially over winter.

The village is divided into two parts: East Bamfield is the part that you drive in to, and has service-oriented businesses like the marina, accommodation, a pub and café, and a grocery store. The old original town is on the west side of the inlet, on the Mills Peninsula, with a waterfront boardwalk that links all of the homes and docks. Here in West Bamfield are galleries, lodges and B&Bs, a café and a grocery store, and the post office.

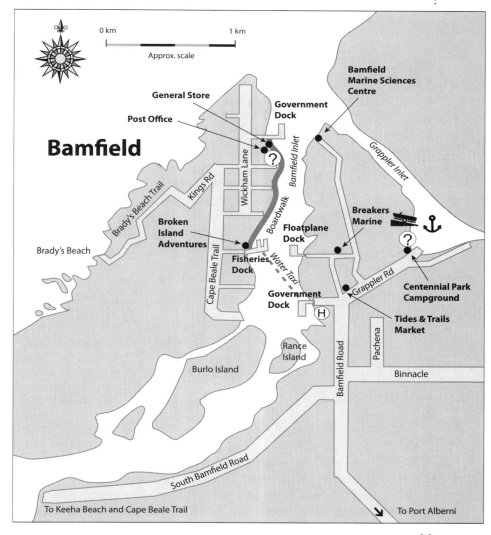

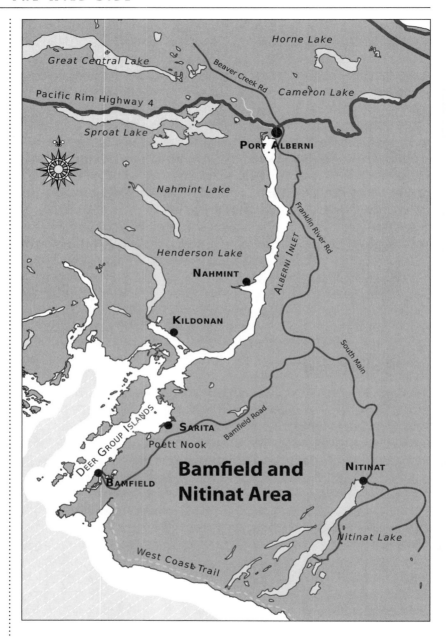

The narrow isthmus of the Mills Peninsula was the site of a significant Native village called Keeshan. The traditional territory of the Huu-ay-aht extends eastward from here, along the southeastern shores of Barkley Sound and southward along the coast toward Nitinat Lake. Today, Huu-ay-aht's main village is Anacla, commonly called Pachena Bay, located about 4 km out of Bamfield near the West Coast Trailhead. Anacla has no visitor facilities, although people are welcome to pop in. Since Bamfield's gas station closed, it is the only place to buy car fuel in the area.

The village of Bamfield got its start as a fur trading post. Fur trader W.E. Banfield had been working and trading along Vancouver Island's west coast, north of the newly founded settlement of Victoria, for years. Around 1860 he established a trading post at the present site of Bamfield, but he died under mysterious circumstances only a few years later. Early accounts were that he had drowned while out in his canoe, but later versions indicated that he had been killed by a Huu-ay-aht man on shore. A Native man was taken to Victoria for trial, but was acquitted for lack of evidence. Banfield's trading post survived, though, and misspellings of his name repeated over the years give the town its present name.

GETTING HERE AND AROUND

You can get to Bamfield by car from Port Alberni (80 km/49.7 mi of gravel logging roads, about 1½ to 2 hours) or directly from Victoria on the backroads (180 km/111.8 mi, half on gravel logging roads, about 4 hours). See page 54 for driving information. For current updates on road conditions, contact the Bamfield Road Safety Association, 731-3223, www.brsa.ca/recent-road-conditions.

Over summer, you can also get to Bamfield by **bus**. The **West Coast Trail Express** runs May through September serving Victoria, Nanaimo, Port Alberni, Nitinat, Port Renfrew, Bamfield and Pachena Bay. 477-8700, 1-888-999-2288, www.trailbus.com. The **Pachena Bay Express** operates a taxi-like charter bus service May to October out of Bamfield, 728-1290, 1-877-728-1290, http://pachenabayexpress.pachena.ca.

You can also get to Bamfield from Port Alberni and, with more difficulty from Ucuelet, by **boat**. **Lady Rose Marine Services** makes daily runs from Port Alberni ($34 one-way, 723-8313 year-round, or 1-800-663-7192 April through September, www.ladyrosemarine.com). **Seaway Express** offered daily scheduled water taxi service between Ucluelet and Bamfield in 2008, and claim that they will resume that service at some point; visit their website for updates, www.barkleysoundmarine.com. **Broken Island Adventures,** based in Bamfield, is available for custom charters for groups, and may be of help in arranging creative boat transport for adventurous individuals (hooking up on the water with other boat transport running between Ucluelet and the Broken Group), 728-3500, 1-888-728-6200, www.brokenislandadventures.com. Other water taxis that will service Bamfield are based out of Ucluelet (page 113). The **Juan de Fuca Express** runs nearly daily boat service between Port Renfrew and Bamfield—the two ends of the West Coast Trail—from May through October, $125 one-way, advance reservations necessary, 1-888-755-6578, 1-877-332-5333, http://members.shaw.ca/berry5868/juanfuca.htm.

FRESH SEAFOOD
There is no seafood market here, but ask around when you get to town. There may be commercial fishermen at the docks with fresh fish or shellfish.

There is no float plane based in Bamfield, but you can book one from elsewhere to take you in. For groups, this often works out to a very economical as well as time-efficient option. Try **West Coast Wild Adventures** in Ucluelet (726-7715) or **Harbour Air** from Vancouver (604-274-1277 or 1-800-665-0212).

Bamfield is a small village, and for the most part you can get around town on foot, but to travel from West to East Bamfield you must get a **water taxi**. There is a phone to call for service located at the government dock, (**Pirate Water Taxi**, 728-1212). For taxi-like road service, you can charter the **Pachena Bay Express**, listed above, 728-1290.

SERVICES

Although you can find basic supplies here, you should count on arriving well equipped with most of what you need; the nearest centre with any range of supplies is Port Alberni. There is no real year-round restaurant in Bamfield, but if you plan in advance you can usually arrange for a fine meal at one of the lodges.

Tourism information is available at the Centennial Park Campground office, open daily over summer and closed for the rest of the year, 728-3006 (not answered over winter) or check out www.bamfieldchamber.com.

There is no bank here, but there is an **ATM machine** at the **Tides & Trails Market**—its cash supply is not consistent, so don't count on withdrawing large amounts. (Both grocery stores take debit cards and can usually give you cash back with a purchase, and credit cards are accepted most everywhere around town.) The **post office** is in West Bamfield, 728-3400.

For **gas**, you must drive to the village of Anacla (Pachena Bay), about 4 km out of Bamfield—available at the Pachena Bay Campground over summer, and when the campground is closed through the Huu-ay-aht Band Office, Monday to Friday 8:30-4, 728-3414. (Gas is also available at **Poett Nook Marina**, 20 km out of Bamfield). Boaters can fuel up at the McKay Bay Lodge in West Bamfield. There is a **laundromat** at the **Bamfield Trails Motel**.

There are two **grocery stores**, both of which are also licensed **liquor outlets**. In West Bamfield, the **Bamfield General Store** has groceries (including a reasonable selection of fresh produce), snacks and ice cream, and is open daily year-round, 728-3351. In East Bamfield, the **Tides & Trails Market** has groceries and snacks, and is open daily year-round with a café open May to October, 728-2000.

Breakers Marine, East Bamfield, stocks a range of **camping supplies** and **fishing tackle**, and also services and repairs cars and outboard motors and sells propane. Open daily year-round except Sundays and Mondays over winter, 728-3281, www.breakersmarine.com. Outside of Bamfield, the **Poett Nook Marina and Campground** about 70 km/43.5 mi south of Port Alberni, 20 km/12.4 mi north of Bamfield by road also has a store and sells **oil and gas**, **tackle**, **bait** and **ice and some groceries**. Marina 720-9572, office 758-4440, www.poettnook.com.

There is wireless internet coverage throughout Bamfield village (password required, check with your accommodation provider), but the service is a bit patchy, and at times slow and unreliable. Don't count on seamless connectivity. You may also be able to get access through the Bamfield Community School.

THINGS TO DO

Bamfield is a pretty little town to stroll around—especially on the boardwalk that runs along the waterfront, past the historic old houses and the docks in the old part of town, West Bamfield. You can visit the galleries along here, and stop in at **The Bistro** in the **Bamfield Lodge** for a cappuccino. Remember that many Bamfield businesses are one-person operations, and hours may be erratic.

There is not much to do here in the way of bopping entertainment, but the locals almost always have a few things going on. Take the time to chat with them (they're pretty friendly) to get yourself into the loop about potluck dinners, dances or visiting speakers. Look for listings of upcoming Community Events on www.bamfieldchamber.org.

For a spectacular and memorable evening, grab a picnic dinner and stroll down to **Brady's Beach** to watch the sunset. This beach is an easy 20- to 30-minute walk from town, along the gravel trail signposted from the boardwalk.

Be sure you make time for the **Bamfield Marine Sciences Centre**, a research facility that includes laboratories, aquaria and a scientific library. They provide custom educational programs for schools, colleges and adult learning programs. Tours for the public also run daily in July and August, weekdays 3pm and weekends 11am. Interested groups can also visit by appointment, 728-3301, www.bms.bc.ca.

The Bamfield Marine Sciences Centre is a research facility that also provides educational programs for the public.

Annual festivals

Music by the Sea is a week-long festival taking place in July, featuring live classical music performed by internationally renowned musicians in the Bamfield Marine Station's scallop-shell theatre overlooking Barkley Sound. Contact 888-7772, www.musicbythesea.ca.

The **Mushroom Festival** is held on a weekend in early October. Festival events include guided interpretive forest walks, a monster mushroom derby, and a forest feast supper followed by the Toadstool Stomp dance, 728-3132, www.mushroomfestival.ca.

The Sproat Lake Loggers **Winter-Spring Fishing Derby** has been taking place annually for over two decades now. Hundreds of fishers congregate at Poett Nook for a weekend of fishing in early March, all moorage and camping free for the weekend, 720-9572, www.poettnook.com.

Some "annual" events are not actualy held every year; look for current info about Community Events on www.bamfieldchamber.com.

Nightlife

Hawk's Nest Marine Pub at the Bamfield Trails Hotel (main intersection entering Bamfield) features a fully stocked bar and pool tables. 728-3231 or 728-3228, www.hawkeyemarinegroup.com.

Beach walks and day hikes

Brady's Beach is easily accessible from town, a 15- to 20-minute walk from the boardwalk in West Bamfield. This is a top spot for a romantic sunset picnic dinner in summer, or for storm-watching in winter. When the tide is low, you can work your way westward along the beach for up to an hour, exploring tide pools and rock formations, including a blowhole. Just make sure that you head out on a falling tide, so that you don't get trapped by the rising water.

From East Bamfield you can hike out to **Tapaltos Beach**, **Cape Beale Lighthouse** or **Keeha Beach**. These trails are all rough hiking routes, suited to experienced hikers. Access is from South Bamfield Rd., just south of town, and there is a parking area 400 m/1,300' before the trailhead at the end of the road. About 1.5 km/0.9 mi along the trail you will come to a junction: turn right for Tapaltos Beach and Cape Beale, and left for Keeha Bay.

From the junction it is another 2 km/1.2 mi to **Tapaltos Beach**, a lovely crescent-shaped sand beach with views toward the **Deer Group** islands. From here it is another rough 3 km/1.9 mi, passing in part through muddy bog to get to the lighthouse. **Cape Beale** is on a tidal island—you cannot cross the sand flats at high tide, so check the tide tables. The return trip to Tapaltos Beach is 7 km/4.4 mi (allow 4 hours, or more if you are going to stay at the beach a while), and to Cape Beale is 12 km/7.5 mi (allow 8 hours). The trail to **Keeha Bay** takes you to a large curved south-facing beach exposed to big Pacific swell. From the Tapaltos junction, this trail continues another 2 km/1.2 mi, crossing a floating bridge and climbing up a steep hill before descending to the beach. This route is 7 km/4.4 mi round trip (allow 4 hours, plus any time you spend at the beach).

You can also hike the first 10 km/6.2 mi of the **West Coast Trail** to **Pachena Point lighthouse**. The lighthouse keepers are usually happy to have visitors (although the keeper who used to make fudge for backpackers is no longer there). Since this trip is 20 km/12.4 mi return, make sure that you are physically prepared and have appropriate equipment. You do not need a National Parks permit.

There are many other interesting and unique walks and hikes to do in Bamfield, along routes that are not marked and sometimes cross private land. Some locals do casual guiding work; inquire around town, and you may find someone who will take you exploring.

Overnight hikes

The **West Coast Trail** unit is the largest unit in Pacific Rim National Park Reserve (page 41). The West Coast Trail is a 75 km/46.6 mi hiking route following the rugged outer coast, originally constructed in 1890 as a rescue route for shipwrecked sailors. Extending from Bamfield to Port Renfrew, this remote wilderness trail is only for fit and experienced hikers. Although some have been known to hike it quickly (or even run it), it is best to allow between five and eight days to complete the route.

The terrain is both rugged and remote, and the route includes about 70 ladders, 130 bridges, 4 cable cars and 2 boat crossings—not so easy when carrying a heavy pack! There are as many as 100 emergency evacuations on this trail each season (a large number of which are related to untreated blisters!). It is important that groups have appropriate equipment, clothing and footwear, and first-aid kits—and know how to use them all. An unofficial, privately run website, www.i-needtoknow.com/wct/, provides a wealth of information including detailed route information and maps, campsites and recommended gear to take.

The trail is open for hiking from May 1 to September 30. Through the peak season (June 15 to September 15) there is a daily quota for hikers setting

---

STORM-WATCHING

Be extremely cautious when approaching the shoreline. Storm waves can easily wash you off the rocks and into the ocean. When the swell is big, watch the rocks for at least 15 minutes, so you can start to understand the wave patterns before you decide whether it is safe to venture out on them. Watch waves carefully before you venture out on to the rocks, and do not turn your back on the sea.

out, although a few spaces are made available each day to people who just show up. Reservations are recommended during the peak season, though the trail is actually not as busy as it used to be. Reservations are not accepted outside of the peak season; hikers just need to show in time for the midday orientation on the day they intend to head out. Fees to hike the trail are $127.50 per person plus a $25 reservation fee, as well the two ferry boat fees for Nitinat and Gordon River at about $15 each. For trail reservations call 387-1642, 1-800-435-5622 (or from Vancouver 604-435-5622).

You can also hike just the first section of the trail as a return trip, from Bamfield/Pachena Bay to Nitinat Narrows and back. This avoids having to deal with car shuttles and organizing boat transport over the narrows, but it is a long and strenuous 64 km/39.7 mi round trip; allow at least three to four days.

Access to the trailheads in Bamfield and Port Renfrew is by car, by daily bus or by boat. You can take public transport both ways, or you can leave your car at one end of the trail, then travel back to your car by bus or by boat.

The **West Coast Trail Express** serves both trailheads from May through September, as well as Victoria, Nanaimo, Nitinat and Port Alberni, 477-8700 or 1-888-999-2288 or www.trailbus.com. The **Pachena Bay Express** operates a charter bus service May to October out of Bamfield, with service on request to anywhere on Vancouver Island, including transporting hikers the 7 km/4.4 mi from Bamfield town to the West Coast Trail trailhead. Contact 728-1290, 1-877-728-1290, http://pachenabayexpress.pachena.ca.

The **Juan de Fuca Express** runs nearly daily (dependent both upon bookings and weather) boat service between Port Renfrew and Bamfield from May through October. This is an absolutely great way to overview the whole route and a higly recommended trip; it is strongly recommended to take the transport first and then hike back towards your car in order to avoid any uncertainties in pick-up caused by weather. $125 one-way, advance reservations necessary, 1-888-755-6578, 1-877-332-5333, http://members.shaw.ca/berry5868/juanfuca.htm.

Storm-watching

Brady's Beach, only a short walk from town, is a great storm-watching spot, with views across the entrance of Barkley Sound and out to sea. Any of the other beach or lighthouse hikes listed above will also get you to spectacular places to see giant rollers coming in from the open ocean, but they may be hard to get to in storm conditions. If you are into toughing it out, the view can be worth the challenge—just wear lots of rubber.

Kayaking

Bamfield is a great place to start your explorations of **Barkley Sound**. All of the waters are exposed to changing wind and currents, and many areas

THE DEER GROUP (BARKLEY SOUND)

This group of large islands, in the eastern part of Barkley Sound near Bamfield, is famous for the abundance of arches and sea caves and for its beautiful shell beaches. Since it is outside of the National Park, it is a little quieter and less crowded than the nearby Broken Group. The islands are strung out more or less in a line, so the Deer Group is also less protected from weather and swell than the Broken Group—therefore not the best choice for beginner paddlers. The line of islands extends about 20 km/12.4 mi from northeast to southeast, so there is plenty of scope for exploration on trips ranging from a few days to a week in length.

The nearest land access to the Deer Group is from Bamfield. You can get to Bamfield by rough logging roads from Port Alberni, or make the trip a bit easier by loading your kayaks and gear on to the MV *Frances Barkley* in Port Alberni, and travelling to Bamfield via Alberni Inlet. Paddlers experienced in navigating in tidal currents and through fog can make the 3 km/1.9 mi crossing from Bamfield to the Deer Group in under an hour in calm conditions, but this stretch of open water can also be rough and unnavigable at times. There is also a water taxi in Bamfield that can transport paddlers and kayaks over to the islands (below). You can also arrange water taxi transport for paddlers and kayaks from Ucluelet (page 105), though it is a much longer boat trip. For guided trips of the Deer Group, contact **Majestic Ocean Kayaking** in Ucluelet (page 123), **Batstar Adventures** in Port Alberni (page 68) or **Barkley Sound Kayak Centre** (page 98).

are also exposed to large ocean swell. A few routes are suitable for beginning paddlers when conditions are calm.

You can launch kayaks right in Bamfield, and head out on a day trip to explore the harbour and the adjacent shorelines in **Bamfield Inlet** and **Grappler Inlet**. Even close to town, you will have a good chance of seeing wildlife such as deer, raccoons and birds.

Farther up the inlet, 20 km/12.4 mi along the road back toward Port Alberni, the sheltered waters of **Numukamis Bay** are a great choice for paddlers of all experience levels. But even this protected bay can get rough in any wind direction, especially on a southwesterly. The bay is accessible from **Poett Nook Recreational Site** (see page 102) with a small kayak launching fee charged.

More advanced paddlers may cross over to the **Deer Group**, but check the weather forecast first. You can also head southwest toward the open ocean, depending upon wind and wave conditions, but avoid going past Cape Beale, where big ocean swell, turbulence, strong currents and thick kelp beds make these waters dangerous.

The nearest islands of the Deer Group are only a short 3 km/1.9 mi crossing from Bamfield—in most conditions this should take you less than an hour. From the Deer Group, it is a minimum 10 km/6.2 mi crossing through extremely exposed waters to the nearest parts of the Broken Group. This crossing is not recommended to kayakers. The MV *Frances Barkley* will transport paddlers and kayaks on her scheduled runs through Port Alberni, Bamfield, Ucluelet and the Broken Group, and there are also water taxis from both Bamfield and Ucluelet that will transport paddlers with their kayaks to the Broken Group. For information about the Deer Group and the Broken Group islands, please see pages 97 and 122.

The rest of Barkley Sound is not beginner kayak country. If you are not well versed in rough-water skills, navigation in fog and currents, and kayak rescues, please travel with a guide.

KAYAKERS!

Always check weather forecasts and tide tables before heading out, because conditions can change on you quickly. If possible, chat with the townsfolk for that invaluable "local knowledge" about your intended route. Remember, even in seemingly protected inlets wind and water conditions can change rapidly. The cold water here is unforgiving. If you have not practised kayak rescues in the kinds of conditions that you might encounter, paddle with a trained guide. See "Kayaking on the ocean," page 68.

Barkley Sound Kayak Centre operates a summer base for kayak rentals from the Deer Group as well as offers multi-day guided trips to the Deer Group ($675 for 6 days). They can arrange water taxi transport to other locations for renters as well. Rentals: single $45, doubles $55, 403-678-4102, 403-678-8108, www.barkleykayakcentre.com. **Broken Island Adventures** rents kayaks, and can transport you and your boats out to the Broken Group or the Deer Group in their water taxi. They do not rent boats to kayakers who intend to paddle from Bamfield to the Broken Group, but do rent to groups with sufficient experience to make the shorter crossing to the Deer Group. They also rent extra gear including charts, tents, first-aid kits and dry bags. Single kayaks $45/day, doubles $65, half-day rentals also available. 728-3500, 1-888-728-6200, www.brokenislandadventures.com.

Lady Rose Marine Services, with their boat that services Bamfield from Port Alberni several times a week, also rents kayaks and canoes that you can collect in Bamfield or the Broken Group. Singles $45, doubles $60, 723-8313 year-round, or 1-800-663-7192 April through September, www.ladyrosemarine.com. **McKay Bay Lodge** has kayaks for rent for inlet use only, free for their guests and $40/day for others, 728-3323, www.bamfield-travel.com.

Whale-watching and other wildlife-viewing boat tours

Many outfits in Bamfield offer combined wildlife viewing and scenic cruises. Depending upon when and where you go, you may see **grey whales**, **humpbacks**, **orcas**, **seals**, **sea lions**, **sea otters**, **eagles**, **bears**, **wolves**, **deer** and any number of **seabirds**.

Broken Island Adventures offers 3-hour whale-watching and wildlife viewing tours in their 27' covered and heated cruiser or their 33' Viking sailboat. The route is customized according to what you want to see, $75-95, tours run year-round, 728-3500, 1-888-728-6200, www.brokenislandadventures. com. **McKay Bay Lodge** offers a "marine safari," a 2½- to 3-hour whale-watching and scenic trip for up to 6 people, $250, May through September only, 728-3323, www.bamfield-travel.com.

Mills Landing Cottages and Charters offers 2-hour whale-watching tours and Broken Group tours, $75–100. 728-2300, 1-877-728-2301, www. millslanding.com. **Sea Otter Charters** offers custom "adventure tours" in their 30' cruiser Coastal Rover, which include wildlife viewing, scenic tours of the Broken Group islands and kayaking from the boat and fishing tours, 728-3419, www.bamfieldlodge.com.

Spotted sandpipers are seasonal visitors to the Pacific Rim.

Birdwatching

Bamfield is a great spot for watching shorebirds and seabirds. You may see **bald eagles**, **blue herons**, **kingfishers**, **cormorants**, **crows**, **ravens**, **gulls**, **loons** and a variety of **ducks** right from the boardwalk in town. **Brady's Beach** is also worth checking out during the spring shorebird migration, in late April and early May, for the varieties of sandpipers that may stop here to feed before continuing northward. Getting out on the water on a scenic boat tour, you are likely to see a range of seabirds, including **common murres**, **rhinocerous auklets**, **murrelets**, and **diving ducks** and **loons**.

Sport fishing and recreational boating

Fishing here is mainly for **chinook salmon** and **halibut**. The best fishing in Bamfield runs from February to October, both offshore and within the more protected waters of Barkley Sound. In February, small chinook move in, following the spawning herring.

Larger migratory chinook start showing up in June, and fish weighing 66 kg/30 lbs or more are regularly caught over summer. **Sockeye** also appear in the early summer, on their way up Alberni Inlet toward their spawning streams, and coho can be caught throughout the summer and fall.

You can buy **tackle, bait** and **ice** at the Bamfield General Store, Breakers Marine, Island Fish Camp, and at the Poett Nook Marina, 20 km/12.4 mi back toward Port Alberni from Bamfield. Breakers Marine (728-3281) has **licences**.

There are many **fishing charter operators** out of Bamfield, many of whom provide all-inclusive packages including accommodation, meals and freezers. You can rent **fishing boats** from **Mills Landing Cottages and Charters**, 728-2300, 1-877-728-2301, www.millslanding.com or **Seabeam Charters** (728-3286, www.seabeamcanada.ca) and from **Harbourside Lodge** (728-3330, guests only).

Fishing charters and lodges

Fishing charters and accommodation are usually packaged together. Contact the operators listed below for fishing charters, accommodation, or combination deals.

Bamfield Lodge and Cottages & Sea Otter Charters, cottages $100 double, 2-br house for up to 5 people $230 (bedding extra), kitchens, BBQ and freezers, moorage available, fishing charter packages including accommodation $350/day or $450/day including meals, 728-3419, www.bamfieldlodge.com.

Harbourside Lodge has rooms and bunkhouses $40–65, suites $160, recreational rooms, boat rentals for guests $300/d, fishing charters $100/hr plus fuel surcharge, open June to mid-September, 728-3330, www.harboursidelodge.com.

Imperial Eagle Lodge & Charters, West Bamfield, room and breakfast $66-102, 2-br cottage for up to 4 people $160–230 including boat moorage. In-house restaurant with harbour view, gourmet picnic lunches and dinners to go with advance booking $12–25. 23' charter boats, day charters $125/hr. Fishing charter/accommodation packages start at $526 per person per day. Open year-round except December 15 to January 3, 728-3430, www.imperialeaglelodge.com.

McKay Bay Lodge, West Bamfield, rooms and suites $125 per person, communal kitchen, hot tub, restaurant with fresh local seafood and fresh herbs and greens from their own garden. Custom fishing charters in 27' boat can be arranged for guests. Open daily May through September, then every other week (Tuesday to Tuesday) for the off-season, 728-3323, www.bamfield-travel.com.

Mills Landing Cottages & Charters, at government dock, 1br ($120-190/night) and 2-br cottages ($150–230/night) overlooking water with kitchenettes and gas BBQs, moorage available, inshore charters $400, full-day offshore $850, half- and full-day boat rentals and fishing gear also available, open year-round, 728-2300, 1-877-728-2301, www.millslanding.com.

Rocky Point Charters Waterfront Lodge, on Grappler Inlet, 3-br suite sleeps up to 9 from $150/day, accommodation and fishing open year-round, half-day charters start st $550, 728-3678, www.rockypointcharters.ca.

Seabeam Fishing Resort/Bamfield Fishing Charters in Grappler Inlet (beside East Bamfield), hostel-style lodge for up to 20 with shared kitchen, $30/night, trailers with cooking facilities that sleep 2 to 4 people, $50–90/

UNDERWATER WILDLIFE
The two best environments for viewing sea life in the Pacific Rim are kelp beds and shallow rocky reefs, especially around the mouths of large inlets where daily tidal currents move lots of nutrients through the water. The many fish include rock cod, kelp greenlings and myriad tiny fish that hide in the seaweed or in crevices. On the reefs, giant Pacific octopus cower in crevices, and many bivalves can be seen including purple-hinged rock scallops and swimming scallops. There are three types of urchins, several different nudibranchs, anemones in shades of green, white, orange and pink, and unusual crustaceans such as decorator crabs, which stick bits of rock, shell or seaweed over their mucousy bodies. Giant acorn barnacles stick to rocks around the edges of the kelp beds. Some shellfish-collecting is permitted with an appropriate fishing licence (page 73). From land, you can get a preview of what can be seen underwater by visiting the Ucluelet Aquarium (page 115).

night. Bring your own bedding (some is available for a fee). 8-hour charters for salmon and halibut in offshore waters are $800-900, 6-hour charters for salmon and bottomfish in inshore waters $600–700, boat rentals 15–21' with downrigger and necessary safety equipment, $150–275/day. Rods and tackle boxes also available to rent, open May through September, will open for groups by special appointment, 728-3286, www.seabeamcanada.ca.

Tyee Resort, West Bamfield, sunset views off deck, hot tub, lodge sleeps 22 people, restaurant, rooms with private bathrooms, $160–195/room, room and meal packages from $150/person, rental houses available year-round $365–400. Lodge available in summer or by special arrangement, all-inclusive fishing packages from $450/person with rate discounted in off season, 728-3296, 1-888-493-8933, www.tyeeresort.com.

Boating

There is a public boat launch near town in Centennial Park, at the end of Grappler Rd.. You must pay a fee at the Information Centre to launch here, but those aiming for an early morning start may be frustrated to find the Centre closed. There is also a launch for a fee at the marina at Poett Nook (see page 102).

Diving

Bamfield is the perfect base for experienced and self-contained divers from which to access the great diving in the Broken Group. The water is clearest in winter, though storms can sometimes disrupt plans at this time of year. There are a few shipwrecks in the area, but the area is best known for shallow rock reefs teeming with abundant marine life. Most of the diving here is relatively shallow, between 9 and 19.8 m (30 and 65').

There is no dive shop in Bamfield (or in Port Alberni). **Broken Island Adventures** has a 27' dive boat that can accommodate up to 6 certified divers.

They will dive with you if you don't have a buddy, and can fill air tanks. $85 per dive (no gear rental available, they supply weight belts and tanks), cheaper for groups, 728-3500, 1-888-728-6200, www.brokenislandadventures.com. You can also fill air out on the water at **Rendezvous Dive Adventures** in Rainy Bay (page 74).

WHERE TO STAY

Bamfield accommodation consists mainly of family-run campgrounds, lodges and cabins. Most of the lodges focus on fishing, and are listed in the sports fishing section on pages 99–100. For up-to-date accommodation information, contact the Bamfield Chamber of Commerce, 728-3006, www.bamfieldchamber.com, or have a look at http://bamfield.travel.bc.ca/.

Over the last few years, a number of Bamfield's hotels and lodges have been bought up by the Hawkeye Marine Group, who seem to be somewhat unpredictable about keeping their businesses open (you can tell the members of this group in the listings below by the web address). People who have booked into one lodge may find their reservation moved elsewhere once they arrive in town. Keep this in mind when booking, and reconfirm your reservations.

Campgrounds

Centennial Park at the end of Grappler Rd. in East Bamfield has basic unserviced campsites with showers and toilets, RV-oriented with a few private tent sites, rates vary seasonally (but are cheap), open year-round but more self-serve over winter, 728-3006.

Pachena Campground, Anacla Reserve, Pachena Bay, 3 km/1.9 mi from Bamfield, $18 tents, $18–25 RVs with/without hookup, coin-operated hot showers, flush toilets, open April through August, 728-1287. http://huuayaht.com/campground.htm.

Poett Nook Marina and Campground, 70 km/43.5 mi south of Port Alberni, 20 km/12.4 mi north of Bamfield by road, has sites with water and limited power $18 (half-price in winter), pay showers. Also on site are a marina, boat launch and basic store. Marina 720-9572, office 758-4440, www.poettnook.com.

Hostels

Bamfield Trails Motel, East Bamfield, has a "backpackers bunkhouse", beds $50, 728-3231 or 728-3228, 1-877-728-3474, www.hawkeyemarinegroup.com.

Cloudbreak Bamfield Summer Rentals, West Bamfield, is an artistically built home on a 5-acre forested property on top of the hill on the way to Brady's Beach, dorm-like rooms downstairs $35/p (min. 2), 720-1808, www.cloudbreakbamfield.com.

Poett Nook Marina and Campground, 70 km/43.5 mi south of Port Alberni, 20 km/12.4 mi north of Bamfield by road, has beds in the bunkhouse ranging from $25-80 pp. Also on site are a marina, boat launch and basic store. Marina 720-9572, office 758-4440, www.poettnook.com.

Seabeam Fishing Resort has hostel-like accommodation in a shared lodge for $25/night (see pages 100–01).

Bed and breakfasts, cabins and cottages

Bamfield Lodge, cottages $100 double, 2-br house for up to 5 people $230 (bedding and towels $20), kitchens, BBQ and freezers, moorage available, Boardwalk Bistro Restaurant onsite, 728-3419, www.bamfieldlodge.com.

Boots & Anchor B&B, East Bamfield, hot tub, water view, big cooked breakfast, double $100-110, open year-round, 728-3608, agathaed@telus.net.

Broken Island Adventures, West Bamfield, 2-br suite with kitchen, hot tub, can sleep up to 6 people, double $75-240, open year-round, 728-3500, 1-888-728-6200, www.brokenislandadventures.com.

Cloudbreak Bamfield Summer Rentals, West Bamfield, is an artistically built home on a 5-acre forested property on top of the hill on the way to Brady's Beach, $200 for 2 people and cheaper for groups, 720-1808, www.cloudbreakbamfield.com.

Hawkeye House, East Bamfield, sleeps 2 people, $700/night, moorage available, open year-round, 728-3231 or 728-3228, 1-877-728-3474, www.hawkeyemarinegroup.com.

Kingfisher Lodge, East Bamfield, waterfront cabins sleeping up to 10 people, $400-800, moorage available, summer only, 728-3231 or 728-3228, 1-877-728-3474, www.hawkeyemarinegroup.com.

Marie's Bed & Breakfast, East Bamfield, adult-oriented B&B with homey feel, inlet and mountain views, mountain bikes available for guest use, $80-90, 728-3091, open year-round, www3.telus.net/marie/index.html.

Tracy's Bed and Breakfast, 246 Binnacle Rd., East Bamfield, continental breakfast, RV access, open open year-round, single $50-75, double $80-100, 728-3370, www.bamfieldadventures.com.

West Coast Magic B&B, West Bamfield, on a cliff overlooking Brady's Beach, open year-round, packed lunch and evening picnic supplies on request, $120 double (max. 3 people), open over summer, 728-3132, www.westcoastmagic.com.

Woods End Landing Cottages, West Bamfield, little wooden houses and big gardens, two 2-br cottages and duplex suites, decorated with local marine and beachcombed paraphernalia, full kitchens, gas BBQ, cottages for 2-4 $135-260, suite that sleeps 6 $210-350. Open year-round, 728-3383, 1-877-828-3383, www.woodsend.travel.bc.ca.

Motels and Inns

Bamfield Trails Hotel, East Bamfield, rooms $145, 1-br suites $190, pets welcome, restaurant, moorage available, reports are that it has become a bit run-down, open year-round, 728-3231 or 728-3228, 1-877-728-3474, www.hawkeyemarinegroup.com.

Lodges

See also the lodges listed under fishing charters on page 100.

The Bay Lodge, East Bamfield, waterfront home sleeps up to 10 people, from $1300, moorage available, summer only, 728-3231 or 728-3228, 1-877-728-3474, www.hawkeyemarinegroup.com.

Ostrom's Lodge, East Bamfield, waterfront lodge with kitchen facilities sleeps up to 26 people, $200/per person, moorage available, summer only. 728-3231 or 728-3228, 1-877-728-3474, www. hawkeyemarinegroup.com.

WHERE TO EAT

Some of Bamfield's best dining is at the lodges, whose chefs generally make a point to use local ingredients including fresh seafood. It's best to reserve well in advance.

Locals' top choices are marked with ✪.

Boardwalk Bistro, at the Bamfield Lodge, West Bamfield, is closed some winters, and generally open in summers for lunch and dinner. Live jazz music several times a month in summer. 728-3419, www. bamfieldlodge.com.

Hawk's Nest Pub, in the Bamfield Trails Hotel, East Bamfield, generally open year-round but subject to change, offers burgers and pub-style meals specializing in seafood when in season, $8–15. 728-3231 or 728-3228, 1-877-728-3474, www.hawkeyemarinegroup.com.

McKay Bay Lodge, West Bamfield, restaurant serving fresh local seafood and herbs and greens from their own garden. Open for breakfast, lunch and dinner by prior reservation only, full dinners about $35 including dessert. Open daily May through September, then every other week (Tuesday to Tuesday) for the off-season, 728-3323, www.bamfield-travel.com.

✪ **Tides & Trails Café**, East Bamfield, breakfasts, burgers, fries, sandwiches, fish and chips, $8–19. Open daily from May to October, 728-3464.

✪ **Tyee Resort**, West Bamfield, lunch 11:30am–3:30pm and dinner by advance reservation only, open from late May to early September, 728-3296, www.tyeeresort.com.

Nitinat

Nitinat is a tiny First Nations village inhabited by about 220 members of the Ditidaht tribe, located at the head of Nitinat Lake. (Nitinat and Ditidaht are different pronunciations of the same word). Until recently, the village has not had much to offer visitors in terms of activities, or even accommodation. It was visited mainly by self-contained travellers: windsurfers who take advantage of the strong and predictable winds over **Nitinat Lake**, and adventurers passing through on their way to the **West Coast Trail** or **Carmanah Walbran Provincial Park**. The new Nitinaht Visitors Centre is changing that, however, so keep an eye on their website for new activities and services as they become offered.

SERVICES

It is best to arrive essentially supplied and self-contained. The **Nitinaht Visitors Centre**, open daily year-round 8am–10pm, is the hub for all tourism

Bald eagles, endangered in many parts of North America, are common residents of the Pacific Rim.

activities in the area, as well as site of the grocery store, gas bar (ice available) and restaurant, 745-3375, www.nitinaht.ca. There is no cellphone coverage in Nitinat, but there is internet (both computers and wireless access) available at the Visitors Centre.

THINGS TO DO

The Nitinat experience is about raw adventure. There is not a lot programmed here, and not much of anything happening inside. But for those who live for the great outdoors, the unbeatable combination of wind, water, and woodland provide numerous adventure possibilities.

Annual festivals

Nitinaht proclaims itself the "windsurfing and kiteboarding capital of North America". The **Nitinaht Wind Fest** has been held annually since 2006 and consists of two weekends of competition in both windsurfing and kiteboarding. It normally takes place in August, and attracts many top international competitors, www.nitinaht.ca.

Hiking

There are eight short hiking trails in **Carmanah Walbran Provincial Park**, a 40 km/25 mi drive from Nitinat. You can also hike with caution along the steep river banks in **Nitinat River Provincial Park**, about 6 km /4 mi from Nitinat village (see "Provincial Parks", below).

Mountain biking

There are no bike rentals available here, but if you can bring your own bikes, there are three great mountain bike trails as well as numerous logging roads to ride on. Check in at the Nitinaht Visitors Centre for maps and information.

Kayaking and Canoeing

There is a reason that windsurfing is so big here. Kayakers and canoers who plan on venturing out on Nitinat Lake should be well prepared, in terms of both gear and experience, for strong winds, big waves, and rapidly changing conditions. You can rent short plastic kayaks from the Nitinaht Visitors Centre in the summer and early fall. These are not proper touring kayaks, but they are good for getting out on the water and exploring nearby, $45/day plus deposit. The Nitinaht Visitors Centre also offers short but beautiful guided kayak trips on the Nitinat River, in summer if there is enough water, and September through November to view bears and spawning salmon.

Serious wilderness adventurers can canoe the **Nitinat Triangle**, a multi-day mixed paddling/portage and hiking trip that takes you from Nitinat Lake to the outer coast via Tsusiat Falls. This remote wilderness route is actually more of a "vee" than a "triangle"; the triangular idea comes from the notion of a third leg that requires launching the loaded canoe through breaking surf at Tsusiat Falls, paddling 6 km/3.7 mi of exposed ocean coast, then paddling in through the notorious tidal rapids of Nitinat Narrows. The narrows connecting Nitinat Lake to the open ocean are the locus for big breaking ocean swells as well as for strong and changeable tidal currents, and there have been numerous fatalities here. Avoid this leg—the long leg of the route is far more interesting for canoers anyway!

Launching at Nitinat Lake, a combination of paddling and two portages (1 km/0.6 mi and 3 km/1.9 mi) takes you to two remote lakes, Hobiton Lake and Tsusiat Lake. This is a multi-day wilderness route, suitable for experienced canoers; remember to pack light for the portages. From Tsusiat Lake you can paddle down to Little Tsusiat Lake and then day-hike down Tsusiat River to Tsusiat Falls and the open coast. Tsusiat Falls lies within Pacific Rim National Park Reserve and is one of the West Coast Trail campsites; you may meet hikers here, but camping is only with a valid permit. You must have a permit to canoe this route; call Parks Canada, 726-7721.

Other watersports

The campground at **Nitinat Lake Recreation Site** is a great hangout for **windsurfers** and **kite boarders**, who can launch right there.

For those who have not brought their own windsurfers or kiteboards, both **rentals** and **lessons** can be arranged through the Nitinaht Visitors Centre. They are also the only place in the region that offers rentals of the newest watersport trend, **stand-up paddle boards**. What you give up in terms of balance, you make up for by getting a whole-body workout. And for those with a need for speed, they also have jet-skis on offer, $120/hr, 745-3375, www.nitinaht.ca.

Wildlife viewing

To witness **spawning salmon**, visit the **Nitinat Hatchery** on the Nitinat River about 11 km/6.8 mi toward Port Alberni from Nitinat village, where you can see returning coho, spring, chum and steelhead from August to October.

Or, get out on the river yourself. The **Nitinaht Visitors Centre** offers short flatwater river kayak tours on the Nitinat River to view spawning salmon and bears, from September through November. This may be your best chance to get face to face with a bear (they are very mellow when there is so much food around), 745-3375, www.nitinaht.ca.

Nitinat Wilderness Charters runs **whale-watching** and **birdwatching** tours, as well as the ferry for West Coast Trail hikers crossing Nitinat Narrows, and fishing charters. Run by Ditidaht band member Carl Edgar; inquire about cultural tourism, 745-3509, 715-7248.

Boating

There are two **boat launches** into the lake: one on the north side of Nitinat village, and one on the east side of the lake at Doobah about 45 minutes from the village down the road toward South Carmanah Park. The old launch at Knob Point, on the northwest side of Nitinat Lake, is no longer accessible because the road has washed out. Although it is possible to get to the ocean from Nitinat Lake, this should only be attempted by (or accompanied by) experienced navigators—otherwise, do not go! Boaters have died here, and safe passage is contingent upon passing through the turbulent narrows either on slack tide (which lasts mere minutes) or on an incoming tide, and then through breaking surf.

PROVINCIAL PARKS

The **West Coast Trail** unit of Pacific Rim National Park Reserve covers the area from the southern half of Nitinat Lake right out to the coast. It is accessible only by foot along the West Coast Trail, or by water—either by sea or via Nitinat Lake. There are also several remote and undeveloped provincial parks near Nitinat.

Carmanah Walbran Provincial Park. The Carmanah Walbran is one of the largest tracts of old-growth spruce forest remaining in British Columbia, and at 16,450 ha (40,648 ac), one of Vancouver Island's largest parks. It is accessible by a logging road 20 km/12.4 mi south of Nitinat. The lower Carmanah Valley was declared a park in 1990, as a result of environmental protests against plans to log it, and the upper Carmanah and Walbran Valleys were added to the park in 1995. There are eight forest hiking trails here, ranging in length from 1 km/0.6 mi to 7.5 km/4.7 mi (one-way), some of which follow the Carmanah River or take you to groves of spruce trees that tower 80 m/262′ in height or more. (The BC Parks website provides detailed trail information, www.env.gov.bc.ca/bcparks/explore/parkpgs/carmanah. html.) There is no vehicle-accessible campsite in the park, but wilderness camping is permitted for a fee of $5/night. Campfires are permitted in select campsites, but nowhere else in the park. Rainbird Excursions offers day-trips to Carmanah from Port Alberni (page 70).

Hitchie Creek Provincial Park. This remote 226 ha/558 ac park is primarily of interest to backcountry explorers and anglers, and is important habitat for wildlife, including Roosevelt elk. Bordering on the West Coast Trail unit of Pacific Rim National Park Reserve, it is located on the northwest side of Nitinat Lake. Access is hike-in only, from the national park. There are no facilities, but backcountry camping is permitted; fires are discouraged in order to protect the fragile environment.

Nitinat River Provincial Park. This undeveloped park consists of two segments, both accessible by logging road from Nitinat or Cowichan Lake, totalling 160 ha (395 ac). The Nitinat River is picturesque, with canyons and waterfalls cutting through old-growth forest. Some of the pools in the river are lovely (but chilly) swimming spots in summer. The river hosts populations of steelhead, salmon and trout; fishing is prohibited in the deep pools on the river, but it is permitted in the Nitinat River bridge pool, in the southern section of the park. Camping permitted, fires discouraged.

WHERE TO STAY

The **campground at Nitinat Lake Recreational Site,** open April through October, is managed by the Nitinaht Visitors Centre, 745-3375. There are tent sites and unserviced trailer sites, $10, and outhouses. You can get fresh water at the visitors centre, so make sure you travel with sufficient containers. Some maps show the Knob Point Recreational Site on the west side of the lake as a campsite, but the road here has been washed out.

The **Nitinaht Lake Motel** has 9 rooms, some with kitchen units, coin showers and laundry, $60–80, open year-round, 745-3375.

WHERE TO EAT

The restaurant at the **Nitinaht Visitors Centre** serves basic diner meals, burgers and sandwiches, and is open daily year-round 8am–10pm, $5–10, 745-3375.

Ucluelet and Barkley Sound

Ucluelet

Once in the shadow of its neighbouring village of Tofino, Ucluelet is now a destination recognized on its own merits.

In the 1990s, downturns in Ucluelet's primary industries of mining, fishing and logging forced the town to look elsewhere for survival. It didn't have to look far—only up the road to Tofino and its growing tourism-based economy. In just a few years, hard-luck Ucluelet has turned itself around. It can now offer pretty much anything that Tofino can, from resorts, spas and restaurants to galleries and wilderness tours—and often at a much better price!

Ucluelet's Wild Pacific Trail is one of the gems of the Pacific Rim; there are many lovely outer coastal beaches here, as well as spectacular rocky

Some of Ucluelet's waterfront homes date back to the arrival of early settlers nearly a century ago.

UNIQUELY UCLUELET: WHAT TO DO
- Hike the Wild Pacific Trail through majestic rainforest, rocky headlands and crashing surf.
- Go cruising through the Broken Group of islands at sunset.
- Get your hands wet at the Ucluelet Aquarium.
- Go on a bear-watching tour—by kayak, canoe or tour boat.
- Storm-watch from the restaurant at the Black Rock Resort.
- Watch strapping bushmen competing in logging sports at "Ukee Days" in July.
- Head out on Port Albion Rd. for an eye-opening fall salmon-spawning tour.
- Hit the logging roads for a dip in refreshingly remote Kennedy Lake.
- Hop on a float plane for a scenic tour from above.

THREE MAGIC MOMENTS:
1. The Wild Pacific Trail right after a storm.
2. Thornton Creek during the autumn salmon spawn.
3. Big Beach at sunset.

headlands that make for great storm-watching. A small but very complete aquarium with both common and unusual types of aquatic life and hands-on displays is located right in town. It is open only through the summer months; in the fall, the creatures are returned to the wild, and new specimens are collected for the following year. And, in 2009, the Black Rock Resort opened its doors, rivalling anything to be found in Tofino for its luxurious suites and sweeping views of wave-washed rocky coastline.

The name "Ucluelet" is derived from the Nuu-chah-nulth word *ucluth*, which means "safe harbour." For millennia this narrow, protected harbour, as well as the land extending northward up the coast toward Long Beach and inland toward Kennedy Lake, has been home of the Ucluth-itl-aht (or Ucluelet) people. Around the point to the south and extending northeastward into Barkley Sound, lies the territory of the Toquaht.

The strategic value of this safe harbour was recognized early by English explorers and traders. Around 1860, as William Banfield established his trading post at Barkley Sound's southern entrance, Captain Peter Francis set up a post at the northern entrance. The Sutton brothers arrived soon after, and set up a lumber mill at the top of the inlet.

Around 1920, Japanese settlers started to arrive on the West Coast. Most were families that had been fishing on the BC mainland for years. By the 1930s, along the stretch of coast from Tofino to Bamfield, there were more Japanese than white settlers. For the most part, relations between white Canadians, Japanese-Canadians and First Nations peoples were friendly and cooperative.

After the bombing of Pearl Harbor by Japan in 1941, the Canadian government ordered the removal of all people of Japanese descent from the

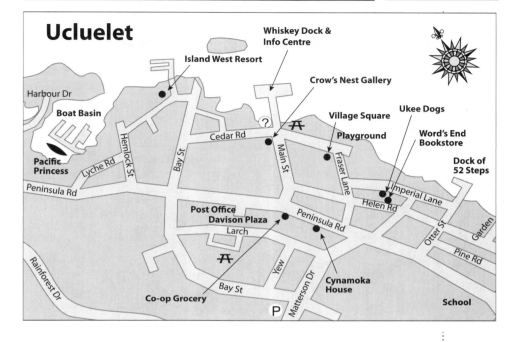

West Coast. Ucluelet's Japanese residents were sent to internment camps inland along with the rest. Following the war, although Japanese-Canadians were permitted to return to Ucluelet, very few actually returned. A few descendents still live here today as honoured and respected members of the old-town community.

Ucluelet was incorporated as a village in 1952. The road from Port Alberni was completed in 1959—a labyrinth of rough logging roads connected to make a through passage, open to the public only outside the active logging workday. In the 1960s the road was paved and a power line supplying electricity was constructed.

GETTING HERE AND AROUND

Most people arrive in "Ukee" by car, passing through Port Alberni, but you can also get here by bus, boat or plane (pages 49–56). Highway 4 is a narrow and winding road, with great sightseeing but few opportunities to pass slower vehicles such as logging trucks or sightseers. Although it is only 100 km/62 mi of paved "highway," allow at least 1½ hours for the drive from Port Alberni, and more if the weather is poor or if there is a lot of summer traffic. For current driving conditions on Highway 4, contact 1-800-550-4997, www.drivebc.ca.

Ucluelet town is small, and you can walk the commercial area end to end in about 10 minutes. Walking southward from the town centre around Main Street to Terrace Beach and the start of the Wild Pacific Trail (at the tip

111

of the Ucluth Peninsula) takes 20 to 30 minutes. The main shopping areas are within a few hundred metres of one another: the **Whiskey Dock** at the bottom of Main St.; the **Ucluelet Village Square Shops** at 1576 Imperial Lane, just above the docks; the **Coop Grocery** supermarket at the top of

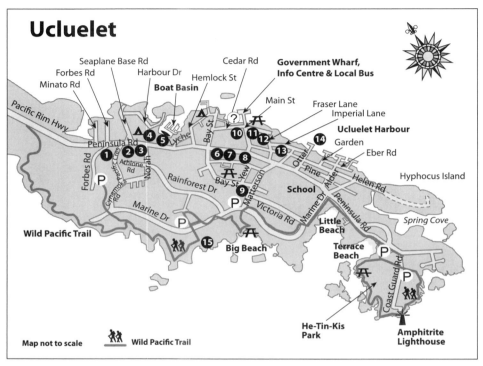

Ucluelet

1. Co-op Gas
2. PetroCan Gas
3. Offshore Restaurant
4. Du-Quah Gallery
5. Pacific Princess
6. Norwoods
7. Post Office & Davison Plaza
8. Co-op Grocery
9. Skate Park
10. Crow's Nest Gallery
11. Bank
12. Village Square
13. Ucluelet Village Square Shops
14. Dock of 52 Steps
15. Black Rock Resort

Seafood fresh off the boat is one of the attractions of the Ucluelet waterfront.

Main St. at Peninsula, and **Davison Plaza** just on the north side of the Coop. There are also many shops along Peninsula Road on the way northward out of town.

You can **rent a car** from **Budget Car & Truck Rental**, located at the airport near Long Beach, 725-2060, 1-800-268-8900, www.budget.ca, or you can call the **Ucluelet Taxi**, 726-4415. For luxury road transport to anywhere that wheels can get you, **Pacific Rim Five Star Navigators** runs a limo-like service in premium 4WDs, and they can get you around on the paved roads as well as out on the rough logging roads, 725-8393, www.pacificrimnavigators. com.

If you don't have a car, the **Beach Bus** is a great option for getting around—no extra charge for bikes and surfboards. The bus runs between Tofino and Ucluelet several times a day over the summer months, with stops at most of the beaches and trails in the National Park around Long Beach (including the airport). The schedule changes from year to year, contact 725-2871, www.tofinobus.com.

For leisurely boat travel from Port Alberni, **Lady Rose Marine Services** sails the 200-passenger MV *Frances Barkley* to Ucluelet Mondays, Wednesdays and Fridays, June through mid-September. The 5-hour trip is $37 one-way, and is as much a tour as transport, 723-8313 year-round, or 1-800-663-7192 April through September, www.ladyrosemarine.com.

For transport on the water, call a **water taxi**. Both **Beachcomber Charters** (726-8921, 1-877-363-2288, www.wildedgewhales.com) and **Bostrom Charters** (726-8166, 726-7266) run charter water taxi service throughout Barkley Sound (including Bamfield and the Broken Group) and can carry kayaks. **Broken Island Adventures Water Taxi** (based in Bamfield) is also available for charters between Bamfield and Ucluelet and can transport kayaks and bikes; they may be able to offer creative solutions for people trying to make their way to Bamfield by water over summer, 728-3500, 1-888-728-6200, www.brokenislandadventures.com. You can also go to most places that a water taxi would get you to on a **float plane**; call **West Coast Wild Adventures**, 726-7715, 726-8668, 1-877-992-9453, www. wcwild.com.

SERVICES

The **Ucluelet Visitor Information Centre** is located at the bottom of Main Street by the dock, and is open daily in summer, weekdays only for the rest of the year, 726-4641, www.uclueletinfo.com. The **Pacific Rim Visitor Centre** is 8 km/5 mi north of town at the Tofino–Ucluelet junction and open daily year-round, 726-4600, www.pacificrimvisitor.ca.

To find out what **special events** are going on, check out the notice boards at the **Post Office** and at the **Co-op Grocery Store**, both on Peninsula Rd., or look for the free **Tofino Time magazine**, www.tofinotime.com.

FRESH SEAFOOD

Pick up some plump, local side-striped shrimp, frozen at sea, at **Radford's**, 1983 Athlone Rd., 726-2662, www.radfords.ca. The shrimp come with the heads already removed, frozen in a little tub, and need a bit of time to defrost. Or check out **Fishfull Thinking**, for both fresh and smoked salmon as well as halibut and a range of shellfish, all purchased locally and processed on site, open year-round. Look for their sign at 1914 Peninsula Rd., across from The Moorage, 726-2000. You can also try your luck at the Inner Basin government dock (beside the *Pacific Princess* boat) and see what boats are in with fresh seafood for sale. Look for signs around town or on the dock itself, and you may come up with freshly caught salmon, tuna, shrimp or crab.

There is one **bank**, a CIBC, downtown on Main Street, 726-7701. The **post office** is located at Davison Plaza, 726-4441, and there are two **pharmacies**, **Barry's Drug Mart**, 1685 Peninsula Rd., 726-4342, and **Peoples Drug Mart**, 1892 Peninsula Rd., 726-2733.

Ucluelet has two **gas stations** on the edge of town. The **Petro-Canada** gas station, 2040 Peninsula, is open daily 6am to 9pm daily, to 10pm in summer, and has a garage open weekdays, 726-2001, and the **Co-op** gas station, 2076 Peninsula, is open daily 6am to 10pm, 726-2006. For **laundry**, **Gerry's Bubblemat**, downtown at Davison Plaza, is open daily 9am to 10pm.

You will find a pretty good range of **groceries** at the **Ucluelet Consumers' Co-op** downtown at Peninsula and Bay, 726-4231. For a wider range of **ethnic food items**, **health foods** and **organic produce**, pay a visit to **Shearwaters**, 1701 Peninsula Rd., open daily except Mondays year-round, 726-7425. The **liquor store** is downtown on Main Street, beside the bank.

For basic **camping supplies**, check out the **Ucluelet Consumers' Co-op** downtown at Peninsula and Bay, 726-4231, or **Camper Jack's** next door at Davison Plaza, 726-2331. There are more complete outdoors stores with a broader range of clothing in Tofino, but don't count on being able to buy much "real" gear, like tents or sleeping bags.

For **fax service** and colour **photocopying**, visit the **Crow's Nest Gallery** on Main Street, open daily, phone 726-4214, fax 726-7303. Many of the cafés and restaurants offer wireless internet access; for actual **computers**, go to **Wild Heather Books**, 726-2655, the **Gray Whale Deli**, 726-2113, or the **Visitors Centre** down by the dock, 726-4641.

THINGS TO DO

As in many coastal villages, one of the most pleasurable things to do is go for a **stroll around town** and past the docks. Head for the corner of Main and Peninsula and walk down the hill to the the Whiskey Dock and harbour. This was the centre of the original town, and the **Crow's Nest Gallery** was the old General Store; the original wooden shelving, display cases and floorboards are intact. Heading southward along the waterfront, following alongside the docks, you will come to Imperial Lane and the old weatherboard houses built by Japanese fishermen and their families during the 1920s. Walk down to the dock of the **52 Steps**; the view back to shore from here gives you an idea of what the old town looked like before the roads were put in. There are also several breathtaking beaches a short walk from town.

The **Ucluelet Aquarium**, at the waterfront on the bottom of Main Street, is small but surprisingly rich in both quality and content, with great educational and hands-on displays of local creatures. Open daily March to October, $5 adults $3 children, 522-2782, www.uclueletaquarium.org.

Annual festivals

For more detailed information on events and dates, contact the Ucluelet Visitor Information Centre, 726-4641, www.uclueletinfo.com or Pacific Rim Visitor Centre, 726-4600, www.pacificrimvisitor.ca.

The **Pacific Rim Whale Festival** takes place in Ucluelet and Tofino for a week in mid-March, as thousands of grey whales pass by on their annual northward migration. Events include whale-watching by boat or from shore, talks by local naturalists, artist events, theme dinners, nature films and a whale parade, www.pacificrimwhalefestival.org.

Forest Day, part of Canada's National Forest Week, is held on a weekend in early May, and may include presentations and displays by fisheries biologists, forest ecologists, logging companies, and local First Nations, as well as children's activities and games, logging sport demos, and a salmon BBQ. Check with the visitor information centre for dates and details, 726-4641, www.uclueletinfo.com.

George Fraser Day and Heritage Fair takes place on a weekend in May, celebrating Ucluelet pioneer and rhododendron breeder George Fraser with garden tours, historical displays and music. Check in with the visitor information centre for details, 726-4641, www.uclueletinfo.com.

Ucluelet is one of the stops for the **Van Isle 360 International Yacht Race**, which takes place in June in odd-numbered years. The variety of yachts sailing into the harbour is an impressive sight, www.vanisle360.com.

The **Edge to Edge Marathon**, covering the marathon distance from Tofino to Ucluelet, is becoming well known on the North American marathon circuit and is now an accredited Boston Marathon qualifying race. The event includes one of the prettiest half-marathon courses around, following the Wild Pacific Trail. Takes place on a weekend in early June, and you can run the whole thing or enter as a five-person team, 726-4641, www.edgetoedgemarathon.com.

Ukee Days takes place over a weekend at the end of July, and is a family-oriented weekend including a fair with children's games and events, live music, an oyster and salmon BBQ, and a loggers' sports competition. Look out for the **pirate-theme boat cruise** of the Broken Group the week before, too. Organized by the District of Ucluelet, 726-7744. www.ucluelet.ca.

The **Return of the Salmon Festival** has returned, taking place over one or two days in mid-October. The exact dates are set only weeks beforehand, because they depend upon rainfall and water levels in the rivers that the salmon ascend. Events include an open house at the Thornton Creek hatchery, as well as interpretive programs put on by groups including the Department of Fisheries and Oceans, Tofino Streamkeepers, and the Raincoast Education Society. Contact for info and dates: 726-4641, www.uclueletinfo.com.

There is usually a **Christmas Arts and Craft Fair** featuring local artisans in early December—a great opportunity for unique Christmas gift shopping, as well as **Midnight Madness** the first Friday in December, with shops open late for shopping and offering some bonus Christmas cheer. Check with the visitor information centre for dates and locations, 726-4641, www. uclueletinfo.com.

Amusements

The Long Beach Golf Course, 25 km/15.5 mi north of town, is open year-round, 725-3332 (page 134). A 12 m/40' **indoor swimming pool** $6 and large

gym $8 are open to the public at the **West Coast Motel**, 247 Hemlock St., open 9am–9pm (9-6 Sundays) year-round, gym/pool/sauna passes $11.50, 10-visit passes available 726-7732, www.westcoastfitnesscentre.com. There is a skate park and new BMX track on Matterson Rd., behind the school. There are also community plans to build mountain bike trails here; check in at Ukee Bikes, 726-2453, for current info.

Nightlife

Eagle's Nest Marine Pub at Island West Resort, 1990 Bay Street, 726-7570.

Official Sports Lounge, 250 Main Street, bar with big-screen TVs, 726-4250.

Ucluelet Lodge Pub, 250 Main Street, pub with frequent live music, karaoke and jam nights, 726-4324, www.theuclueletlodge.com.

Galleries

The **Cynamoka Coffee House**, 1536 Peninsula Rd., has a small gallery space with native art, local crafts, and books, open daily year-round, 726-3407, www.cynamoka.ca. **Du-Quah Gallery** on Peninsula Rd. at the north end of town has a fine collection of traditional Nuu-chah-nulth art including prints and carvings, and is open year-round, 726-7223. The **Huu-mees ma-as (Cedar House) Gallery**, by the Whiskey Dock, features fine native art including masks, paintings, knitting and weaving, and books, open daily, 726-2652, www.nativeartcedarhouse.com. The **Huupaquinum Gift Shop and Gallery,** 1861 Peninsula (alongside the Thornton Motel), is operated by the Ucluelet First Nation, and features local native art including carvings, basket weaving, silver jewellery and clothing, open April to October, 726-3492, www.ucluth.ca.

The **Mark Penney Gallery**, at the Whiskey Dock, offers fine art with a focus on larger works: painting, sculpture and photography, open afternoons Tuesday through Saturday, 726-2012, 726-7200, www.markpenneygallery.com. Ucluelet's new **Reflecting Spirit Gallery,** in Davison Plaza, is a new branch of artist Signy Cohen's successful Tofino gallery. Much larger than the Tofino shop, it features quality art including paintings, prints, sculture, woodwork and jewellery, open daily year-round, 726-2422, www.reflectingspirit.ca.

Rubio Gallery at the Whiskey Dock features fine hand-made jewellery with a specialty in multi-coloured Baltic amber, as well as unique Murano (handblown) glass bowls and vases, open daily year-round, 1-866-507-8246, www.rubio.ca.

Specialty shops

Pay a visit to the **Ucluelet Village Square Shops** at 1576 Imperial Lane, just above the docks, for a selection of unique and locally owned shops and boutiques including the book store, bike shop, and Ukee Dogs eatery. Located on the old site of Ucluelet pioneer and rhododendron enthusiast George Fraser's gardens, 726-2103, www.uclueletvillagesquareshops.com. **Crow's Nest Gallery** on Main Street has books, cards, gifts and souvenirs, stationery and photocopying and fax services (fax 726-7303), open daily year-round, 726-4214. **Image West Gallery & Gifts** on Peninsula Rd. sells books, T-shirts, souvenirs, art prints, pottery and sculpture, open daily year-round (also evenings in summer), 726-4487.

Piña, 1627 Peninsula Rd., local clothing designs, printed clothing, focus on organic, hemp, bamboo and recycled fabrics. Open daily year-round 726-7469. **2nd Hand Cargo**, 272 Helen, thrift shop with used treasures—clothing, music, books and more, Monday to Saturday, 726-7225. **Tula Clothing**, 1998 Peninsula (with Relic Surf Shop), clothing and accessories by local west coast designers, also coffee and cold drinks, open daily, 726-4421.

See "Surfing", pages 127–128, for a listing of **surf shops**, most of which also sell clothing, gear, and souvenirs.

Books

Wild Heather Books, at the **Ucluelet Village Square Shops** on Imperial Lane, for new and used books as well as gourmet espresso, open daily (closed Sundays and Mondays in winter), 726-2665, www.wildheatherbooks.ca.

Spas

Pacific Coast Massage Therapy, 243-C Main St., offers deep tissue and relaxation massage by registered therapists, 726-7779. **Drift Spa at the Black Rock Resort** offers esthetic services as well as several types of massage, acupuncture, esthetic treatments, body wraps and more, open daily year-round, 726-4800, 1-877-762-5011, www.blackrockoceanfront.com. West Coast weather can be unpredictable: the only sun you may see could be at the **Beautiful You Beauty Salon**, 1325 Peninsula Rd., with a tanning bed as well as esthetics and hair-dressing, open Tues-Sat year-round, 726-2884, www.beautifulyousalonspa.com.

Beach walks and day hikes

The **Wild Pacific Trail** is Ucluelet's gem. This lovely coastal trail follows the outer coast, passing through rainforest and over high rocky headlands above crashing surf, along the west side of the Ucluth Peninsula. Construction of this trail has been a unique initiative by community members, so the trail is being expanded and improved over the year. Information below may change, so get a trail map from the Ucluelet visitor information centre or look up www.wildpacifictrail.com. The entire trail, including the connecting section by road, is currently 8.5 km in length, and a great full-day trip (conveniently taking you through downtown Ucluelet around lunchtime). Bicycles are not permitted on the trail. Check the trail website for info on guided interpretive walks offered over summer by the **Raincoast Education Society**, www.raincoasteducation.org.

The first segment of the trail, the **Lighthouse Loop** is an easy 2.5 km/1.6 mi loop leaving from the parking lot on Coast Guard Road (turn right at the south end of Peninsula Rd.) with breathtaking views of the open ocean and great lookouts for watching the sunsets or storm-watching. The gravel trail is wide enough for strollers or wheelchairs, but some of the hills are rather steep. There is one single step near the top of a hill just on the north side of the lighthouse.

From here, it is 2 km/1.2 mi by road to the **Big Beach Section** of the trail; head north along Peninsula Rd. turn left onto Marine Drive, and park at the

---

GREY WHALE FACTS

Grey whales make one of the longest migrations of any mammal. The eastern north Pacific population travels between wintering grounds off Mexico's Pacific coast and summer feeding grounds in the Arctic, a round trip of about 20,000 km (12,427 mi).

Pacific grey whales were hunted to near-extinction in the 1850s, after their calving lagoons in Mexico were discovered. In 1947, they were given full protection by the International Whaling Commission. Since then their population has recovered to over 20,000 animals—roughly their original population size. In the Atlantic Ocean, grey whales have been hunted to extinction.

Adult greys measure about 14 m (46') and weigh about 30 tonnes (33 tons). They reach sexual maturity between five and 11 years. Mating often involves three whales—one male supporting the other from beneath so he can couple with the female.

---

corner with Matterson. The great views continue along this 1 km section, which includes some boardwalk and stairs, and takes you to another parking area just past the Black Rock Resort. The final **Brown's Beach Section** is 3 km in length, leaving from the Black Rock Resort and heading north to the current trail-end at the highway. More wild views from the top of the rocks here, and keep your eyes peeled for bald eagles that frequent this part of the trail. You can return to town along the same trail (recommended) or by walking the bike path alongside the highway (only slightly faster). The gravel trail is smooth and wide and there are no stairs on this section, but there are a lot of steep hilly parts. Planned expansions will continue the trail 14 km/8.7 mi northward to Florencia Bay.

There are also some lovely outer coastal beaches located within a 15-minute walk from the town centre. **Little Beach** and **Terrace Beach** are accessed from Peninsula Rd., just south of the town centre, and Big Beach from Matterson Rd., just behind the school. There are parking areas and picnic tables at both Big Beach and Terrace Beach. Little Beach and Terrace Beach are more protected from the open ocean swell, but be cautious of breaking waves that can sweep you off the rocks around all of these beaches. These are great storm-watching spots in winter.

There are also a number of short and medium-length walking trails, some of them wheelchair accessible, nearby in **Pacific Rim National Park Reserve** (see pages 144–45). Just north of town, 1 km/0.6 mi along the highway east of the Tofino–Ucluelet junction, is a 1 km/0.6 mi loop-trail called **A Walk in the Forest.** Constructed by the Ministry of Forests and the District of Ucluelet, this little trail takes you on a self-guided interpretive tour of the rainforest and explains about current logging practices and reforestation. It had fallen into disrepair, but there have been recent efforts to fix this trail up. Boardwalk sections may be slippery when wet, so walk with care.

Storm-watching

The best storm-watching here by far is from the lofty rock ledges of the **Wild Pacific Trail.** From the southern sections of the trail you get many different, spectacular views both southward across the entrance to Barkley Sound and westward to the open sea. You can get close to the action, but you are high enough to not be in danger from the waves. **Big Beach** is also a great spot to witness giant winter-storm swell breaking on the rocks. However, here you are at wave level, so you must be very cautious—storm-watchers have been swept off the rocks.

If you really don't want to get wet while witnessing Nature's fury, head over to the **Black Rock Resort** for lunch (it's dark by dinner time in winter!) at their **Fetch Restaurant** or a drink at their **Float Lounge**—or book in there for the night.

There are also some great storm-watching spots a short drive away at **Long Beach**, page 145. Former park ranger, naturalist Bill McIntyre specializes in leading guided storm-watching hikes October and April; he can get you to the best viewing spots for the conditions, 726-7099, www. longbeachnaturetours.com.

Biking

There is biking for all tastes around Ucluelet. It is easy to bike around town and to the various trailheads of the Wild Pacific Trail, and a paved bike path heads out of town for 8 km to the Tofino-Ucluelet junction and Pacific Rim Visitors Centre. (Biking is not permitted on the Wild Pacific Trail). For those looking for gentle offroad cycling, there is an extensive network of gravel logging roads in the hills behind town; get the **Tofino-Ucluelet-Pacific Rim Backroad Map**, available at local info centres or Ukee Bikes, for routes. Hard-core downhill mountain-bikers will appreciate the trails on the flanks of Mt.

Ozzard; check in at Ukee Bikes for access info. There is also a BMX bike track on Matterson Road, behind the school.

Ukee Bikes, behind the **Ucluelet Village Square Shops** at 1559 Imperial Lane, offers rentals of all sorts of bikes, including specialty items like tandem bikes and baby trailers, as well as sales and repairs. Bike rentals from $5/hr or $25/day. They are also friendly and knowledgeable, and if you let them know what kind of cycling you prefer, they are sure to come up with a suggestion. Open Tuesday to Saturday except January, 726-2453, www.ukeebikes.com.

Kayaking and canoeing

Ucluelet is a great base for day trips on the inlet, as well as a staging point to access the **Broken Group** of islands, a lovely and somewhat protected kayaking destination at the entrance to Barkley Sound in Pacific Rim National Park Reserve.

You cannot rent kayaks in Ucluelet, but you can from from **Lady Rose Marine Services** in Port Alberni, who will transport them out to the Broken Group (page 68). A number of companies that offer guided day trips and overnight tours of Ucluelet Harbour, the Broken Group and the Deer Group are listed below.

There are two easy places to launch kayaks in Ucluelet: at the **government dock** at the base of Main Street, and a little bit up the inlet at the **Island West boat ramp**, at the bottom of Bay Street. Even though you are paddling near town, there is a good chance of seeing wildlife here: sea lions or seals in the harbour and bears along the shoreline—especially around Thornton Creek during the autumn salmon spawn. The inlet is protected from ocean swell

Ucluelet's Wild Pacific Trail offers stunning views of some of the most rugged parts of Vancouver Island's shoreline.

THE BROKEN GROUP (BARKLEY SOUND)

The Broken Group is a cluster of small islands, covering an area about 8 km by 12 km (5 mi by 7.5 mi) in size, located at the broad mouth of Barkley Sound between Ucluelet and Bamfield. These islands make up the central section of Pacific Rim National Park Reserve (page 37). Access is by boat only. The closest boat launch is at Toquart Bay, but you can also launch from Port Alberni, Alberni Inlet, Bamfield or Ucluelet. Road access to Toquart Bay is by a 16 km/9.9 mi rough gravel road; the turnoff from Highway 4 is about 12 km/7.5 mi northeast of the Tofino–Ucluelet junction. Fishing charters and scenic day cruises to the Broken Group are available out of Port Alberni (pages 70–71), Bamfield (pages 98–101) and Ucluelet (page 113).

The Broken Group is a prime paddling destination for its myriad rocky and forested islands, with lots of tiny bays and coves to explore. My favourite spot is the Tiny Group, a cluster of tiny rock islets in the centre of the group. Since it is located at the entrance of Barkley Sound, the Broken Group provides opportunities for paddlers to experience open ocean conditions in the south, but also to duck behind the islands for more sheltered paddling. **Tent camping** is at designated camping areas located on **Hand, Turret, Gibraltar, Willis, Dodd, Clarke** and **Gilbert** islands. Camping is no longer permitted on Benson Island. You must pay to camp ($9/night); camping is on a first-come, first-served basis, no reservations. Solar composting toilets are provided at the campsites. Campers must bring in their own fresh water and pack out all garbage. The camping areas can be crowded in the summer months.

Toquart Bay offers the best access and most sheltered route for kayakers paddling in. In some weather conditions, experienced open-ocean paddlers may be able to make the 15 km/9.3 mi crossing directly from Ucluelet, but for the most part this exposed paddle is not recommended. For those who want to paddle in, the 8 km/5 mi crossing from Toquart Bay is much more sheltered.

There are many possibilities for transporting kayaks to the Broken Group. In the summer the MV *Frances Barkley* transports paddlers and kayaks from Port Alberni, Bamfield or Ucluelet on its scheduled sailings four times a week, and also has kayaks available to rent. From October to May it will do kayak drops from Port Alberni to the Broken Group by special request. There are also water taxis that can carry kayaks running out of Bamfield (page 92) and Ucluelet (page 113).

and strong currents, but pay attention to the weather forecast before you head out because it can still get windy here. If you dare to leave the inlet you will quickly find yourself in unprotected open ocean—beware. For kayaking safety tips, see "Kayaking on the ocean," page 68.

Paddling directly to the Broken Group from Ucluelet, even when conditions are good, is not recommended except to very experienced outer coastal paddlers. The 15 km/9.3 mi open-ocean crossing is exposed to both wind and swell, and conditions can change abruptly. It is a more sheltered 8 km/5 mi paddle from Toquart Bay (36 km/22.3 mi by road from Ucluelet, page 1). Water taxis from Ucluelet and Bamfield can get you and your kayaks to the Broken Group, or you can take the scheduled boat service from Ucluelet (in summer) or from Port Alberni (year-round) offered by **Lady Rose Marine Services**, page 68.

You can also get to the Deer Group islands from Ucluelet on a water taxi, but Bamfield is a closer (and therefore cheaper) access point than Ucluelet. For more information on paddling the Deer Group, see page 97.

For water taxis that take kayaks, call **Beachcomber Charters**, 726-8921, 1-877-363-2288, www.wildedgewhales.com; **Majestic Ocean Kayaking**, 726-2868, 1-800-889-7644, www.oceankayaking.com; or **Broken Island Adventures Water Taxi** (based in Bamfield), 728-3500, 1-888-728-6200, www.brokenislandadventures.com.

Barkley Sound Kayak Centre operates throughout the summer from their seasonal base in the Deer Group, and offer multi-day guided trips there ($675 for 6 days) as well as rentals: single $45, doubles $55, 403-678-4102, www.barkleykayakcentre.com. **Coastal Knights Kayaking** conducts guided day trips in and around Ucluelet Harbour, including bear-watching kayak tours, and offers lessons, from $55, 726-4202, 1-877-726-4202, www.coastalknights.com. **Lady Rose Marine Services** rents kayaks and canoes that you can collect in Bamfield or the Broken Group, singles $40-45/day, doubles $60. **Majestic Ocean Kayaking** has been operating out of Ucluelet since 1993, and offers guided day trips and courses both in sheltered Ucluelet Harbour ($67), and on Ucluelet's exposed outer coast, Barkley Sound and the Broken Group ($145–245), as well as a range of overnight expeditions to the Broken Group and Deer Group, from $1060 for 4 days, 726-2868, 1-800-889-7644, www.oceankayaking.com.

Pacific Rim Informative Adventures runs kayaking courses, including introductory lessons and rolling clinics, from $60, as well as longer multi-day instructional courses including rescues, navigation and guide training, from $220, 726-2773, www.priaoutback.com. **Pristine Adventures** offers guided 2- to 5-hour canoe trips oriented toward wildlife viewing on the inlet, from $100, March through November, 266-0226, www.darylspristineadventures.com.

Nature tours and wildlife viewing

It is only a short drive from town, heading out along the Port Albion Rd., to some of the important salmon spawning creeks. At **Salmon Creek**, on the Port Albion Rd. at the culvert about 1 km/0.6 mi in from the main Tofino–Ucluelet highway, chum salmon can be seen ascending the creek in mid- to late October. Continuing along the road and following the signs to the **Thornton Creek Hatchery**, you will find a great place to view returning salmon. A boardwalk trail and viewing area allow you to look down into the water at the congregating fish. Coho, chinook and a few chum come up the creek in late September and through October. Best viewing is when the creek level is higher, after a heavy rain, at a medium or low tide.

Farther from town, toward Kennedy Lake, are other salmon spawning sites. **Kennedy Lake** has two different sockeye runs. The river run passes through the lake in September on the way upstream. The lake run can be seen spawning in early November in shallow water right at the lakeshore near the boat ramp in Kennedy Lake Provincial Park, close to the highway. Best viewing is on a calm windless day. This is a very sensitive area—please do not wade around in the water or otherwise disturb the fish while they are spawning.

Between Tofino and Ucluelet, at **Kootowis Creek**, big chum and coho can be seen ascending the stream from the third week of October to early November. You will need one of the backroad maps to get out here. Turn east from the highway 23 km/14.3 mi south of Tofino, 10 km/6.2 mi north of the junction, go past the dump, and use the map to get to the Kootowis Bridge, approximately 7 km/4.4 mi north of the highway turnoff. Use extreme caution—the gravel road is rough. At **Staghorn Creek**, along the West Main logging road 1 km/0.6 mi before the Kennedy River bridge, a small wooden bridge over the creek provides good viewing of chinook and coho if water levels are low in October and early November.

To add some depth and education to your outdoor experience, sign up for a tour with an experienced local naturalist through **Long Beach Nature Tours**. Former national park naturalist Bill McIntyre and his team of guides lead half- and full-day land-based hikes with themes such as **birdwatching**, **tidepools**, **rainforest ecology** and **storm-watching**, 726-7099, www.longbeachnaturetours.com. **Coastal Knights Kayaking** offers **bear-watching** tours by kayak or dory, from $59, 726-4202, www.coastalknights.com.

Pristine Adventures offers guided 4- to 8-hour canoe and hiking trips oriented toward **bear-watching** and **wildlife viewing** on the inlet and rivers, $100-350, inquire about overnight tours, March through November, 266-0226, www.darylspristineadventures.com.

Scenic cruises and whale-watching

The main tour-boat season runs from March, with the beginning of the grey whale migration, to October. Although some operators will run tours through the winter, Mother Nature usually demands some flexibility in scheduling.

Aquamarine Adventures runs 2½-hour whale-watching tours in Zodiacs with hydrophones, $80, April through October, 726-7727, 1-888-726-7727, www.westcoastwhales.com. **Archipelago Nature Cruise** runs 5-hour trips to the Broken Group ($140-160) and 3-hour sunset tours ($100) on its 53' canoe cove cruising yacht, which can take up to 23 people, hosted by friendly and knowledgeable owners/crew Allan and Toddy Landry. Scheduled tours run March to October, 726-8289, www.archipelagocruises.

com. **Beachcomber Charters**, 3- and 6-hour whale-watching tours from $89, custom charter trips throughout Barkley Sound in their 12-passenger covered boat, 726-8921, 1-877-363-2288, www.wildedgewhales.com.

Jamie's Whaling Station offers whale-watching and other scenic and wildlife viewing tours, in Zodiacs or on their 65' cruiser, from March 15 to September 30, $80–100, 726-7444, 1-877-726-7444, www.jamies.com.

Majestic Ocean Kayaking offers 3-hour whale-watching trips in a covered heated boat, $99, 726-2868, 1-800-889-7644, www.oceankayaking.com.

Subtidal Adventures runs scenic and wildlife-viewing 2½- and 4-hour tours year-round, by Zodiac or in their covered vessel, $70–100, and winter tours (conditions permitting). 1½-hour storm-watching from the sea $50, 2½-hour winter sunset cruise to the Broken Group $89, 726-7336, 1-877-444-1134, www.subtidaladventures.com.

The sheltered cove called Boat Basin provides refuge for both fishing and pleasure boats.

Birdwatching

The beaches and forests around Ucluelet, and even right in town, are good spots for birdwatching. In addition, there are great birding environments around Long Beach (page 146) and Tofino (page 174). Tofino-based **Just Birding** (page 155 for more information) provides guided birdwatching tours from $80, 725-2520, www.justbirding.com. **Long Beach Nature Tours** offers guided nature walks year-round that include custom birdwatching tours in the Tofino–Ucluelet area, and are licensed to operate within Pacific Rim National Park Reserve, group rates available, 726-7099, www.longbeachnaturetours.com. There are also several very experienced birders in Tofino who offer guiding services throughout the region, page 175.

Fishing

Ucluelet could give Port Alberni a challenge on its claim as "Salmon Capital of the World" (as could Bamfield and Tofino). Fishing offshore and in Barkley Sound starts in March and April with the first feeder chinook and halibut, and continues throughout the summer and early fall for the larger trophy chinook, coho and sockeye. Fishing licences are available from the Government Agent Office, 726-7025 or Camper Jack's, 726-2331 (both in Davison Plaza, 1620 Peninsula Rd); and Toquart Bay Store, Toquart Bay, 726-8306.

Alan Boyd's Wild Fishing Charters, 25' cruiser for salmon and halibut, 4- 6- and 8-hour trips, 2-4 people from $475, 735-9453, www. wildpacificcharters.com. **Albion Charters,** 24' hard-top cruiser, 6- and 8-hour trips, 2–4 people from $665, accommodation packages available, 726-2410, www.albioncharters.com. Barkley Adventure Station, 38' fishing yacht, **Canadian Princess Resort**, late April to late September, 43' and 52' cabin cruisers, salmon, halibut and bottom fish, 3-hour trips from $59 per person, 3–5 day accommodation/fishing packages starting at $240, fly-in packages from Vancouver also available, 726-7771, 1-800-663-7090, www. canadianprincess.com. **Castaway Charters**, 32' sport-cruising yacht, 4-, 6- and 8-hour trips for salmon and halibut, from $400 for 2 people, 726-2628, 720-7970, www.castawaycharter.com.

High Roller Charters, full-day trips for 2-4 people from $800, 266-2624, www.highrollercharters.com. **Island West Resort**, offer 4-, 6- and 8-hour charters in boats from 24–30' in length, from $525 for 2 people, also fishing and accommodation packages, year-round, 726-7515, www. islandwestresort.com. **Long Beach Charters**, well-equipped 24' cabin cruisers, fishing/whale-watching combinations from $525 for 2 people, multi-day and accommodation packages available, 726-3474, 1-877-726-2878, www.longbeachcharters.com. **Pacific Rim Fishing Charters**, more than 20 years operating from Ucluelet, closed heated 30' and 36' boats can take up to 6 people, 4-, 6- and 8- hour trips for salmon and halibut, from $540 for 2 people, February through September, 726-5032, 1-877-871-8771, www.pacificrimfishingcharters.ca.

Roanne Sea Adventures, 8- and 12-hour charters in 40' wooden troller, 726-4494, 266-1943, from $550 for 3 people for 8 hours, www.alberni.net/ roanne. **Salmon Eye Charters**, 3-hour whalewatching-fishing combo $530 for up to 5 people, 4-, 6- and 8-hour trips, from $500 for 2 people, accommodation packages available, 719-229-5063, 1-877-777-4344, www. salmoneye.net. **Tight Lines Fishing**, salmon and halibut fishing, full-day trips from $1000 for 3 people, 266-8000, 726-2407, www.tightlinesfishing. ca. **Westcoast Fish Expeditions**, half- and full-day trips year-round for salmon and halibut, from $600 for up to 4 people, 1-877-333-8221, www. westcoastfish.com.

Boating

There are two public boat launches right in town, one at the end of **Sea Plane Base Rd.** and one at the end of **Bay Street**. In the area, there are also boat launches at **Toquart Bay** (page 134), **Kennedy Lake** (page 136–37), **Grice Bay** near Long Beach (page 147) and **Tofino** (page 177).

FLOAT PLANE INTO THE WILDS
West Coast Wild Adventures, based in Ucluelet, specializes in float plane tours, including a full-day tour, with several stops along the way, to visit the "seven wonders of Vancouver Island," $1,750 for up to three people. They will also organize custom multi-day float plane safaris for you. 726-7715, 726-8668, 1-877-992-9453, www.wcwild.com.

Diving

There are no companies offering diving instruction here. Although most of Barkley Sound's best diving is accessible only by boat, there are a few locations where those with experience can do an interesting shore dive. Good diving with abundant marine life at shallow levels can be found right near town at **Terrace Beach** and **Little Beach**, and also from **Hyphocus Island**, which you can drive to at the end of Helen Rd. All of these locations may have surf.

You can refill your tanks (air only) at **Subtidal Adventures**, 1950 Peninsula St., 726-7336, www.subtidaladventures.com. A few companies may offer trips for certified divers. You can try your luck at contracting a boat to take you and your group out. In general, you will have better luck organizing a boat if you are a larger group, which makes things more economical, and if you go during the winter months. Charter rates range from about $110 to $180/hr, depending upon the boat and the season.

Bostrom Charters has a 33' aluminum water taxi that can take up to 12 certified divers, 726-8166, 726-7266. **Subtidal Adventures**, a company with more knowledge about diving but sometimes busy on other contracts, operates a 26' Zodiac and 36' covered boat, diving trips $99/certified diver for 2 dives (if minimum group numbers are met), or charters $175/hr, 726-7336, 1-877-444-1134, www.subtidaladventures.com.

Surfing

The scene is not as developed in Tofino, but it's growing quickly. Ucluelet is a great base for getting access to some big (and cold) waves. The many beaches in the national park to the north, especially Wickaninnish Beach and Long Beach, are popular destinations. If you are not experienced, it is strongly recommended that you take a lesson or two before heading out—both for your own safety as well as to acquaint you with local surfing etiquette. If you are already a hot surfer, there are some great world-class waves around here that go off in very specific wind/wave conditions. Ask around—if you can convince the locals of your credentials, you may get let in on some of the secrets. **Inner Rhythm Surf Shop**, 1685 Peninsula, offers private and group lessons (from $79), daily rentals of surfboards ($15/half-day, $20/day), as well as wetsuits, skimboards and roof racks. The surf shop handles rentals, as well as sells boards, surfwear and skateboards, and does board repair, 726-

3456, 1-877-393-7873, www.innerrhythm.net. **Long Beach Surf Shop**, 2060 Peninsula near the entrance to town, surfboard and wetsuit rentals from $15 each, shop sells boards, surfwear, skateboards and accessories, 726-2700, www.longbeachsurfshop.com. **Relic Surf Shop and Surf School**, 1998 Peninsula at the north end of town, lessons from $65, board+wetsuit rental $35/day, shop shared with Tula Clothing stocks surfwear and other clothing, also has coffee and cold drinks, open daily, evening rental pick-ups/drop-offs can be arranged, 726-4421, www.relicsurfshop.com. You can also rent surfboards and wetsuits at the **Surf Junction Campground**.

WHERE TO STAY

There is a great range of accommodation available in and around Ucluelet, and it is impossible to list everything. A representative sampling appears here; for a more complete listing and current rate information, check out the Ucluelet Visitor Information Centre's website, www.uclueletinfo.com, or www.uclueletlodging.worldweb.com. If you email the visitor information centre in advance with your dates and the type of accommodation you're looking for, they will forward your request to appropriate accommodation businesses, who will reply to you directly. Most places have wireless internet access but, if this is important to you, it's best to double-check.

Don't risk showing up in town with nothing booked over the busy summer months, Christmas and spring break, or long weekends. Tofino will be booked out too, and it is a long drive back across the island! There are also a number of B&Bs on the inlet within 10 km/6 mi of town, listed in the Around Ucluelet section, page 139, as well as remote, water-accessed lodges out on Barkley Sound; they are listed in the Port Alberni section, page 86. All quoted room rates are based upon double occupancy unless otherwise stated.

Campgrounds

Island West Resort, in town overlooking boat harbour at 1990 Bay St., RV sites $29-35, non- or partial or full hookup, open year-round, 726-7515, www.islandwestresort.com.

Surf Junction Campground, 2650 Pacific Rim Hwy, 500 m/1,640' south of the Tofino–Ucluelet junction. Tent and RV sites $26-35 with full and partial hookup, hot tub and hot showers, recreation facilities, $20–30, open April to October, 726-7214, 1-877-922-6722, www.surfjunction.com.

Ucluelet Campground, 260 Sea Plane Base Rd., full and partial hookup RV sites $22-38, open March to September, 726-4355, www.uclueletcampground.com

Hostels

C&N Backpackers, 2081 Peninsula Rd. on waterfront, bedding included, internet access, single beds $25, private rooms $65, 726-7416, 1-888-434-6060, www.cnnbackpackers.com.

Surf's Inn Backpackers Lodge, 1874 Peninsula Rd., adult-oriented shared rooms $20-27/person, private rooms, $55-125, 726-4426, www.surfsinn.ca.

Ucluelet Lodge, right downtown on Peninsula and Main above the pub and The Official Sports Bar, $35–55 double, $45–75 with private bathroom, open year-round, 726-7022, www.ucluelethotel.com.

Bed and breakfasts

Boathouse B&B, 303 Reef Pt. Rd. near Wild Pacific Trail, 2 suite-style rooms in adult-oriented home, $80-125 with 2-night minimum, 726-7278, www.theboathousebb.com.

Bostrom's B&B on Little Beach Bay, 358 Marine Dr., 3 rooms, hot tub, games and exercise rooms, ocean view, $130-250/night, 726-7266 www.bostromsbandb.com.

Radford's Bed & Breakfast, 1983 Athlone Rd., child-friendly home in a residential neighbourhood, also sells locally caught fresh and frozen shrimp, 2-br suite available year-round (no breakfast) sleeps 5 people, $75-115, 2 private rooms $50/single, April to September only, 726-2662, www.radfords.ca.

Hertel's Beach House Bed & Breakfast, 1191 Coral Way, unique handcrafted wooden home in the rainforest with ocean views, $120–180, open April through October, 726-3649, www.hertelsbeachhouse.ca.

Horizons West Bed & Breakfast, 364 Marine Drive, private decks with open ocean views, full breakfast, $130-170 double, open year-round, 726-2271, 1-877-726-2271, www.horizons-west.com.

Majestic Ocean B&B, 1183 Helen Rd., sheltered kayak launch at doorstep, fireplace, gourmet breakfast, open year-round, $125–160, 726-2868, 1-800-889-7644, www.majesticoceanbb.ca.

Ocean Mist Guesthouse, 966 Peninsula Rd., on Wild Pacific Trail, ocean views, $110-125, open year-round, 726-7199, 1-877-726-6478, www.oceanmistgh.com.

Reefpoint Oceanfront B&B, adult-oriented luxury suites with ocean view and cliff-top hot tub, $205-285, open year-round, 1166 Coral Way, 726-1230, 1-877-726-1230, www.reefpoint.ca.

Snug Harbour Inn "luxury B&B," listed under "Hotels and Resorts" below.

Cabins, cottages and suites

He-tin-kis Lodge, 366 Reef Point Rd., contemporary post and beam lodge, oceanfront suites with private balconies, $130–250, open year-round, also can arrange in-house fishing charters, 726-2928, www.hetinkislodge.com.

Little Beach Resort, 1187 Peninsula Rd., private beach cabins, some with kitchenettes and Jacuzzis $70-160, 2-br beach house $150–300, BBQs, 726-4202, www.littlebeachresort.com.

Reefpoint Cottages, at the bottom of Peninsula Rd., studio 1-br and 2-br cottages, some with hot tubs and ocean views, $100-310, open year-round, 1-877-726-4425, www.reefpointcottages.com.

Surf's Inn Hostel Style Guesthouse, 1874 Peninsula Rd., private cabins and cottages tucked away in the rainforest, sleep up to 7, $80-250, open year-round, 726-4426, www.surfsinn.ca.

The Cabins at Terrace Beach, 1090 Peninsula Rd., close to Wild Pacific Trail, 12 cabins and 1 condo with Jacuzzis and electric fireplaces, $100–$330, open year-round, pets welcome, 726-2101, 1-866-438-4373, www.thecabins.ca.

Terrace Beach Resort, 1002 Peninsula Rd., close to Wild Pacific Trail, oceanfront cabins $200–$350 and suites $100-350, open year-round, pet friendly, 726-2901, 1-866-726-2901, www.terracebeachresort.ca.

Wild Edge Lodge, 238 Matterson, self-contained suites with kitchettes, BBQ, downtown, 1 br sleeps up to 4 people, $80–115, 2 br sleeps up to 8 people, $160–230 (rate for 4 people), good deals available for groups, also packages that include wildlife-viewing boat tours $155-205/person, 726-3444, 1-877-363-2288, www.wildedgewhales.com.

Wild Pacific Oceanfront Cabins, 277 Boardwalk, Reef Point, self-contained suites with kitchen, fireplace, private deck, ocean and forest views and with hot tub, suites sleep 2–4 people, $115–210, open year-round, 726-2707, www.wildpacificcabins.com.

Motels

Island West Resort, in town overlooking boat harbour at 1990 Bay St., motel rooms with full kitchenettes, $80–110, also lodge that sleeps up to 10, pet friendly, open year-round, 726-7515, www.islandwestresort.com.

Pacific Rim Motel, 1755 Peninsula Rd., some rooms with kitchenettes or kitchens, $85–150, 2-br suites $125–175, open year-round, 726-7728, 1-800-810-0031, www.pacificrimmotel.com.

Thornton Motel, 1861 Peninsula Rd., some rooms with kitchenettes $73–133, 2-br suites $132-190, open year-round, 726-7725, www.thorntonmotel.ca.

West Coast Motel, 247 Hemlock St. beside marina, has gym, indoor pool and sauna, some rooms with kitchenettes, $75–175, open year-round, 726-7732, www.westcoastmotel.com.

Whale's Tail Motel, 1906 Bay St. near marina, suites with kitchenettes, $100–300, 726-2985, www.whalestailmotel.net.

Hotels and resorts

Black Rock Oceanfront Resort, Ucluelet's large new high-end resort, perched on the rocky shores along the Wild Pacific Trail, with restaurant, lounge, spa, outdoor hot tubs, rooms and suites $135-615, 726-4800, 1-877-762-5011, www.blackrockoceanfront.com.

Canadian Princess Resort, a fishing-oriented resort on a ship at dock in Boat Basin, double room on ship $50–140, luxury suites on land $120–285, range of rates and fishing packages (e.g. 3 days $240–475 per person), as well as economical fly-in packages from Vancouver, open June through September, 726-7771, 1-800-663-7090, www.canadianprincess.com.

Snug Harbour Inn, 460 Marine Dr., markets itself as a "luxury B&B," with 6 clifftop oceanfront rooms and a great room serving full breakfast, private fireplaces and hot tub on main deck, a great storm-watching spot, $190-355, 726-2686, 1-888-936-5222, www.awesomeview.com.

Waters Edge Resort (site of former Tauca Lea Resort & Spa) at the end of Harbour Drive operates as mostly unserviced vacation rental units, 1 and 2 br suites with full kitchens and harbour views, $150-200, 726-4625, 1-866-899-2842, www.aviawest.com.

WHERE TO EAT

Ucluelet can be a hard place to find lunch in on a summer weekend. Unlike Tofino, with all locals working hard to earn their meagre seasonal incomes, many Ucluelet residents actually value their time off, and some may close up shop on weekends—even in peak season. If you are having trouble finding lunch, remember you can always head to the deli section at the Coop Grocery store—they've got a great selection including soups, a salad bar, and a few hot main dishes. And if you can't find anywhere open for coffee on a Sunday morning, head to the Cynamoka Coffee House or Tula Clothing/Relic Surf Shop.

Locals' top choices are marked with ✪

✪ **The Cynamoka Coffee House**, up the steep driveway at 1536 Peninsula Rd., coffees, muffins and light meals like soup, wraps, and quiche $5–7, small art gallery inside, open 6am to 5pm year-round, 726-3407, 1-866-880-6652, www.cynamoka.ca.

✪ **Delicados Surfside Café**, Peninsula Rd. at North Rd. at the north edge of town, fresh and tasty Mexican dishes: wraps, salads, soups and baked dishes, $3-12, 726-4246, www.delicados-deli.com.

Driftwood Patio Restaurant, 1672 Cedar Rd. downtown on the waterfront, seafood, pasta, burgers, rice dishes, licensed patio, open daily year-round, 726-2739.

Fetch Restaurant at the Black Rock Resort, with stunning views from above the wave-washed rocks, Chef Andrew Springette focuses on local BC ingredients, especially seafood, lunch $8-13, dinner $26-30—or enjoy the views equally from adjacent **Float Lounge**, cocktails, tapas-style appies $9-12, open 3pm to late, 726-4800, 1-877-762-5011, www.blackrockoceanfront.com.

Gray Whale Ice Cream & Deli, 1950 Peninsula Rd. sandwiches, soups, meat pies, baked goods, and cappucino bar, internet café, $4-15, open early for breakfast, daily til 6 except Sundays in winter, 726-2113.

✪ **Jigger's Fish and Chips**, great fresh local fish and home-cut fries sold from a little truck in the parking lot at Peninsula and Bay, open 3-9pm, may be closed Mondays and Sundays (especially over winter) as well as when no fresh fish is available, fish and chips $12-17, also burgers and hot dogs, $3-9, 726-5400.

✪ **Matterson House Restaurant**, in a historic settler's home at 1682 Peninsula Rd., broad range on menu from eggs Benedict for breakfast, to chowder, burgers and wraps for lunch ($6—9) to pasta, seafood and other enticing main courses for dinner ($13—30), open daily until 8:30pm year-round (except Mondays over winter), 726-2200.

✪ **Norwoods**, 1714 Peninsula Rd., contemporary west coast cuisine with an emphasis on sustainable seafood sources by Chef Richard Norwood (formerly of Boat Basin restaurant at Tauca Lea), daily for dinner, appies $13-18 mains $21-25, reservations recommended, 726-7001, www.norwoods.ca.

✪ **Offshore Restaurant**, 1972 Peninsula Rd., Chef Tina Ostergaard prepares a wide selection in this small venue: sandwiches and wraps for lunch $9-18; seafood focus at dinner including seafood hotpot, mains $20-32, as well as sushi $4-14, open 6 days a week (5 over winter) days vary, dinner reservations recommended especially over summer, 726-2111.

Peninsula Motor Inn and Chinese Restaurant, 1648 Peninsula Rd., standard small-town Chinese food, open daily, 726-7751.

Roman's Pizza & Grill, Davison Plaza, pizza $14-24, also burgers, pasta, steak, fish and chips, soup, sandwiches, wraps, Mexican $6-22, eat-in or takeout and delivery, 726-2888.

✪ **Ukee Dogs**, 1576 Imperial Lane in the Ucluelet Village Square Shops, focus on cheap healthy foods, specialty hot dogs (including vegetarian options), meat pies, vegetarian chili, salads, as well as hearty breakfasts $4-7, Monday to Friday 8:30am–3:30pm year-round, 726-2103, www. uclueletvillagesquareshops.com.

Around Ucluelet

THINGS TO DO

Ucluelet is a great base for exploring Vancouver Island's west coast. Aside from Long Beach and Tofino, which are only a short drive away and covered in the following chapters, you can also head out by gravel road to **Toquart Bay** or **Kennedy Lake**. Roads and junctions are not well marked; travel with either the *Backroads Mapbook* or the *Tofino–Ucluelet–Pacific Rim Backroad Map* sheet by Pacific Rim Informative Adventures, both available at local tourist info centres. Some of these roads are used by logging trucks, so travel with care.

You can also explore from here by water, on your pick of **scenic cruises** or **kayak trips** to the Broken Group, or **whale-watching** tours offshore. Also,

The Amphitrite Point Lighthouse at Ucluelet guards the northern entrance to Barkley Sound.

groups can consider a **day trip to Bamfield**. There is no scheduled boat service, so this is expensive for individuals, but can be quite cost-effective for groups of 8 to 12. A morning run across Barkley Sound, with an afternoon return, gives you a great chance to experience the ocean, with time to either browse the galleries and have lunch in quiet Bamfield, or go for a hike near town. Contact **Broken Island Adventures** in Bamfield, 728-3500, 1-888-728-6200, www.brokenislandadventures.com, or **Beachcomber Charters** in Ucluelet, 725-3955, 726-8921, 1-877-363-2288, www.wildedgewhales.com.

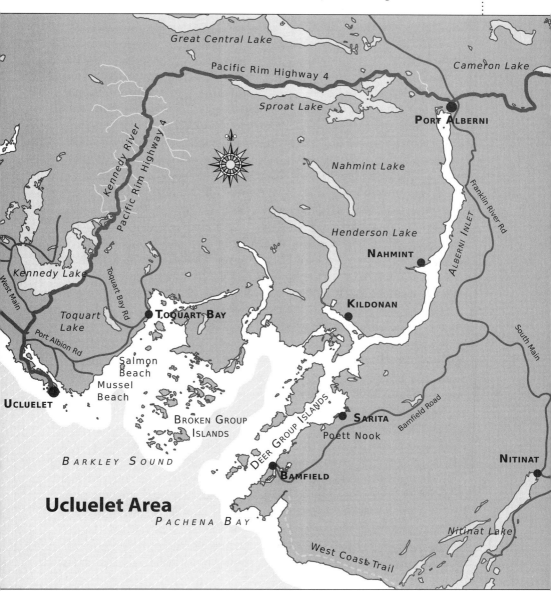

Barkley Sound

Barkley Sound is a maritime playground—a prime destination for **kayaking**, **boat-touring**, **wildlife viewing**, **sports fishing** and **diving**. The broad opening to the sound is dotted with the tiny islets of the Broken Group. Closer to Bamfield are the Deer Group islands, larger and less protected. Eastward, the sound narrows into Alberni Inlet, a winding fjord that cuts its way into Vancouver Island up to the town of Port Alberni. From Ucluelet, you can also drive out to areas near Barkley Sound's northwestern entrance: to Toquart Bay and Mussel Beach.

Toquart Bay

Toquart Bay is a tiny seasonal community about 15 km/9.3 mi as the crow flies northeast of Ucluelet, or 36 km/22.4 mi away by road. The attraction of this place is not so much the spot itself, but that it is the jumping-off point for adventures in Barkley Sound either by motorboat or by kayak. To get there, take the turnoff southward from Highway 4, 12 km/7.5 mi east of the Tofino–Ucluelet junction, and follow this winding gravel road for 16 km/9.9 mi to the coast. Between the **Toquart Bay Marina**, 726-8349, and the **Toquart Bay Store**, 726-8306, you will be able to find basic groceries, fishing licenses and supplies, camping supplies, as well as propane and gas. There is a family-oriented commercial campground with water and toilets (unserviced but open over winter) here and a boat launch. For info, call the marina or visit www.toquartbay.com. **Barkley Sound Kayak Centre** can arrange water taxi transport for paddlers here who are renting from their base camp in the Deer Group, 403-678-4102, 403-678-8108, www.barkleykayakcentre.com.

Mussel Beach and Salmon Beach

Mussel Beach is a pretty spot just inside Barkley Sound's southern entrance, around the corner from the entrance to Ucluelet Harbour. It is most popular for its famous surf break at nearby Twin Rivers, and can be busy with surfers when a big south swell comes up (pros only—people get hurt here!). The **Mussel Beach Campground** is open year-round, with tent and unserviced RV sites, but you must bring your own drinking water. There are propane showers and outhouses but not much else in the way of facilities. Day-visitors can use the site and facilities for $5/day.

From the Tofino–Ucluelet junction, go 1 km/0.6 mi south (toward Ucluelet), then turn east on the gravel Port Albion Rd. and follow the signs for 8 km/5 mi to Mussel Beach. If you continue another 4 km/2.5 mi along the Barkley Main Rd. you will come to **Salmon Beach**, a private resort in the middle of nowhere that boasts being a "secure gated community"—at the moment nothing more than a little collection of private homes and cottages.

Kennedy Lake and Kennedy River

The entire Kennedy watershed was declared a tribal park by the Tla-o-qui-aht First Nation in 2007. Tla-o-qui-aht are working with numerous partners, including Parks Canada and BC Parks, to balance industrial and recreational use with both preservation and local job creation. (Note that Clayoquot Plateau and Kennedy Lake Provincial Parks, as well as a small section of Pacific Rim National Park Reserve, lie within the boundaries of the tribal park). As **Ha'uukmin Tribal Park** becomes more clearly defined, it is possible that some of the access information outlined below may change; contact the tribal parks office at 1-888-425-3350, 725-3350 x27, or visit www.tribalparks.ca.

Kennedy Lake is a favourite spot for locals from both Tofino and Ucluelet, both for freshwater dips and for escaping the fog that smothers the seacoast during late summer. Access to Kennedy Lake is along rough gravel logging roads; make sure your car is sturdy and your spare tire is in good condition.

Access to Kennedy Lake is via gravel roads off of Highway 4. To get to what locals call "Rainbow Beach", turn north on the West Main logging road 1 km/0.6 mi east of the Tofino–Ucluelet junction. Follow the logging road for about 4 km/2.5 mi from the highway, then turn right on the unmarked

Bridge spanning the narrows between Clayoquot Arm and the main part of Kennedy Lake.

SWIMMER'S ITCH

"Swimmer's itch," a skin rash caused by an aquatic parasite, can be a problem in Kennedy Lake. Children are more susceptible because it is more prevalent in the shallows. The rash is not serious, and will go away on its own. Watch for posted warning signs, avoid shallow and marshy areas and towel-dry yourself as soon as you get out of the water.

135

TRIBAL PARKS

The concept of a "tribal park" is a unique initative that stems from the attempt at industrial logging of Meares Island, straight across the water from Tofino, in the early 1980s. In 1984, Tla-o-qui-aht hereditary chiefs declared **Meares Island** a tribal park and logging was temporarily stopped, pending resolution of land claims—which are still on-going today.

Ha'uukmin Tribal Park is also an initative of the Tla-o-qui-aht First Nation, whose traditional territory includes the watersheds of Kennedy Lake and southern Clayoquot Sound. The process of creating this tribal park started in 2007, and partners at various stage in this process have included Ecotrust Canada, the District of Tofino, Parks Canada, the University of Victoria's Geography Department, and the BC Government. The Tla-o-qui-aht word "ha'uukmin" means "feast bowl," and it refers to the richness of the bowl-like watershed of Kennedy Lake.

Tla-o-qui-aht's vision for their tribal parks is somewhat different than that of government parks, which are focused upon preservation and recreation. Rather, the aim of a tribal park is more in keeping with traditional First Nations governance and values, which include both *using* the land as well as *caring for* the ecosystem. Tla-o-qui-aht plan to work in cooperation with all of the stakeholders in the land as much as possible—including those with commercial interests as well as pre-existing national and provincial parks that lie within the tribal park boundaries. There is no implied ban on harvesting, or even on industrial use, provided that those uses are managed and sustainable. In Ha'uukmin Tribal Park, there are plans for businesses that range from ecotourism to run-of-river power generation.

For more information on the Meares Island and Ha'uukmin Tribal Parks, phone 888-425-3350, 725-3350 x27, or visit www.tribalparks.ca.

gravel road and follow it through the gate another 2 km/1.2 mi to the beach. This is a lovely east-facing sand beach with mountain views, sheltered from afternoon westerly winds, and within Kennedy Lake Provincial Park (page 138). Continuing another 6 km/3.7 mi along West Main, you'll come to the Kennedy River Bridge, site of the 1993 environmental protests that saved parts of Clayoquot Sound from clear-cut logging. Nine hundred people were arrested here, in what was the largest act of civil disobedience in Canadian history.

Across the bridge at **Clayoquot Arm Beach Recreational Site** is a pretty beach and a boat launch, a good base for fishing or kayaking, with a short nature trail. To the north of the second bridge is the Clayoquot Arm of Kennedy Lake, inaccessible by road. Paddling northward from here and then ascending Clayoquot River is a tough but worthwhile multi-day journey for hard-core adventurers who thrill at being immersed in pristine ancient rainforest. You will also find the **Norm Godfrey Nature Trail**—one of the best-kept rainforest secrets around! The trailhead is 12.1 km/7.5 mi in from the highway along the West Main Rd.; you will see a little parking area on your left, and the trailhead on your right. From the road, step immediately into ancient rainforest and to a thousand-year-old cedar tree that itself forms the base for other trees—an elegant example of the intricacies of this complex ecosystem. The boardwalk trail is about 1 km/0.6 mi in total, splitting into an "H" shape with both bottom ends leading to a lovely sand beach and swimming spot (considered by some to be clothing-optional). Both top ends of the "H" lead back to the road.

The beach that locals know as "Swim Beach" lies within Pacific Rim National Park Reserve (it is a small, isolated patch of park disconnected from the main Long Beach Section), so park rules apply: no camping, no fires and keep dogs on leash. The turnoff is in a low dip in the highway about 7 km/4.3 mi east of the Tofino-Ucluelet junction. Turn north and follow the short (1.6 km/1 mi) gravel road to the parking lot. This is a large north-facing sand beach with broad shallows in front—a great place for children to splash around or to go for a swim.

There are also **boat launches** to Kennedy Lake at the provincial park site on the highway, on the west side of Log Dump Creek bridge 10 km/6.2 mi east of the Tofino–Ucluelet junction, at the Clayoquot Arm Bridge, and at the far east end of Kennedy Lake on the highway by Cedar Creek. The lake itself is relatively nutrient-poor, so limited in its fish species. Cutthroat trout can be fished here all year round. Many of the creeks in this area, as well as the lake itself, are significant salmon spawning grounds and good places to watch salmon in autumn. Some of the easier-to-access locations are listed on pages 133–34.

Through the **Ha'uukmin Tribal Park** initiative, there are plans for a number of tourism ventures in the upper **Kennedy River** upon which construction has already started. These include zipline tours in the Kennedy River canyon, flat-water river kayak trips, tours of a run-of-river microhydro power generation plant and salmon hatchery, and the development of a network of hiking trails. They will be located on Highway 4, approximately 30 km east of the Tofino-Ucluelet junction. Contact the tribal parks office or visit their website for current information: 1-888-425-3350, 725-3350 x27, or visit www.tribalparks.ca.

Provincial parks around Kennedy Lake

Only a few of the provincial parks around Kennedy Lake are road-accessible. For general information on BC Parks, see page 201.

Clayoquot Arm Provincial Park. This large (3,491 ha/8,626 ac) backcountry park covers the northwest side of the Clayoquot Arm of Kennedy Lake, as well as the pristine rainforest of Clayoquot Lake and the Clayoquot River valley. It can be accessed by boat from Kennedy Lake (there are boat launches near the highway in Kennedy Lake Provincial Park and at the Clayoquot Arm Bridge). When water levels are low, adventurers can make their way into Clayoquot Lake by paddling and dragging a canoe up the river. Accessing this lake at any other time of year is not advisable as heavy rains can flood the lake and river. Backcountry camping is permitted—no fees and no facilities. While fires are allowed, they are discouraged.

Clayoquot Plateau Provincial Park. This large (3,155 ha/7,796 ac), rugged and remote park is an incredible place for adventurers who are experienced in self-contained expeditions and proficient at navigation through rugged terrain by map and compass. From some of the high peaks you can get views westward to Clayoquot Sound. This undeveloped park is barely accessible by a series of non-active logging roads setting off north of Highway 4 from the west side of Sutton Pass. For the most part these roads are inaccessible to vehicles, but you can use them to get into the park on foot or by mountain bike. There are no maintained trails. There is a cave system suitable for exploration by experienced cavers only. Backcountry camping is permitted in the park—no fees and no facilities. Fires are permitted but discouraged.

Kennedy River Bog Provincial Park. This tiny park (11 ha/17 ac) is located on an oxbow bend on the Kennedy River. It is accessible by boat, canoe or kayak 2 km/1.2 mi downstream from the Kennedy River bridge. Popular with birdwatchers, with opportunities to view osprey, bald eagles and many water birds. Day-use area only, no facilities; camping not permitted.

Kennedy Lake Provincial Park. Small (241 ha/595 ac) park consists of two day-use areas on the south side of Kennedy Lake, right on Highway 4, 8 km/5 mi east of the Tofino–Ucluelet junction. This park is a great place in summer for fishing, swimming, canoeing and windsurfing. In late fall there is a sockeye salmon run, separate from the sockeye that pass through the lake on their way up the river, that spawns right here at the beaches. Do not enter the water here during the spawn. Facilities include a picnic area and pit toilets, and a boat launch located beside Log Dump Creek.

WHERE TO STAY

Besides the town of Tofino and Greenpoint Campground at Long Beach, there are few places to stay around Ucluelet itself. There are a couple of B&Bs on the inlet, just outside of town, and a few campgrounds and a couple of rustic wilderness lodges on the water.

Campgrounds

Clayoquot Arm Beach Recreational Site by the Clayoquot Arm Bridge on Kennedy Lake, 11 km/6.8 mi from Highway 4 on West Main logging road, has 12 basic tent and trailer sites and a boat launch, no facilities.

Mussel Beach Campground (follow signs from Port Albion Rd., 1 km/0.6 mi south of Tofino–Ucluelet junction, then 8 km/5 mi gravel road) has wilderness tent and RV sites on the shores of Barkley Sound by famed Twin Rivers surf spot, pit toilets, propane showers, bring your own drinking water, $25–30, open year-round, 537-2081, 893-2267, www.musselbeachcampground.com.

Toquart Bay Campground, RV and tent sites and boat launch, basic services only (water, toilets, firewood) at Toquart Bay, 20 km/12.4 mi by paved road then 16 km/9.9 mi on gravel road from Ucluelet, $12 April through August, free for the rest of the year but unserviced, 726-8349, www.toquartbay.com.

Bed and breakfasts

Evergreen Forest Cabins, Mavis Road (Millstream), 2.5 km/1.5 mi south of Tofino–Ucluelet junction, 2 cabins with hot tubs on decks, each sleeps 2, large forested property, $175-215, open year-round, 726-2811, www.evergreenforestcabins.com.

Harbour House Bed and Breakfast, quiet location out of town on the inlet opposite town, small beach and kayak launch, 6.4 km/4 mi down the Port Albion Rd., self-serve continental breakfast, $80-190, open April to September, 726-7511, www.aharbourhouse.ca.

On the Inlet Bed & Breakfast, 2355 Pacific Rim Highway (Millstream) 2 km/1.2 mi south of Tofino–Ucluelet junction, fronting on to Ucluelet Inlet, hot tub, $90-150, open year-round, 726-7351, 1-866-726-7351, www.ontheinletbandb.com.

Long Beach

BIG SURF, SPARKLING WATERS, EXPANSIVE SANDY BEACHES—when tourists think of the Pacific Rim, they often think of the Pacific Rim National Park Reserve's Long Beach. "Long Beach" is actually made up of a number of different beaches: Schooner Cove and Long Beach proper in the north, Green Point Campground and Combers Beach in the middle, and Wickaninnish Beach in the south. A headland (traversed by the Nuu-chah-nulth Trail) separates these beaches from the southernmost of the large beaches at Florencia Bay. The string of beaches known collectively as "Long Beach" remains largely undeveloped, yet is one of Canada's most visited tourist destinations—the gem of the Pacific Rim.

Combers Beach is part of the vast expanse of sand that makes up Long Beach.

PACIFIC RIM NATIONAL PARK—LONG BEACH UNIT

Just over half of the Long Beach Unit of the Pacific Rim National Park Reserve's 137 square kilometres (52.9 sq mi) are on land; the remainder are on the ocean. The Long Beach Unit of the park is actually a very narrow strip of land fringing the shoreline most of the way from Tofino to Ucluelet, and in some places it is backed by clear-cuts or other industrial development. The park, however, is largely undeveloped, and you don't have to walk too far from the main parking areas to find your own section of wild surf-washed beach. There are eight well-maintained walking trails, some of which are boardwalked or wheelchair-accessible, all described below. There is a somewhat confusing system to pay for the parking and park entry charges during the park's official open season from mid-March to mid-October; look for posted information in the parking areas. The parking lots and trails are still open and access is free for the remainder of the year (subject to change). Please follow the guidelines for sharing the wilderness with wildlife (page 55) and about wilderness etiquette (page 43). There is a very active wolf pack in the Long Beach area, and they have kiilled dogs that owners have brought into the park off-leash. Please obey park regulations that are aimed at protecting and preserving this amazing place both for human visitors and its wild inhabitants. The ultimate rule is *Leave no trace.*

The main park visitor centre is the Wickaninnish Interpretive Centre, 5 km north of the Tofino-Ucluelet junction, but there is also a new staffed national parks information booth in the Pacific Rim Visitors Centre, right at the junction—a recommended stop for anyone driving in.

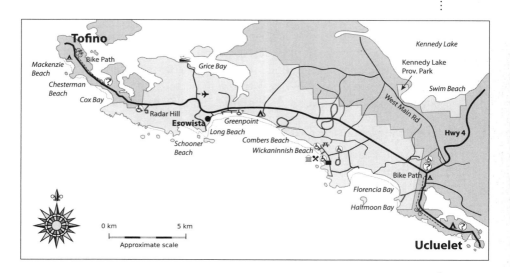

This is the traditional territory of the Tla-o-qui-aht and Ucluelet tribes. A significant Tla-o-qui-aht village site called Esowista, at the north end of Long Beach, is still occupied today.

Even during the 1920s, Long Beach was already a tourism destination of sorts (although on a much smaller scale than today), as residents from the

UNIQUELY LONG BEACH: WHAT TO DO
- Go beachcombing for shells, rocks, polished glass and even Japanese glass fishing floats at Florencia and Combers Beaches.
- Build a sandcastle.
- Go for a long, meandering walk on the beach—and take the dog.
- Take a surfing lesson, go skimboarding, or just sit in the sun by the big rock at Long Beach and watch the surfers.
- Check out tidal pools and overturned rocks for sea stars, anemones, crabs and other intertidal life.
- Walk along both loops of the Rainforest Trail, taking the time to absorb it all.
- Fly a kite! Long Beach is a kite-flyer's dream—lots of wind and no power lines.
- Have a romantic dinner, perched above crashing waves, at the old Wickaninnish Restaurant.

THREE MAGIC MOMENTS:
1. South Beach right after a winter storm, as the sun peeks out of clouds backlighting the waves exploding on the rocks.
2. The lookout at Radar Hill at dusk.
3. A still summer morning, floating in a kayak on Grice Bay with feeding grey whales.

fledgling villages of Tofino and Ucluelet came out for a few days of camping, beachfires and bathing in the sea.

By the 1960s, Ucluelet and Tofino were established villages, and the road from Port Alberni had finally been punched through to the coast. The fresh road drew a new wave of settlers to Long Beach. In the dawning age of free love, hippies and draft-dodgers arrived, setting up tent cities at Florencia Bay and Schooner Cove. These squatters were evicted in 1971, when Long Beach was declared to be part of Pacific Rim National Park Reserve.

GETTING HERE AND AROUND

Long Beach is about a two-hour drive from Port Alberni (see page 54 for more information on the route). Most of this area lies within Pacific Rim National Park Reserve. The small Tla-o-qui-aht village of Esowista, population around 150, is located at the north end of Long Beach. Outside of Esowista and the handful of people who live at the airport/golf course, the area is wild and unsettled by people.

The airport that services Tofino and Ucluelet is located just behind Long Beach, and flights to and from Vancouver operate daily, weather permitting (pages 54–56).

Getting around the Long Beach area is tough without a car. The **Beach Bus**, based out of Tofino, makes regularly scheduled runs several times a day between Tofino and Ucluelet over summer, with stops at the beaches and trails around Long Beach, and has racks for taking your bike or surfboard,

The Wickaninnish Interpretive Centre has many informative displays as well as a restaurant with an unbeatable view.

725-2871, www.tofinobus.com. You can get around here by bike, but it's not recommended; the highway is narrow and without a shoulder.

You can also call for taxi service from Tofino or Ucluelet, but beware—cellphone service is sketchy from Long Beach. **Tofino Taxi** 725-3333, **Ucluelet Taxi** 726-4415, or **Pacific Rim Five Star Navigators** (a premium 4WD taxi service) 725-8393, www.pacificrimnavigators.ca.

Rental cars are available from **Budget Car & Truck Rental**, located at the airport, 725-2060, 1-800-268-8900, www.budget.ca.

SERVICES

The **Pacific Rim Visitor Centre**, located at the Tofino–Ucluelet junction, is open daily March through October, and Thursday through Sunday the rest of the year, 726-4600, www.pacificrimvisitor.ca. You can also get park information at the **Wickaninnish Interpretive Centre** (turnoff 5 km/3.1 mi north of the junction, open from March through October), and the **Administration Office** (take the same turnoff toward Wickaninnish Beach and turn right on Ocean Terrace, open Monday to Friday year-round). For general park information, contact **Pacific Rim National Park Reserve**, 726-7721, info@pc.gc.ca, or take a look at www.pc.gc.ca/pn-np/bc/pacificrim/. The National Park information line is 1-888-773-8888.

There is a **restaurant** at the Long Beach Golf Course, open May to October, 725-3332, and **Surf n' Snack** store in the village of Esowista open most of the year, closed January, 725-2765, 266-2765. For groceries and other supplies, head to Tofino or Ucluelet.

In case of emergencies, the park **Warden's Office** is located just north of Green Point Campground, 14 km/8.7 mi north of the junction. There are no shops or services in the National Park or around Long Beach. The nearest places with any services are the villages of Tofino and Ucluelet. In the case of a **tsunami warning** (or if you experience a strong earthquake, which means that a tsunami is likely imminent) head directly to the airport/golf course, which is actually 24 m/80′ above sea-level.

THINGS TO DO

Walking trails and day hikes

The Bog Trail passes through the coastal bog ecosystem, replete with spongy mosses and carnivorous plants.

There are eight walking trails, of varying difficulty and length, within the park, with parking areas at all trailheads. Trails are listed from south to north.

Willowbrae Trail is 2.8 km/1.7 mi round trip, with difficult footing in places. Follows the old route that early settlers travelling between Ucluelet and Tofino took to get from the head of Ucluth Inlet out to Long Beach. The trailhead at Willowbrae Rd. is about 2 km/1.2 mi south of the Tofino–Ucluelet junction, on the west (ocean) side of the highway. The route starts as a gravel path, then splits into two rougher trails with several steep stairways: turn left for secluded Halfmoon Bay or right for the sweeping crescent beach of Florencia Bay.

South Beach Trail is 1.5 km/0.9 mi round trip, mostly easy but ramp and stairs can be slippery when wet. The trail leaves from the Wickaninnish Centre and passes through rainforest just behind the shoreline, offering glimpses of lovely secluded coves. It ends at South Beach with small pebbles exposed to big ocean waves—a perfect storm-watching spot.

The **Nuu-chah-nulth Trail** links the south end of Long Beach to Florencia Bay, 2.5 km/1.6 mi each way, mixed trail and boardwalk with some stairs. Like the Willowbrae, this trail is part of the old settlers' travel route from a century ago. It starts as the South Beach Trail at the Wickaninnish Centre but turns left at the signpost a short way down the track. The trail passes through pristine rainforest and has a dozen signs explaining local Native culture and natural history.

Bog Trail is 1 km/0.6 mi on a wheelchair-accessible boardwalk. This short trail takes you on an educational tour through the coastal bog ecosystem, where you can see stunted centuries-old shore pines, hummocks of spongy peat moss and carnivorous sundew plants. Free pamphlets at the trailhead provide information about this specialized ecosystem.

Rainforest Trail is made up of two 1 km/0.6 mi boardwalked loops with a few stairs. The parking lot for these trails is on the west side of the highway, 10 km/6.2 mi north of the Tofino–Ucluelet junction. Both pass through ancient and pristine coastal temperate rainforest, with giant cedar trees festooned with mosses and ferns. The western loop explains about the forest structure and wildlife, and the eastern loop talks about forest life cycles.

Combers Beach Trail is a new trail—a short ten-minute forested walk from the large parking lot at the side of the highway to the beach.

Spruce Fringe Trail is closed until further notice.

Schooner Beach Trail is 1 km/0.6 mi each way from parking lot to beach, mixed trail with some muddy sections as well as boardwalk with some stairs. This pretty rainforest trail takes you to lovely Schooner Cove, at the north end of Long Beach—a great place to explore and beachcomb on a sunny afternoon.

Radar Hill is a very short, wheelchair-accessible hilltop loop with panoramic views. A turnoff 10 km/6.2 mi south of Tofino winds up to the top of Radar Hill. There is one lookout perched on a clifftop with views of the open Pacific Ocean looking toward Japan, right at the parking lot. A short walk along the trail takes you to an even higher lookout with panoramic northward views of Clayoquot Sound—great spots to watch the sunset.

The old **Gold Mine Trail** was washed out by a storm, and has been closed until further notice. You can also simply walk the lengths of the beaches— just beware of the distances. The full length of Long Beach (including Long Beach proper, Combers Beach and Wickaninnish Beach) is about 12 km/7.5 mi. You can continue even farther if you time your trip to cross the headlands between beaches around low tide. Just be cautious that you do not get trapped by a rising tide while returning, and always be on the lookout toward the sea for large waves.

Storm-watching

The exposed nature of the coast here makes Long Beach a top storm-watching spot. Any of the beaches here are great places to witness the fury of giant waves rolling into the coast, either during or after a storm. Places where you can get really close to the action are the decks around the **Wickaninnish Interpretive Centre and Restaurant** (not to be confused with Wickaninnish Inn just outside Tofino), where you can get up high and above the waves, and **South Beach**, a 20-minute walk away from the centre. The big rock off South Beach gets some huge waves smashing and exploding on it.

Naturalist Bill McIntyre is licensed to guide within the park, and offers **guided storm-watching hikes** October through April. A a former park ranger, he knows the terrain and can get you to the best viewing spots for the conditions, 726-7099, www.longbeachnaturetours.com.

Kayaking

All beaches here are surf beaches, not suitable for sea kayaks. Sea kayakers can explore **Grice Bay**, a shallow area, although it can be exposed to strong northwesterly winds common in summer. (For kayaking safety tips, see "Kayaking on the ocean," page 63.) The main interest here is to see grey whales which, in some years, use this shallow tidal bay as a summer feeding ground—check with the whale-watching companies in Tofino to see if whales have been in the bay lately. No kayak companies regularly run trips here. If you do not have your own kayaks, you can rent in Tofino, but inquire first.

Grice Bay is also a good launching spot for kayak day trips exploring the "back" (eastern) side of Meares Island. Just pay close attention to the tides—narrow passages around here, especially at Tsapee Narrows and Dawley Passage, make for strong currents during tide changes. You can access Grice Bay via the short road on the east side of the highway by the airport, 15 km/9.3 mi south of Tofino.

If you have your own whitewater or surf kayak and are an experienced **surf kayaker**, you can play on the waves at any of the beaches alongside the surfers. (Just be careful not to get in their way, or you'll hear about it!) If you are just learning, find an area with small waves and keep your distance from the surfers. Long Beach proper is the best spot for surf-kayaking. There are no rentals of whitewater or surf kayaks available anywhere in the region.

Nature tours

Explore the natural and cultural history of the Pacific Rim at the **Wickaninnish Interpretive Centre**, on the shore of the Pacific at the end of Wick Rd. (3.5 km/2.2 mi from Highway 4). The building houses an information centre, gift shop, restaurant and interpretive facility, where you'll find a whaling canoe, ocean life murals and whale bones on display.

In addition, two nearby companies offer interpretive tours. Ucluelet-based **Long Beach Nature Tours**, owned and operated by former national park naturalist Bill McIntyre, offers half- and full-day land-based walking tours with themes such as birdwatching, tidepools, rainforest ecology and storm-watching. They are licensed to operate within the park. Tours are customized for interests, group rates available, 726-7099, www.longbeachnaturetours.com.

Birdwatching

The Long Beach area is great for birdwatching because of its diverse ecological environments: rainforest, beach and mudflats.

Rainforest. Although you may hear many birds singing in the forest, including winter wrens, flycatchers, and three types of thrushes, they are hard to spot in summer. However, through the winter months, those that have not migrated southward descend to lower elevations, and are more often seen flitting through the shrubbery—species such as varied thrushes, winter wrens, rufous-sided towhees and kinglets. Trails such as the Rainforest Loop Trail are good places for winter birdwatching.

Long Beach. The outer coastal beaches, and the rocky headlands in between them, host a variety of bird species. On the beaches you will see a range of shorebirds such as sandpipers, plovers and sanderlings, during their spring migration in late April and early May, and again through the fall and winter. On the headlands you may see oyster-catchers and pigeon guillemots, both of which nest within the park.

Grice Bay. The mudflats here, within the National Park and across the road from Long Beach, are accessible by the Grice Bay Rd. (near the airport). Stop about 3 km/1.9 mi down the road, when you first glimpse water, before the boat ramp. This is a great spot to watch the migrating shorebirds in late April/early May (for a listing of some shorebird species you may see here, see Tofino mudflats section, page 174), and for birds in general throughout the year.

Boating

There is a boat ramp at **Grice Bay**. The turnoff for Grice Bay is the same as for the airport, 17 km/10.6 mi north of the Tofino–Ucluelet junction.

Surfing

The most popular surfing area is Long Beach proper, accessible by the two parking lots located 17 km/10.6 mi south of Tofino. Park lifeguards are stationed here in July and August. **Wickaninnish Beach** can also be a popular surf spot at times, but it is generally subject to bigger waves and stronger currents and so is more suitable for experienced surfers.

Surf n' Snack, in Esowista village, handles rentals of surfboards ($20/day) and wetsuits and booties ($20/day), extended rates available, open most of the year except January, 725-2765, 266-2765. You can rent boards and other equipment in both Tofino (page 178) and Ucluelet (page 127). The **Beach Bus** (summer only) will transport boards at no extra cost, 725-2871, www.tofinobus.com.

The Pacific Rim is one of the few areas in Canada where you can sign up for surfing school.

THINGS TO DO NEARBY

The **Long Beach Golf Course** and its **Pro Shop** are open year-round. There is a 9-hole course ($24) as well as an 18-hole mini-golf course ($5–7), and a restaurant on site open May through October, 725-3332, www. longbeachgolfcourse.com.

SURFING CANADIAN-STYLE

The surf scene that developed in California in the 1960s is well known. What most people *don't* know is that people started surfing Long Beach around the same time. There was even a surf school here back in the 1970s!

Vancouver Island's west coast is undoubtedly Canada's surf capital, and most of our national champs come from right here. The surf video *49°* (the title refers to both the latitude and the Fahrenheit water temperature) is a Canadian surf classic, and features Tofino's famous Bruhwiler surfing family. The more recent video *Numb* (no prizes for guessing what this title refers to) is made by Tofino-based surfer and filmmaker Jeremy Koreski, www.jeremykoreski.com.

Surfing is both a sport and a culture. If you are already an experienced surfer, you will find some world-class waves here in the Pacific Rim. Surfing hot spots include Florencia Bay, Wickaninnish Beach, Long Beach, Chesterman's Beach and Cox Bay. As you will already know, different waves work only in specific conditions, a combination of wind, swell and tide. If you know what you are doing and can handle big water, ask around – the locals will probably share their knowledge and help you get to where it is going off.

If you are a beginner, be cautious! Not only are the waves dangerous – even our pros get injured here – there is also a very defined surf etiquette regarding positioning and right-of-way. If you start to upset the locals, they will make sure that you are not going to have *any* fun out there. Taking a couple of surfing lessons is just plain smart: not only will you be safer, you will find yourself standing up a lot sooner.

Kennedy Lake is only a half-hour short drive from Long Beach along rough gravel logging roads. If you are craving a freshwater dip or a change of scenery, or are trying to escape the coastal fog, this makes a great day trip, see pages 135–37.

WHERE TO STAY

Most people who visit Long Beach find accommodation in either Tofino (pages 180–84) or Ucluelet (pages 128–30), but there are two campgrounds at Long Beach itself, as well as one B&B in Esowista village.

Green Point Campground is operated by Pacific Rim National Park Reserve, and is open from mid-March to mid-October. Unserviced (toilet building only) and primitive campsites $16–21, firewood for purchase. Reservations are required for summer (and recommended for the remainder of the season) and can be made up to three months in advance, 1-877-737-3783, www.pccamping.ca.

Long Beach Golf Course, an unserviced campground mainly in use as overflow accommodation from May long weekend to Labour Day, has basic campsites $30 (no hookup), and a restaurant on-site open May through October, 725-3332 or 725-3314, reservations taken by phone only, www.longbeachgolfcourse.com.

Long Beach Haven, a unique B&B run in a peaceful home right on the beach, 2-br guest suite (sleeps up to 4) $135-275, B&B rooms with ocean views $90-145 double-occupancy, 725-3332, www.longbeachhaven.com.

WHERE TO EAT

If you are staying in Tofino or Ucluelet, your best bet is to get a packed lunch to take with you to Long Beach. Many of the hotels, delis and cafés are happy to pack up a custom meal for you. Around Long Beach, there are only two options—and both are closed over winter.

Long Beach Golf Course has a basic restaurant on-site that serves pub-style meals like burgers, sandwiches and wraps, $8–12, open May through October, 725-3332.

Wickaninnish Restaurant, at the interpretive centre on Wickaninnish Beach (not to be confused with the "new" Wickaninnish Inn on Chesterman Beach just outside Tofino), with spectacular ocean views and a heated outdoor deck, has a focus on seafood and pasta and fine desserts, mains $20–25, open March to September for lunch and dinner, 726-7706, www.wickaninnish.ca.

Tofino and Clayoquot Sound

TOFINO

There's a reason why Tofino is the number-one tourist destination in Vancouver Island's Pacific Rim. Perched on a rocky headland at the tip of the Esowista Peninsula, at the gateway to Clayoquot Sound, it is literally at the end of the road, within easy reach of some of the province's best beaches, parks and recreational opportunities. With a host of internationally renowned resorts, restaurants and spas, galleries and gift shops, tourism is Tofino's main industry. It's the home of the world-class Wickaninnish Inn

The shoreline around Tofino consists of sandy beaches separated by high rocky headlands.

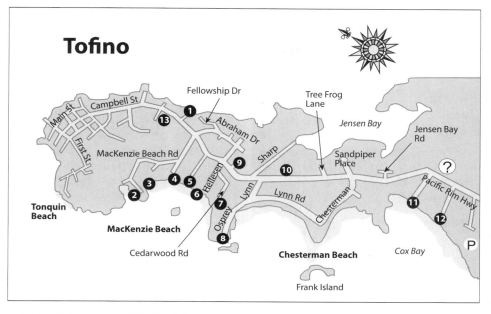

Tofino

1. Tofino Botanical Gardens
2. Middle Beach Lodge
3. Bella Pacifica
4. MacKenzie Beach Resort
5. Tin Wis
6. Ocean Village
7. Crystal Cove
8. Wickaninnish Inn
9. "Outside Break" shops
10. Clayoquot Orca Lodge
11. Pacific Sands
12. Long Beach Lodge
13. The Alternative Climbing Club

UNIQUELY TOFINO: WHAT TO DO

- Paddle a traditional Native dugout canoe on the ocean with Tlaook Cultural Adventures.
- Have a coffee and organic chocolate zucchini muffin at the Common Loaf Bake Shop, and check the bulletin board for upcoming events.
- Do the art gallery stroll, stopping at Driftwood, House of Himwitsa, Reflecting Spirit, Eagle Aerie, Tofino Art Glass and more.
- Hop on a boat for a day trip to Hot Springs Cove. Better yet, stay here for the night, on the *Innchanter*.
- Kayak to Meares Island and walk the Big Tree Trail.
- Enjoy drinks and appies in Long Beach Lodge's luxurious Great Room.
- Get a pair of gumboots at the Co-op and go puddle-jumping.
- Pamper yourself to the extreme in Cedar Sanctuary, the oceanside treatment room of the Wickaninnish Inn's award-winning spa.
- Don all your rubber, and get out on the beach in the middle of a winter storm.

THREE MAGIC MOMENTS:

1. Summer sunset from the First Street Dock (9:30pm).
2. Winter sunset from Tonquin Beach (4:30pm).
3. Chesterman Beach on a moonless night.

Between fishing boats, water taxis and tour boats, there is always some activity down on the Tofino docks.

on Chesterman Beach, the resort that made storm-watching famous. Tofino has an active cultural life with dance performances, films, live music, visiting speakers and more. It's also an excellent destination for birdwatchers: more than 300 bird species have been recorded, from the majestic bald eagle to the tiny rufous hummingbird.

The Native name for this place is Naachaks, which means "lookout." The first white settlement here was a fur-trading post on Clayoquot Island, which opened up around 1860. Over the decades, immigrants mainly from England, Scotland, Norway, China and Japan arrived, settling at Clayoquot and on other surrounding islets. Since there were no roads, the islands with good boat access were soon populated. The earliest settlers worked mainly in resource extraction—fishing, logging and mining—but by the turn of the century homesteaders began to try their luck at farming too.

In 1912 it was recognized that more land was needed for the growing island population, so the townsite of present-day Tofino was chosen. The following year residents constructed the St. Columba Church—a pretty little church that still stands today at the corner of Second and Main. By the 1920s, Tofino had become the main settlement in Clayoquot Sound, although the original settlement on Clayoquot Island still played an important social role to the community; the licensed Clayoquot Hotel was a popular stopping point for sea-traders. Japanese fishermen started to arrive, forming a significant part of the non-aboriginal community until they were evicted and sent to internment camps during the Second World War. Other than a rough road constructed in the 1940s linking Tofino to Ucluelet, Tofino and its outlying communities were accessible only by boat until 1959.

Tofino today is a town that combines its pioneering and maritime heritage with its newfound identity as a world-class tourist destination. Many locals can still be defined as "water people," making their living out on the sea, some of them even living full-time on the water in cabins or floathouses.

GETTING HERE AND AROUND

Tofino is a 2- to 2½-hour drive from Port Alberni. For more information on the route, see page 54. You can also get here by bus or by plane (pages 53–55).

The downtown core of Tofino is very small, and you can walk the four blocks from end to end in about five minutes. Chesterman Beach is 4.5 km/2.8 mi from town, and the paved multi-use path makes it easy to get back and forth between the beach and town either on foot (45 to 60 minutes) or by bike (20 minutes). There are two types of public transit that run in the summer months only: **Tofino Transit** runs every hour or two between downtown Tofino and the Cox Bay Visitors Centre (7 km/4.4 mi out of town, across from the Long Beach Lodge) with stops at most of the beaches and resorts in between. The **Beach Bus** runs twice daily between Tofino and Ucluelet, with stops at the various trailheads around Long Beach along the way, takes bikes or surfboards at no extra charge. For info on both services contact, 725-2871, www.tofinobus.com.

For **taxi service**, call **Tofino Taxi**, 725-3333. You can rent a car from **Budget Car & Truck Rental**, located at the airport near Long Beach, 725-2060, 1-800-268-8900, www.budget.ca.

Bike rentals are available from two places in Tofino (page 168), and some resorts provide bikes for guests. Parking is tight over summer, both in town and at the beaches—biking between town and the beaches is not only good for the environment and good for the body, it often ends up being more convenient than trying to drive.

For transport on the water you can call a **water taxi**. The **Ahousaht Pride** runs twice-daily scheduled service to Ahousat on Flores Island, $20, 670-9563. The **Matlahaw** runs daily between Tofino and Hot Springs village, $50, 670-1100. (Many of Tofino's whale-watching companies also offer one-way service to Hot Springs, see below). For water taxi service to the islands, contact **Tofino Water Taxi** (covered boat, as well as 24' open herring skiff good for kayaks and other gear), 726-5485, 1-877-726-5485, www.tofinowatertaxi.com, or Opitsaht-based **John Tom** (covered boats), 725-3747, or **Marcel Theriault** (open herring skiff, good for transporting kayaks and other gear), 726-8438. For boat transport between Tofino and Hesquiat Harbour call **Dave Ignace**, (covered boat), 670-1164.

You can also get to some remote places on a float plane; call **Atleo River**

Air Service, 725-2205, www.atleoair.com or **Tofino Air**, 725-4454, 1-866-486-3247, www.tofinoair.ca. Tofino Air also runs daily scheduled service between Tofino and Hot Springs Cove, $80 one-way.

SERVICES

The main **Tofino Visitor Centre** is now located in town at 455 Campbell, open daily year-round, 725-3414, 1-888-720-3414, www.tourismtofino.com. A secondary office, open daily March through October, is located on the highway as you approach Tofino, 7 km/4.4 mi outside of town, 725-3429. The **Pacific Rim Visitor Centre** is at the Tofino–Ucluelet junction, 33 km/20.5 mi south of town, open daily year-round, and hosts a staffed National Park info centre within it as well, 726-4600, www.pacificrimvisitor.ca.

Keep an eye out for signs alerting you to the freshest seafood you will ever find.

Tofino's one **bank**, **CIBC**, is located downtown at First and Campbell, 725-3321. The **post office** is located across the street, open weekdays and Saturday mornings. The **Tofino Pharmacy** is downtown at 360 Campbell, and open daily year-round, 725-3101.

There are two **gas stations** on the highway at the edge of town. The **Co-op** gas station is open daily 6am to 8pm (till 10pm in summer), 725-3225, and the **Esso** daily from 6:30am to 10:30pm, 725-2050. For **auto repairs** contact **Long Beach Automotive**, 671 Industrial Way, 725-2030. The local **marina and fuel dock** is **Method Marine**, 380 Main St., and they also stock fishing supplies and can refill dive tanks, open daily year-round, 725-3251. A coin-operated **laundromat** and **shower** is located on Fourth Street at Campbell, behind **Tuff Beans**, open daily 8am–8pm.

Tofino has one reasonably well-stocked **supermarket** right downtown, the **Co-op Grocery Store** at First and Campbell, open daily year-round, 725-3226. Across the street, **LA Grocery** in town, open daily till 11pm, and

---

FRESH SEAFOOD

For fresh local fish, locally smoked salmon, and shellfish ranging from oysters to crab, try out Tofino's two seafood shops: Trilogy Fish Co., down the hill at 630 Campbell, open year-round, 725-2233, and The Fish Store, 564B Campbell, open daily except January and February, 725-2264. For salmon, shrimp and prawns fresh-frozen at sea, contact local commercial fisherman Jeff Mikus, 266-9453.

You also usually get local crab at 900 Pacific Rim Highway, across from the Esso gas station—check if their sign is hanging up by the driveway—or at the Crab Dock, down Olsen Rd., 1 km/0.6 mi from downtown. Sometimes fishermen will sell fresh salmon or fresh-frozen tuna right off the boat at the Fourth Street dock too—go for a wander on the dock or keep an eye out for signs around town.

Long Beach Market at the Esso station, daily till 10:30 pm, both stock basic food supplies and snacks. Closer to Chesterman Beach, **Beaches Grocery** at Outside Break shops (1184 Pacific Rim Highway) is open daily 8am to 10pm, and stocks staples as well as ethnic food ingredients and fresh produce, and stocks fresh sandwiches, pizzas, and baked goods, 725-2237. The **liquor store** is on Neil Street behind the Bakery. For **organic food and health food**, go to **Green Soul Organics**, on Fourth at Campbell, open daily year-round, 725-4202.

For **camping and outdoors gear**, there are a few options. **Storm Light Outfitters**, 390 Main St., has a range of outdoors gear including rainwear, boots, tents, sleeping bags and other specialty equipment, as well as rentals of camping equipment and hand-held VHF radios, 725-3342. For higher-end outdoor clothing and footwear, camping equipment and local books check out **Tofino Fishing and Trading Co.**, on the corner of Fourth and Campbell, 725-2622. **Tofino Sea Kayaking Company**, 320 Main, 725-4222, stocks smaller camping items and clothing, especially gear oriented toward sea kayaking and backpacking. The **Co-op Hardware Store** at Main and First, 725-3436, has more basic camping and BBQ supplies.

Fax service is available at **Tofino Pharmacy**, phone 725-3101, fax 725-

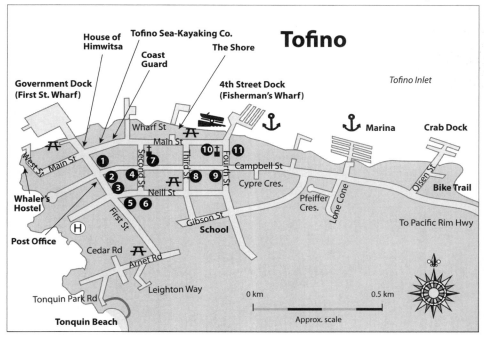

Tofino

House of Himwitsa
Tofino Sea-Kayaking Co.
The Shore
Coast Guard
Government Dock (First St. Wharf)
4th Street Dock (Fisherman's Wharf)
Tofino Inlet
Wharf St
Main St
Marina
Crab Dock
West St. Main St
Second St
Third St
Fourth St
Campbell St
Cypre Cres.
Olsen St
Bike Trail
Whaler's Hostel
Neill St
Pfeiffer Cres.
Lone Cone
Post Office
First St
Gibson St
School
To Pacific Rim Hwy
Cedar Rd
Arnet Rd
Leighton Way
0 km   0.5 km
Tonquin Park Rd
Approx. scale
Tonquin Beach

1. Co-op Grocery
2. Bank
3. Bakery
4. Schooner Restaurant
5. Sobo
6. Friends of Clayoquot Sound
7. Eagle Aerie Gallery
8. Whale Centre Museum
9. Tuff Beans
10. Jupiter's
11. Spotted Bear

4491, and you can send faxes from the post office downtown (phone 725-3734). Many cafés and restaurants have wireless internet for customers; for actual **computers** go to **Caffé Vincente**, downtown Tofino, 725-2599, or **The Tofitian**, at Outside Break shops near Chesterman Beach, 725-2631, www.tofitian.com.

THINGS TO DO

The House of Himwitsa Native Art Gallery features works by Native artists from all over BC and Canada's Arctic.

If you are a boat person, you will probably find that just watching the comings and goings at the First Street and Fourth Street docks can keep you occupied for hours. The **First Street dock** provides the best sunset view in summer (in winter the sun sets too far south). If you are interested in the village's historical buildings, go on the **self-guided tour** "A Walk Through Time" around town; this booklet is available at the Raincoast Education Society interpretive centre in the Botanical Gardens. History buffs should check out the archival photos of old Tofino hanging on the outside of the drug store.

In spite of Tofino's small size (only four blocks by two), you can easily while away a whole day at the docks and in town, browsing the many galleries and specialty shops and sipping cappuccino. Most of the shopping is in Tofino proper; there is a small but growing collection of funky local businesses

out near Chesterman Beach, too, at "Outside Break", on the east side of the highway, just town-side of the North Chestermans turn-off.

Tofino's dedicated locals ensure there are many events throughout the year, such as slide shows, movie nights, dance performances and talks by visiting scientists. Check the bulletin boards at the **Co-op Grocery Store** and **Common Loaf Bakery**, both on First St., and pick up the free magazine **Tofino Time** or look at its community listings online www.tofinotime.com.

Most of the things to do just outside of Tofino are water-based: sea kayaking, whale-watching and other boat tours, sport fishing and surfing. There are also a number of lovely sand beaches within the town area: Tonquin Beach, Mackenzie Beach, Chesterman Beach and Cox Bay. Although there is limited parking, you will probably find at least one of them within walking distance.

Annual festivals

The best resource for up-to-date listings of events around Tofino and Ucluelet, as well as exact festival dates, is www.tofinotime.com. You can also contact the visitors centres.

The **Pacific Rim Whale Festival** takes place in Ucluelet and Tofino for one week during mid-March, as thousands of grey whales pass by on their annual northward migration. Events include whale-watching by boat or from shore, talks by local naturalists, artist events, theme dinners, nature films and a whale parade, www.pacificrimwhalefestival.org.

ArtSplash! WestCoast Visual Art Show is held in conjunction with the Whale Festival in March, and showcases the work of numerous talented local artists, www.pacificrimarts.ca.

The annual **Shorebird Festival** celebrates the migrating birds that pass through by the tens of thousands on their northward spring migration. It is held on a weekend in late April or early May, and includes interpretive talks by visiting experts as well as opportunities to view birds through spotting scopes with local naturalists. Organized by the Rainforest Interpretive Centre, 725-2560, www.raincoasteducation.org.

In May and June, the rhodos are in full bloom around town! Clayoquot Island, now privately owned, invites the public to visit its private gardens for a **Clayoquot Days** weekend in mid-May. Contact the Tofino Visitor's Centre for information, 725-3414, www.tourismtofino.com.

The **Edge to Edge Marathon**, covers the near perfect 42 km marathon distance from Tofino to Ucluelet. It is now an accredited qualifier for the Boston Marathon. It takes place on a weekend in early June, and you can run the whole thing or enter as a five-person team. It is run in conjunction with a half-marathon route on Ucluelet's Wild Pacific Trail. 726-4641, www.edgetoedgemarathon.com.

The **Tofino Food and Wine Festival** takes place on a weekend in June, with restaurants, food producers and wineries from all over Vancouver Island; live music and arts events, 266-0724, www.tofinofoodandwinefestival.com.

The **Pacific Rim Summer Festival**, held in early July, consists of two weeks of live music (jazz, classical, world music and more) and First Nations performances, with different events taking place in Tofino, Ucluelet and Long Beach. Contact the local info centres for current information or www.pacificrimarts.ca.

The **Lantern Festival** takes place on a weekend around the end of August at the Tofino Botanical Gardens. Hundreds of candle-lit lanterns light up the night. Organized by the Raincoast Education Society, 725-2560, www.raincoasteducation.org.

The **O'Neill Coldwater Classic** is part of the qualifying series for the Association of Surfing Professionals World Tour. In October 2009, the competition was held in Tofino, marking the first time that that an international pro surf competition has ever taken place on Canadian shores. Organizers have indicated that they intend to have the Coldwater Classic return to Tofino in coming years, so watch their website for future plans, www.oneill.com/cwc.

Tofino's annual **Oyster Festival** is one of the most anticipated events of the year. The weekend-long event in mid-November includes the Mermaid's Ball, followed by a night of oyster-tasting as local restaurants vie for the coveted juried and people's choice awards. Other events include presentations about oysters and boat tours to operating oyster farms. Tickets for this popular event sell out early! For information, call 725-4222, 1-800-863-4664, www.oystergala.com.

Museums and educational displays

The **Whale Centre Museum** at Third and Campbell is open to the public year-round. This free display showcases rare objects from Tofino's early history, including a whale skeleton, old whaling harpoons and Nuu-chah-nulth artifacts, 725-2132, 1-888-474-2288, www.tofinowhalecentre.com.

Friends of Clayoquot Sound, behind the Bakery at 331 Neill, is a local grassroots environmental group founded in the early 1980s, when Meares Island was threatened by logging. Operating mostly by volunteer labour and funded by private donations, over the past two decades they have saved huge tracts of Clayoquot's pristine rainforest from clear-cut logging. Open to the public on weekdays, they have many displays about the rainforest and logging practices and are happy to provide information, 725-4218, www.focs.ca.

Tofino Botanical Gardens, 1084 Pacific Rim Highway 3 km/1.9 mi from town, theme gardens and rainforest trails fronting on the inlet (good birdwatching too), great on-site café, admission good for three days: $10

> ## WHALE RESEARCH
> The old wooden boat perched up upon the rocks, across the channel from the Weigh West resort, is mission central for **Strawberry Island Marine Research Society**. The society, funded in part by donations from local whale-watching companies, is a field-based research station that does the work that universities cannot. Ongoing projects include photo-identification of transient orcas (killer whales), deep-sea transects to identify and count marine mammals and birds that pass by, measuring and monitoring of eelgrass ecosystems, and investigation of the feeding patterns of both grey and humpback whales. For more information or to help support their research, contact Strawberry Island, 725-2211, www.strawberryisle.org.

adults, $6 students, children free (car-free arrivals discounted by $1), open daily year-round, 725-1220, www.tbgf.org.

The **Raincoast Education Society**, is now housed within the Botanical Gardens, below the Field Station. It has displays and exhibits about local wildlife, ecosystems and communities, and organizes indoor and outdoor programs for both adults and children. Although the building itself is closed over winter, programs are organized year-round; contact them for current information, 725-2560, www.raincoasteducation.org.

Amusements and activities

There is a **skate park** at the Village Green, downtown by Third and Campbell. A small **indoor swimming pool** with a **hot tub** is open to the public, $7, at **Mackenzie Beach Resort**, 3 km/1.9 mi from town, 725-3439. There is a **gym** with a good selection of weights and a few cardio machines, $8 entry; there is no front desk though, so contact **Tofino Fitness** for access and they will let you in, 725-8081. There is also a new **Alternative Indoor Climbing Gym**, 681 Industrial Way, open days and evenings year-round, 725-8777, www.climbtofino.com.

Yoga is big in Tofino—far too many options to list here. Check out the community calendar in TofinoTime magazine or online at www.tofinotime.com, for a selection of drop-in classes as well as courses and retreats. **Groovy Movie** at Outside Break shops near Chesterman Beach is a cool video store with a great selection of old and new films, open daily year-round, 725-2722; you can also rent videos at **LA Grocery** in town.

The **Long Beach Golf Course**, 15 km/9.3 mi out of town, with a 9-hole course as well as mini-golf, is open year-round, 725-3332 (page 135).

Nightlife

The Maquinna, known to locals as "the devil bar" with good reason, is the only bar in town. Cold beer and wine shop below. 120 First Street, 725-3261.

Dockside Pub overlooking the water at the Weigh West Marine Resort, 634 Campbell, 725-3277.

Tofino Legion Hall at Main and Second hosts live bands most weekends, open to the public—check Tofino Time magazine for listings.

Galleries

Cedar Corner Art Gallery, upstairs at Fourth and Campbell, a large gallery with a broad corss-section of local Vancouver Island original art, including painting, photography, sculpture, jewellery, open daily except for a few weeks in January, 725-2182, www.cedarcornerartgallery.com. **Driftwood**, 131 First St., souvenirs and gifts, beachware, jewellery, T-shirts and other clothing, open daily year-round, 725-3905. **Eagle Aerie Gallery**, 350 Campbell, gallery housed in a longhouse featuring prints, carvings, posters and books by Tsimshian artist Roy Henry Vickers, open daily year-round, 725-3235, 1-800-663-0669, www.royhenryvickers.com. **House of Himwitsa Native Art Gallery**, First and Main, sells traditional native art including paintings, prints, carvings, and jewellery, and is known especially for its impressive collection of exceptional masks. Open daily year-round, 725-2017, www.himwitsa.com.

Covet (at Ocean Oufitters), 368 Main, souvenirs, clothing, jewellery, books, art prints, nautical theme gifts, open daily year-round, 725-2860, www.covettofino.com. **Reflecting Spirit Gallery**, upstairs at 411 Campbell, featuring work of local artist/owner Signy Cohen as well as many other regional artists: paintings, sculpture, wood carvings, pottery, jewellery and other gifts, open daily year-round, 725-2472, www.reflectingspirit.ca. **Sandstone**

Ancient Cedars Spa offers massage for two in oceanfront treatment rooms.

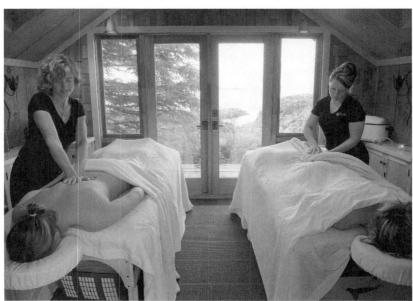

Jewellery and Gifts, at Second and Campbell, jewellery, glassware, local art including First Nations art, open daily year-round except for Mondays and Tuesdays in winter, 725-4482. **Shorewind Gallery**, 120 Fourth St., paintings, pottery, textiles, photography and jewellery by west coast artists, featuring the wildlife paintings of Mark Hobson, open daily year-round (closed Mondays over winter), 725-1222, www.shorewindgallery.com. **Spirit of Fire**, Outside Break shops near Chesterman Beach, watch artist Sol Maya create bowls and other large pieces from hand-blown glass using ancient traditional techniques, open Thursday through Monday year-round, 725-3122, www.solmaya.com. **The Treehouse**, 305 Campbell, various gifts and souvenirs including books and postcards, T-shirts and other clothing, open daily (except closed a few days of the week in January and February), 725-4254. **Tofino Art Glass**, 264 First St., artist Kevin Midgley's hand-crafted kiln-formed glass art pieces include bowls, trays, jewellery and custom art, open daily year-round, 725-3929, www.tofinoartglass.com. **Village Gallery**, 321 Main, in a historic 1920s former home, original paintings, fine-art prints, cards, pottery, jewellery and stained glass, open daily year-round, 725-4229.

No matter where you stay in Tofino, you are within walking distance of a beach.

Specialty shops

Also check out the surf shops, page 178. Aside from surfboard rentals and sales, most of them have large retail shops with a large selection of clothing and accessories.

Bella Boutique and Gallery, at Outside Break shops near Chesterman Beach, clothing and jewellery with a focus on local BC designers and products, open daily (may be closed some days in January and February), 725-3421.

Boutique Upstairs, upstairs from the Whale Centre at 411 Campbell, jewellery, stemware, lingerie and trendy clothing by Canadian designers, open daily year-round, 725-2132.

Castaways, 455 Campbell (behind the Info Centre), second-hand clothing, books, open daily over summer, weekends only in winter, 725-2004.

Celestial Sphere, 305 Campbell (behind the bank), natural fibre clothing, jewellery, crystals, health products, open daily except Mondays in winter, 483-5980.

Chocolate Tofino, Outside Break shops near Chesterman Beach, fine handmade Belgian chocolates crafted on-site, gourmet ice cream, open daily year-round, closed January, 725-2526, 725-2594.

Eco Everything on Fourth and Campbell, clothing and accessories made from hemp, organic cotton and merino wool, as well as eco-friendly household goods including treefree paper and cards and natural bodycare and aromatherapy products, open daily year-round, 725-2193, www.ecoeverything.com.

Habit Clothing and Apparel, 430 Campbell, unique clothing, mostly Canadian, focus on jeans, shoes, accessories, open daily year-round, 725-2906.

Tofino Sea Kayaking Company, located in the original Tofino Hotel at 320 Main, an intriguing selection of books ranging from fiction to nature guides to nautical themes, as well as great cappuccino and a range of kayak gear, open daily year-round, 725-4222, 1-800-863-4664, www.tofino-kayaking.com.

Mermaid's Tale Bookshop, 455 Campbell Street, eclectic book selection includes fiction, local authors, health and wellness, inspiration; also sells kites and children's games and models, open year-round (daily over summer), 725-2125, www.mermaidbooks.ca.

The Studio House, 451 Main, shared art studio with Cheeky Chic Boutique, clothing and other products made by local designer Lisa Jewell, and Project Munster paintings by Julie Robinson and other local artists (www.julierobinsonart.com), open daily year-round, 725-2631.

The **Tofino Botanical Gardens Giftshop**, 1084 Pacific Rim Highway, sells souvenirs as well as books with a focus

The Tofino Botanical Gardens boast several theme gardens and outdoor sculptures, and are home to the award-winning SoBo café.

on natural history, gardening, and field guides, open daily over summer, 725-1220.

The Tofitian, Outside Break shops near Chesterman Beach, is one of those hard-to-peg businesses, offering espresso, baked goods, high-speed internet access, and sales of clothing and herbal remedies, open daily year-round, 725-2631, www.tofitian.com.

Spas and Massage

Arbutus Health, Outside Break shops near Chesterman Beach, acupuncture, massage, private yoga, 725-2212, www.arbutusacupuncture.com.

Ancient Cedars Spa, the award-winning spa at the Wickaninnish Inn on Chesterman Beach, a wide range of massage treatments including hot stone and lomi lomi, body wraps, esthetic treatments, with exclusive oceanfront treatment rooms, 725-3113, www.wickinn.com.

Sacred Stone Spa, 421 Main, massage, body therapies, Chinese medicine, esthetic services, infrared sauna, open year-round, 725-3341, www.sacredstone.ca.

Solwood Studio Spa, 1298 Lynn Rd., massage, raindrop and hot stone therapy, aromatherapy, esthetics, open year-round, 725-2112, 1-866-725-2112, www.solwood.ca.

Thérèse Bouchard, longterm local massage therapist with a peaceful private rainforest studio, 725-4278.

Walks and day hikes

There are some lovely walks and short hikes to do in the national park around Long Beach (page 144), as well as several pretty walks to do right from Tofino.

For an educational and historical walk around town, pick up the booklet "A Walk Through Time" from the **Rainforest Education Society** (located in the Botanical Gardens, open over summer, 725-2560) or **Tofino Sea-Kayaking**

GREY WHALE MIGRATION

Grey whales are the most common whale species off Vancouver Island's coast. They pass by here in the thousands during the spring, as they head northward on their annual migration.

Grey whales make one of the longest migrations of any mammal. The round trip, between their winter calving grounds in lagoons off Mexico's Pacific coast and summer feeding grounds in the Bering and Chukchi Seas, is about 20,000 km (12,427 mi).

While most grey whales simply pass by Vancouver Island as they head northward, a few stop to feed for the summer. One whale, known to researchers and whale-watching drivers as "Two-dot-star," has been returning to the waters off of Clayoquot Sound and Long Beach to feed every summer for 30 years.

Co. (320 Main, 725-4222) and take yourself on a tour of the historic buildings that date back to the settlers' era.

Tonquin Beach is a charming little municipal park, a tiny wave-washed beach with open ocean views close to downtown Tofino. The beach is about a 20-minute walk from downtown: head to the end of First Street (away from the water) and turn right on Arnet and then left on Tonquin Park Rd. You will see a sign for the park on the left, and from here a pretty (but slippery) boardwalk trail through the rainforest takes you to the beach. This is a great

Some of the largest and oldest western red cedar trees in Canada may be seen along Meares Island's Big Tree Trail.

place to watch the sunset in winter, and in summer you can sometimes see grey whales playing in the tidal currents right near shore (best chance to see them is on a big ebb tide).

Beach-goers lean back into the winter wind as sea foam races across the beach.

If you are up for a longer walk, jog or bike ride, it is 4.5 km/2.8 mi from Tofino to **Chesterman Beach**, all along the paved multi-use path beside the highway; turn right when you get to Lynn Rd., just past Beaches Grocery, for the beach. Chesterman Beach itself is 2 km/1.2 mi in length, and makes for a lovely walk at any time of day or night and in any weather. However, parking is extremely limited, so it is best if you can arrive here by foot, bike or the Beach Bus. At the north end of the beach, the **Carving Shed** beside the Wickaninnish Inn is open to visitors who want to watch highly skilled local artists at work. Call 726-5062 for more information.

Hiking in Meares Island Tribal Park: Meares Island was declared a **Tribal Park** by Tla-o-qui-aht hereditary chiefs in 1984 (see info box, p. 136). There are two hiking trails here. Don't be put off by the fact that they are on

HOPING FOR BAD WEATHER

Storm-watching has become such a popular winter aim of visitors that we Tofino locals now get a good chuckle on those spectacular crisp sunny days that also just randomly appear throughout winter. As we flood to the beaches to soak in the sun, the tourists complain about the fine weather: "Well, we had really hoped for a storm. . ." The moral is "Be prepared for anything, and take what you get." It can be sunny in winter, and it can storm in summer—either way, some people complain.

The many inlets of Clayoquot Sound are best explored in silence, by sea kayak.

an island—a short, easy-to-arrange (and scenic) boat ride gets you to either trailhead, see information below. There is a $5 ecosystem service fee for trail use; for current information on how to pay the fee, contact the tribal park office 888-425-3350, 725-3350 x27, www.tribalparks.ca or stop in at the Tla-o-qui-aht Treaty Office at 1118 Pacific Rim Hwy (top of the Tin Wis Resort driveway).

The **Big Tree Trail** is not to be missed. This trail is part of a network of paths put in by concerned citizens when Meares Island was threatened with logging in the early 1980s. Most of the paths have overgrown, but here you can walk 1 km/0.62 mi along a boardwalk trail under the shadows of some of Canada's largest and oldest western red cedar trees. If you don't mind trudging through mud, you can continue off the end of the boardwalk to complete a 5 km/3.1 mi loop through more of this unique intact ancient old-growth – or just double back to the trailhead along the boardwalk (which can be very slippery when damp!). Even though the trails are short, there is lots to see, so plan on spending at east an hour or two to do the boardwalk, or at least 3 hours if hiking the loop.

Hiking up **Lone Cone**, the prominent mountain that dominates the view from the Tofino docks, is a challenging but rewarding experience. Lone Cone, on the southwestern section of Meares Island, was long rumoured to be an extinct volcano but its symmetrical shape is actually just a result of erosion. A steep and gruelling hike up a narrow rainforest trail, with the occasional fallen log to scramble over along the way, takes you to the peak which, at 725 m (2375'), provides spectacular 180° views southwestward from Long Beach to Vargas Island. Allow 3 to 4 hours for the ascent, and 2 to 3 hours to come down.

If you are an experienced sea kayaker, it is only a short paddle across Tofino Harbour to either trailhead on Meares Island; contact **Tofino Sea Kayaking Co**. for kayak rentals and route information, 725-4222, www.tofino-kayaking.com. Most of Tofino's kayak companies offer guided half-day trips that include an interpretive walk along the boardwalked section of Big Tree Trail. Several companies offer return motorboat transport to and from the trailheads for about $25-30; e.g. **Tofino Water Taxi**, 877-726-5485, 726-5485, www.tofinowatertaxi.com; **Joe Martin Custom Tours**, 726-5062; or **Clayoquot Connections**, booking through Jamie's Whaling Station, 725-3919 or 726-8789.

Storm-watching

From Tofino, you can really get right out into the storm. Some of the best storm-watching is from **Chesterman Beach**, especially near the rocks at the north and south ends. If the tide is low you can walk out to **Frank Island**, but be very cautious on the rocks here during a storm. **Cox Bay** is also a great storm-watching spot. Giant waves roar into this unprotected bay, so there is lots of action both along the beach and on the rocks at both ends. Also, check out the great storm viewing spots nearby at Long Beach (page 145). Storm-watching is best done from outside, so that it is a full sensory experience. If you really must do it from behind glass, the restaurants at the **Wickaninnish Inn** and the **Long Beach Lodge** are the places to be.

Naturalist Bill McIntyre offers **guided storm-watching hikes** October through April, and his company, **Long Beach Nature Tours**, is licensed to guide within the national park. A former park ranger, he knows the terrain and can get you to the best viewing spots for the conditions, 726-7099, www.longbeachnaturetours.com.

Bike tours

There are no organized bike tours here, but you can rent bikes. A paved path continues for 7 km/4.4 mi south of town, past Chesterman Beach and out to the info centre by Cox Bay, and it is possible to ride on either of these beaches. Although you can continue all the way to Long Beach, past Cox Bay there is no bike path and the highway is narrow without a shoulder. However, you can get your bike out to Long Beach on the **Beach Bus** for no extra charge and from here, if you have a *Backroads Mapbook*, you can also head off-road to explore the logging roads in the area.

Eco Everything, by the stop sign at Fourth and Campbell, rents mountain bikes, beach cruisers and surfboard racks, from $25/day, 725-2192. **Groovy Movie**, at Outside Break near Chesterman Beach, rents beach cruisers, $8/hr or $25 for 24 hours, open daily year-round, noon to 10pm, 725-2722. **TOF Cycle**, at 660 Sharp Road (200 m down from the Dolphin Motel, near Chesterman Beach) rents mountain bikes, beach cruisers, tandem bikes, and has a range of gear for families such as kids' bikes, trail-a-bikes, trikes, and baby seats, starting from $15/day. Can drop bikes off to renters, also offers repairs and sales. Open daily except January, 725-2453.

Kayaking

The combination of open surf-washed beaches, sheltered inlets and bays, and pristine rainforest makes **Clayoquot Sound** one of the world's best-known sea kayaking destinations. Launching from Tofino, you will find many options for poking around the islands on day trips or for heading out on longer overnight tours. (For kayaking safety tips, see "Kayaking on the ocean," page 68.)

Whether you are heading out on a day trip or a multi-day kayak expedition, plan on checking in with **Tofino Sea Kayaking Co.** on Main Street. They offer a wealth of "local knowledge" type information in the form of maps and books, compiled by their guides over the years and available for visitors to browse through on their back deck. For more information on planning your own kayak expedition through Clayoquot Sound, see above.

There is a public **kayak launch** at the bottom of **First Street**, beside the dock. (There is also a launch to access the southern part of the Sound at Grice Bay, in Pacific Rim National Park Reserve, page 147.) Beware of Tofino Harbour: it is often glassy and calm in the morning, and then turns to a raging sea of whitecaps in the afternoon, especially if the westerly wind is opposing an ebb tide. The harbour is also very busy; for your own safety, make sure you know where the boat channels are and where the float planes are landing before you set out, and avoid those areas.

CLAYOQUOT SOUND: MULTI-DAY KAYAKING ADVENTURES

Clayoquot became a household word after the protests in the 1990s that succeeded in preserving much of its old-growth stands of forest from the logging industry. All of Clayoquot is now designated as a UNESCO World Biosphere Reserve—which does not mean that it is preserved—and within it are many small provincial parks that really are accessible only by kayak or other small boat (pages 188–92).

Three of the largest islands off Vancouver Island's coast are here, **Flores**, **Meares** and **Vargas** islands, and there are many smaller islets and deep fjords around and behind them. Circumnavigating **Meares Island** is a 2–5-day trip in waters protected from ocean swell, but still subject to strong winds at times. This route is quiet—you won't run into a lot of boat traffic or even other kayakers, and it offers lots of opportunities to see wildlife (especially bears), but choices in camping spots are limited, especially if tides are very high. The sweeping surfswept sand beaches on the outer shores of **Vargas** and **Flores** islands are spectacular to paddle around and to camp on, but they are all subject to ocean swell (as well as wind and current), so good technical skills including surf landings are essential. You can design trips to take in these beaches that range anywhere from 2 days to 2 weeks. **Hot Springs Cove** is also a popular destination. It normally takes between 2 and 6 days each way to paddle there from Tofino, depending upon your exact choice of route: the longer but more protected "inside," or the slightly shorter "outside" route along Flores Island's unforgiving, rocky and surf-bashed west coast—for expert paddlers only! This trip requires lots of contingency planning, because in some conditions you cannot get there (or perhaps back) at all, and there are few places to camp or even land on the northern half of this route.

There are several water taxis that can take kayaks, so it is possible to plan one-way paddling trips. The scheduled taxis, the Matlahaw which services Hot Springs Cove (670-1106) and the Ahousaht Pride which runs to Ahousat on Flores Island (670-9563), both can take kayaks, but you would do best to book in advance to be sure they have room. Some of the whale-watching boats might transport you and your kayaks one-way to or from Hot Springs Cove if they have space; try **The Whale Centre** or **Ocean Outfitters** (page 173). For custom charter service in an open herring skiff that can drop you and your gear at almost any location in the Sound, call **Tofino Water Taxi**, 726-5485, 1-877-726-5485, or **Marcel Theriault**, 726-8438. There are also a number of remote lodges and hostels on several islands and points around Clayoquot Sound (page 193)—on Vargas Island, in the village of Ahousat on Flores Island, and at Hot Springs Cove—so it is possible to plan a wilderness kayak trip here that does not require camping every night.

Tofino's sea kayaking companies have come up with a pretty similar menu of day trips: a two-and-a-half-hour harbour islands tour and a four-hour trip with a stop for a rainforest walk on Meares Island. **Tofino Sea Kayaking Co.** also offers longer, full-day trips along the shores of Meares or Vargas Island, as well as overnight trips and rentals.

Paddle West Kayaking (at Jamie's Whaling Station), offers guided day trips from $59, 725-3919, www.jamies.com. **Remote Passages**, downtown on Main Street, guided day trips from $64, March through November, 725-

3330, 1-800-666-9833, www.remotepassages.com. **Tofino Sea Kayaking Co.**, downtown on Main Street, in operation since 1988, Tofino's oldest and largest sea kayaking company and the only local company that offers rentals (experienced paddlers only), guided day trips from $59, daily rentals from $40 (singles) and $74 (doubles). Open year-round, 725-4222, 1-800-863-4664, www.tofino-kayaking.com.

Tofino Sea Kayaking Co. is the only local kayak company that offers overnight trips. 3-day lodge-based trips to Vargas Island run from May to October, $780, and longer wilderness 4- to 6-day trips start at $900, 725-4222, 1-800-863-4664, www.tofino-kayaking.com.

For **kayaking courses**, **Tofino Sea Kayaking Co**. runs day clinics and weekend courses as well as week-long courses that provide the fundamentals of expedition planning in addition to paddling. **Rainforest Kayak Adventures** no longer has a storefront in Tofino, but local kayak gurus Dan Lewis and Bonny Glambeck still offer multi-day kayak courses oriented towards advanced paddlers and those seeking guide certification, 1-877-422-9453, www.rainforestkayak.com.

Canoeing

Clayoquot Sound is probably North America's only top paddling destination where you can choose between a sea kayak or a traditional dugout Native canoe. **Tla-o-qui-aht canoes**, carved from a single cedar log, have been used on Clayoquot Sound for millennia. Brothers Carl and Joe Martin, who hail from Opitsaht, are actively carving traditional canoes using techniques handed down to them by their father and their grandfathers. **Tlaook Cultural Adventures**, run by Joe's daughter Gisele Martin, offers guided canoe day trips led by Tla-o-qui-aht guides, ranging from short paddles around Tofino harbour to interpretive trips to Meares Island Tribal Park, from $55, May through October, 725-2656, 1-877-942-2663, www.tlaook.com.

Nature tours and wildlife viewing

You can witness the annual **salmon spawn** at some of the creeks around Ucluelet, about a 45-minute drive from Tofino (page 123), or you can head out to Meares Island. Some of the small creeks in Lemmens Inlet—accessible only by kayak on a short paddle from Tofino—have runs of chum around the end of October. The fish congregate in the estuaries, but can only be seen going up the tiny creeks after recent rains have raised water levels. If you are an experienced sea kayaker, this makes a nice day trip—just go exploring the small creeks on the chart (but beware of bears!). If you prefer to travel with a guide, you may be able to get the folks at Tofino Sea Kayaking Co. to arrange a custom tour for you.

Ucluelet-based **Long Beach Nature Tours** also offers guided interpretive walking tours in the Tofino area as well as in the national park and around Ucluelet, group rates available, 726-7099, www.longbeachnaturetours.com.

See also tour operators listed in the Birdwatching section, page 174.

Whale-watching, bear-watching and hot springs trips

Trips generally run from March to October, with a few companies remaining open year-round. Boat trips out of Tofino have a pretty standard format, with most companies offering 2½- to 3-hour **whale-watching** and **bear-watching** trips, and 6- to 7-hour trips to **Hot Springs Cove**. The big difference to look out for is the type of boat; some may prefer the rough and bouncy ride of a Zodiac while others will look for a larger covered boat.

In addition to whales or bears, most of these tours get you to places where you may see **sea lions**, **seals**, **porpoises** and a variety of **unusual seabirds**. **Grey whales** can be seen throughout most of the season, while the more active **humpback whales** are more likely to be seen from July onward. Although it is possible to see **orcas** here, their movements are unpredictable. Many operators post information about what wildlife they have been seeing lately.

For a completely different viewing experience, consider **whale-watching by plane**. In the water, you only see the parts of the whale that are above the water surface (usually the back and the tail). Although you don't quite get the feeling of being at one with nature from a noisy plane, you can often get views of the entire whales, and see the paths that they are tracking. Scenic float plane tours start at $80 per person. Call **Atleo River Air**, 725-2205, 1-866-662-8536 or **Tofino Air**, 725-4454, 1-866-486-3247.

Bear-watching tours up the inlets run for most of the summer season. Look for an operator that schedules trips with the tide. For the best chance of seeing bears, you want to be out in the morning on a low tide; this generally occurs around, or during the few days just after, the full or new moon.

Hot Springs Cove is one of the world's natural wonders: geothermally heated waters pour out from a steaming vent in the rainforest, and trickle down over a hot waterfall and through a series of natural rock pools to the sea. See page 195 for more information on Hot Springs Cove.

THE HUMPBACKS ARE BACK!

By the early 1900s, humpback whales had been hunted to near-extinction all around Vancouver Island. Happily, they have started to return. In the mid-1990s, local whale-watchers were surprised to see humpbacks in both Barkley and Clayoquot Sounds. Since then, the whales have become regular summer residents. They are far more active than the resident grey whales, which feed on the bottom. Humpbacks feed alone and in groups on small fish or krill, lunging and occasionally leaping clear out of the water. These days, you are likely to see both grey and humpback whales when whale-watching over the summer months, and there is a possibility of seeing orcas year-round.

Huge wooden dugouts used by Tlaook Cultural Adventures are identical to the sea-going canoes once used to hunt whales far offshore.

For trips to the springs, try to avoid weekends in summer. The natural hot pools are very small, and at times they can be so crowded that there is a throng of people hovering around the rocks just waiting for a turn to get in the water. The pools are undeveloped, and the rocks around them are steep and uneven, so this is not a good trip for people who are not steady on their feet. The springs are not always "hot." Heavy rain can chill them down, and high tides and big swell can also flood the pools with cold ocean water and surf, making it impossible to get in. If a peaceful dip at the Hot Springs matters a lot to you, look into an overnight stay (page 197) so you can hit the pools after the day-trippers leave.

The **Browning Passage**, a 36' Canoe Cove Cruiser with a kitchen and cabin, operated by a former Tofino Coast Guard employee, is available for bear-watching and whale-watching trips ($85) and Hot Springs charters and other custom tours, as well as a trip to a remote floating artists' studio and sunset cruises, 725-3435, 726-8605, www.browningpass.com. **li-wuss Wildlife Charters** is run by long-time Clayoquot Sound seafarer Moses Martin, who offers custom wildlife-viewing and scenic charters for up to 4 people for $125/hour, 726-2765, 266-2765.

Jamie's Whaling Station and Adventure Centre, 606 Campbell, runs whale-watching, bear-watching and other scenic trips on Zodiacs or on their 65' covered vessel (Tofino's largest tour boat), $80–100, and Hot Springs trips on covered boats $110 (including their "Sea-to-Sky" Hot Springs option,

by boat one way and float plane the other $175), March through October, 725-3919, 1-800-667-9913, www.jamies.com. **Joe Martin Custom Tours** is a chance to learn from a local Tla-o-qui-aht guide, canoe carver Joe Martin, custom bear-watching trips $75 and private tours from an open boat that can take up to 8 people $95/hr, March through November, 726-5062. **Ocean Outfitters**, on Main Street between Second and Third, whale-watching and bear-watching tours in a Zodiac or covered boat, from $79, daily Hot Springs trips in a comfortable covered boat from $80, year-round, 725-2866, 1-877-906-2326, www.oceanoutfitters.bc.ca. **Remote Passages**, at the bottom of Wharf Street beside the Coast Guard Station, whale-watching and bear-watching in Zodiacs, $70, and covered boats, $75, and Hot Springs tours in Zodiacs and covered boats, $110-120, March through November, 725-3330, 1-800-666-9833, www.remotepassages.com.

Tofino Water Taxi provides tours of Tofino Harbour and surroundings in their zero-emissions electric boat, 1-2 hours from $35 per person, as well as custom tours in their covered boat that seats up to 8 passengers from $150/ hour, 726-5485, 1-877-726-5485, www.tofinowatertaxi.com. **The Whale Centre**, 411 Campbell Street, with its free whaling museum, whale-watching, bear-watching and marine birdwatching trips in open or covered boats $70, and Hot Springs trips in covered boats, $90-100, open year-round, 725-2132, 1-888-474-2288, www.tofinowhalecentre.com. **West Coast Aquatic Safaris,** 101A Fourth St., runs whale-watching, bear-watching and other scenic trips in a covered boat, $80, and Hot Springs trips $110 (as well as a fly/boat Hot Springs day-trips, $165), 725-9227, 1-877-594-2537, www.whalesafaris.com.

Birdwatching

Tofino and Clayoquot Sound are prime birdwatching territory. In Tofino alone, more than 300 bird species have been recorded, from the majestic bald eagle to the tiny rufous hummingbird. This is one of the few places where you can relatively easily boat out to the open sea, far from shore, to look for pelagic species such as the **puffin**, **albatross** and **petrel**. A favoured birdwatching spot right in town is along Second Street between Main and Campbell. Birdfeeders in private yards on both sides of the road attract a range of songbirds and hummingbirds year-round, including a range of **sparrows** and **finches**, as well as both **rufous** and **Anna's hummingbirds**.

The beaches. The outer coastal beaches (Chesterman, Mackenzie and Middle Beach around Tofino, as well as nearby Long Beach) are great places to see migratory birds, especially the many species of shorebirds that pass through in April/May and again through the fall and winter. You may also see **peregrine falcons** and other **raptors** that prey on the migrating shorebirds here.

Tofino's mudflats are a rewarding stop for birdwatchers during the spring shorebird migration.

Tofino mudflats. There are few places in the world where this incredibly productive intertidal ecosystem is so easily accessible. You can access the Tofino mudflats via Sharp Rd. (turn east off the highway 4 km/2.5 mi out of Tofino), from the Tofino Botanical Gardens, or from the Orca Lodge's waterfront property (private, guest access only) that backs onto the mudflats. During the spring shorebird migration, in late April and early May, flocks of **western sandpipers** and **dunlin** on the mudflats may number in

the tens of thousands, and you will also see other species such as **plovers, dowitchers, whimbrels, marbled godwits** and **greater yellowlegs**.

Offshore. Seabirds such as **marbled murrelets, rhinoceros auklets** and sometimes **tufted puffins**, as well as a variety of **gulls**, can be spotted from boats along the open coasts. Many of these birds nest on the tiny offshore islands. Seabirds can be seen on commercial whale-watching tours from Bamfield (page 98), Tofino (page 171) or Ucluelet (page 124). If you tell your driver that you have a special interest in birds, you may get taken to a few special places. If you are really keen on seeing pelagic species, you will probably have to privately charter a boat to get you far offshore, but you stand a good chance of seeing **black-footed albatrosses, least storm petrels, northern fulmars**, and several species of **shearwaters**—as well as perhaps a few surprises!

The semipalmated plover is one of many shorebird species that stop to feed on Pacific Rim beaches during their annual migration.

Local specialist guides who know seasonal bird movements and best viewing spots can help find rare species. On forested slopes, you may see mountain birds like the **red-breasted sapsucker, blue grouse** and **screech owl**. Summer trips to the shores of the rivers and lakes may reveal close encounters with **bald eagles, pied-billed grebes, loons, pileated woodpeckers** and a variety of **warblers**. Ocean tours along the coast or farther out to sea may encounter **tufted puffins, harlequin ducks** and various uncommon **gulls**, and, farther from shore, possible sightings of **albatross, petrels, fulmars** and **shearwaters**. Tofino-based naturalist and birder **Adrian Dorst** has studied birds here for 40 years and is a co-author of *Birds of Pacific Rim National Park*. He leads custom guided nature tours and bird-viewing tours, $100 per person for 4 hours, 725-1243, www.adriandorst.com. **Just Birding** is run by Tofino-based but internationally-experienced birding guide **George Bradd**, who offers walking tours as well as boat-based and canoe-based trips oriented both to beginning and experienced birders, from $100, 725-2520, www.justbirding.com.

Ucluelet-based **Long Beach Nature Tours** offers guided nature walks year-round that include birdwatching in the Tofino–Ucluelet area, and are licensed to operate within Pacific Rim National Park Reserve, private guided hikes for up to 5 people $180, group rates available, 726-7099, www.oceansedge.bc.ca.

Scenic cruises

Many of the whale-watching companies listed above include scenic

A fly fisherman displays a river-caught steelhead.

Photo courtesy of Jay Mohl

tours as part of their trips, especially on the Hot Springs run. The ones with slower-paced options are:

The ***Browning Passage***, a 36' Canoe Cove Cruiser that sleeps 6 people, is available for scheduled tours including short trips to view wildlife, visit a remote floating artist's studio, or watch the sunset, $85, as well as for evening party cruises and other longer custom trips, e.g. Hot Springs day-charter for up to 12 people, $1000, 725-3435, 726-8605, www.browningpass.com.

Clayoquot Connections offers a range of slow-paced custom tours on their 26' red lifeboat, including harbour and sunset cruises $20, drop-offs to the Meares Island Big Tree Trail $30, and longer wilderness cruises including Lennard Island lighthouse from $70. Book through Jamie's Adventure Centre, 725-3919, 726-8789, 1-800-667-9913, www.jamies.com.

Tofino Water Taxi provides tours of Tofino Harbour and surroundings in their zero-emissions electric boat, 1-2 hours from $35 per person, 726-5485, 1-877-726-5485, www.tofinowatertaxi.com.

Fishing

The waters in and around Clayoquot Sound offer a range of activities for fishers—**offshore fishing** for salmon and halibut, the best **saltwater fly fishing** on the coast, and float-plane accessible **freshwater fishing** in rivers and lakes all year.

The salmon season extends throughout the whole year, with smaller chinook remaining in the area for the entire winter. From May to July large chinook ranging from 6.8 to 18.2 kg (15 to 40 lbs) can be got offshore, and then from July to September even larger chinook are found around kelp beds. Coho are caught offshore during the middle and late summer. Halibut and rockfish can be fished from March through October.

The relatively sheltered waters of Clayoquot Sound are becoming known

CLAYOQUOT SOUND WORLD BIOSPHERE RESERVE

Clayoquot Sound was designated by UNESCO as a World Biosphere Reserve in 2000. This designation resulted from years of work spearheaded by local citizens who were dedicated to preserving Clayoquot for generations to come. The phrase Biosphere "Reserve" seems to be misunderstood by many. A "reserve" is not a "preserve," and in actual fact UNESCO has absolutely no jurisdiction here, and cannot tell the federal or local government, or even companies or land owners, what to do. Designation as a "World Biosphere Reserve" is intended to draw attention to a place on our planet that is special and unique. The aims of a Biosphere Reserve are not to stop all industry and protect everything. Rather, they are to find a way to promote a balanced relationship between humans and nature, that can include communities and industry while still maintaining wilderness areas and promoting values of conservation.

Industries including industrial logging and fish farming are still taking place within the region, and our communities are still working on achieving the balance of people living and working here without destroying those same opportunities for future generations.

For more information, contact:

Clayoquot Biosphere Trust, 316 Main St, Tofino, 725-2219, www.clayoquotbiosphere.org.
Friends of Clayoquot Sound, 331 Neill St., Tofino, 725-4218, www.focs.ca.

as Canada's premier saltwater fly fishing destination. Fly fishers target coho salmon and sea-run cutthroat trout from March to October, with the main cutthroat fishing from March to June and the best salmon in September and October. Bottomfish and chinook can also be caught up the inlets, with fishing for smaller "feeder" chinook continuing throughout the winter months.

Freshwater fishing is a year-round activity. In the rivers, steelhead are around from January to June, and rainbow and cutthroat trout can be found March to December. Rainbow and cutthroat trout are also fished from the lakes from March through October. For guided freshwater fishing trips contact **Jay's Clayoquot Ventures**, listed below.

Most of the charter companies offer both half- and full-day ocean trips with all gear provided. Minimum trip length is normally 4 to 5 hours; many companies offer accommodation packages as well. **Fishing licences** are available at Clayoquot Ventures, Method Marine Supply, 725-3251, and Tofino Consumers Co-op Hardware Store, 725-3436.

Biggar Fish Charters, inshore and offshore charters $100-110/hr, 726-8987, 1-800-307-0277, www.biggarfish.com. **Chinook Charters**, 30' boat for offshore and inlets takes up to 8 passengers, $600/half-day (up to 4 people), $950/day, 725-3431, 726-5221, www.chinookcharters.com. **Hymax Charters**, fly fishing and offshore charters in 40' fishing yacht, from $125/hr, 266-0146, www.hymaxcharters.com. **Jay's Clayoquot Ventures**, a wide range of trips, including offshore half- and full-day trips for salmon and halibut, $110/hr, saltwater fly fishing, $95/hr, and remote river and lake fly-in excursions from $1350/day for 2 people, as well as overnight lake packages, 725-2700, 1-888-534-7422, www.tofinofishing.com.

Ii-wuss Wildlife Charters, offshore and inlet fishing in 24' covered boat with onboard toilet, with Tla-o-qui-aht guide Moses Martin, $125/hr for up to 4 people, 725-2765, 255-2765. **Ospray Charters**, 4- to 10-hour ocean charters for up to 6 people, from $475, 725-2133, 1-888-286-3466, www.ospray.com. **Shallow Water Ventures**, inlet fishing from 18' Boston Whaler, $80/hr maximum 2 passengers, 725-1259, 1-877-725-1264, www.shallowwaterventures.com. **Tofino Charters**, custom charters and offshore fishing in 23' boat, from $100/hr for up to 6 people, 522-0994, 725-3767, www.tofinocharters.com. **Weigh West Marine Resort**, 21–26' offshore charter boats and smaller fly fishing boats, $110-115/hr maximum 4 passengers, meal and accommodation packages available, open year-round, 725-3277, 1-800-665-8922 www.weighwest.com.

Boating

There is a public boat launch right in town, at the **Fourth Street dock**. Nearby, there are also launches at **Grice Bay** within Pacific Rim National Park Reserve (16 km/9.9 mi out of town, page 147), at **Kennedy Lake** (pages 136–37), and in **Ucluelet** (page 126). There is also a **public kayak launch** in Tofino, beside the First Street dock.

Diving

There is great diving around shallow rocky reefs and kelp beds in Clayoquot Sound. This is an area for experienced divers only; strong tidal currents and cold water can quickly create dangerous situations.

WATER SHORTAGE IN THE RAINFOREST

In a part of the world that receives 4 m (13 feet) of rain annually, it may be surprising that Tofino is subject to water shortages. Part of the problem lies in the fact that Tofino is located on the tip of a narrow peninsula. Even though a lot of precipitation falls here, there are no creeks and no place to contain all that water. At the moment, Tofino gets most of its water supplies from the tiny rainforest creeks on Meares Island – a pristine patch of old-growth forest that was protected from logging in the 1980s by a group of concerned local citizens (many of whom did jail time for their protest actions).

A severe water shortage in the summer of 2006 resulted in closure of the town to visitors at the end of that summer. Since then, another reservoir has been dug on Meares Island in order to increase storage capacity – but the treatment and delivery infrastructure is still not up to what the town's temporary population of 20,000 or more may require during the peak summer months.

There is talk of eventually constructing a pipeline to bring water in from Kennedy Lake. Until that happens, please treat our fresh water like the precious resource that it is – even when the rain is pouring all around you.

Tofino is without doubt Canada's surfing capital.

Tofino finally has a dive shop. **Ocean Planet Adventures**, 564 Campbell, offers custom programs for all experience levels, ranging from introductory dives for people wanting to try diving, $99, to PADI open water and advanced certification courses and specialty certificates. For experienced divers, custom half-day charters which include equipment rental and a Divemaster guide are available from $199, 725-2221, 1-888-725-2220, www.divetofino.com. Tank refills are air only.

You can also refill scuba tanks (air only, no mixed gases) at **Method Marine**, 380 Main St., open daily year-round, 725-3251..

Surfing

Tofino has long been regarded as Canada's surfing capital. But when Tofino local-boy Pete Devries won Canada's first international pro surf contest, against a field of 120 of the world's best in October, 2009, Tofino show-cased itself as a world-class surf destination. The waves off Tofino's many beaches are full most days, with surfers who have come from across Canada to learn, as well as those who have come from around the world to check out the cold-water action.

Where that action is depends upon the exact size and direction of the swell. Chesterman Beach is long enough that there is usually some surf going off on one end or the other, although it is sometimes too small to surf over summer. Cox Bay tends to get bigger surf, but it can get extremely rough and also often has strong rip currents. Watch the conditions carefully for at least a few sets before deciding whether or not to go in. There are also many good surf beaches in the national park at and around Long Beach.

Several Tofino companies offer rentals of boards, wetsuits and other gear, and provide surfing instruction.

Bruhwiler Surf School, run by Raph Bruhwiler who, for years, has been one of Canada's top-ranked surfers, group and private lessons, $75/100 and surf day-camps from $135, and multi-day camps, 726-5481, www.bruhwilersurf.com. **Live to Surf**, at Ocean Break shops near Chesterman Beach is Tofino's first surf shop, established 1984, sales, daily rentals of surfboards ($25/6 hrs) as well as bodyboards, skimboards, wetsuits and roof racks, 725-4464, www.livetosurf.com. **Long Beach Surf Shop**, 630 Campbell, surfboard and wetsuit rentals from $15 each, shop sells boards, surfwear, skateboards and accessories, 725-3800, www.longbeachsurfshop.com. **Pacific Surf School**, 430 Campbell (beside Storm Surf Shop) group and private lessons 79/130, 2- to 4-day camps from $450, 725-2155, 1-888-777-9961, www.pacificsurfschool.com. **Storm Surf**, sales of surfboards, bodyboards, skimboards, wetsuits and roofracks, large retail shop also sells clothing and accessories, 725-3344, www.stormsurfshop.com. **Surf Sister**, started by former Canadian women's surf champ Jenny Stewart and still locally owned, group and lessons from $75/130, also family and kids' lessons, weekend clinics $195, camps, 725-4456, 1-877-724-7873, www.surfsister.com. **Westside Surf School** at Ocean Break shops near Chesterman Beach, operated by another member of Tofino's surfing dynasty, Sepp Bruhwiler, group and private lessons $75/90, daily surf camps $150, also youth camps, 725-2404, www.westsidesurfschool.com.

Float plane tours

Two float plane companies operate out of Tofino. Both provide scenic tours of the area—Long Beach, the isles and fjords of Clayoquot Sound, and the snowy peaks of Strathcona Provincial Park—and can also be chartered for drops to outlying areas such as remote mountain lakes or Hot Springs Cove. Prices are surprisingly economical if your group can fill up a plane; Cessnas hold 3 people and Beavers can take 7. Charters start at $550/hr.

Atleo River Air Service, dock on Wingen Lane, down the hill from Main and Second and beside "The Shore", custom charters and scenic tours, 725-2205, 1-866-662-8536, www.atleoair.com. **Tofino Air**, on the First Street dock, custom charters and scenic tours as well as daily scheduled flights to Hot Springs Cove $80 each way, 725-4454, 1-866-486-3247, www.tofinoair.ca.

WHERE TO STAY

You will find that accommodation prices in Tofino are a notch or two higher than elsewhere on the Pacific Rim. Tofino has a preponderance of vacation rental units, ranging from oceanview condos to magnificent beachfront homes, available for nightly, or in some cases weekly, bookings. The two main local companies that manage vacation rental units are **Tofino Beach Homes**, 725-2570, www.tofinobeach.com, and **Tofino Vacation Rentals Inc.**, 725-2779, 1-877-799-2779, www.tofinovr.com.

For the most complete and current listings of all available accommodation, contact the **Tofino Visitor Centre**, 725-3414, www.tourismtofino.com. Email info@tourism.com with your dates and what you are looking for and they will circulate your request to accommodation businesses. The website www.tofinolodging.worldweb.com also keeps an up-to-date listing of accommodation and prices.

Accommodation in Tofino tends to book up weeks or even months in advance, especially over summer and long weekends and holidays. Don't risk showing up in town without a confirmed booking—it is a long drive back across the island. Rates quoted below are based on double occupancy unless otherwise noted; most of the accommodation listed here is open year-round. There are also more remote B&Bs and lodges located out on the waters of Clayoquot Sound; see page 193.

Campgrounds

Bella Pacifica Resort and Campground, 400 Mackenzie Beach Rd., forested sites on and near beach, pay showers, unserviced sites $24-28, partial hookup $27-48, open most of the year but may close for a few months over winter, 725-3400, www.bellapacifica.com.

Crystal Cove Beach Resort, 1165 Cedarwood Place, at the south end of Mackenzie Beach, forested sites by the beach, free hot showers and firewood, RV sites with hookup $48-55, cottages also available, open year-round, 725-4213, www.crystalcove.cc.

Mackenzie Beach Resort, basic tent and RV sites behind beach (a few with beach view), tent sites $30-56, RV sites with power $40-56, indoor pool and hot tub, gift shop, suites and cottages also available, pet friendly, 725-3439, www.mackenziebeach.com.

There are also campgrounds at **Green Point** and the **Long Beach Golf Course**, both located at Long Beach, around 16 km/9.9 mi south of Tofino, see page 148.

Hostels

C&N Backpackers Hostel Tofino, 241 Campbell, private rooms $65 sleep 2, suite with 3 queens $329, 725-2288, 1-888-434-6060, www.cnnbackpackers.com.

Clayoquot Field Station at Tofino Botanical Gardens, shared dorm rooms $20-32 per person (linen provided), private rooms for 2 $60-85, suites with private bath $70-120, open year-round, 725-1220, www.tofinobotanicalgardens.com.

Tofino Surf Hostel (at the Clayoquot-Orca Lodge near Chesterman Beach) has surf-friendly facilites including outdoor showers for wetsuits and boards, drying racks, and daily surf reports at front desk, dorms and private rooms, 725-2323, 1-888-611-1988, www.clayoquot-orca.com.

Tofino Trek Inn, downtown at 231 Main, advertises itself as a "champagne view on a beer budget," beds in shared rooms $25–35, private rooms $60-95, inlcudes breakfast, whole house rental $250-400, 725-2791, www.tofinotrekinn.com.

Whalers on the Point Guesthouse, 81 West St. (at the north end of Main St.) is a new hostel a few notches above the rest, situated on the water with a communal lounge complete with stone fireplace, kitchen and laundry facilities and internet access, bed in shared room $24-32, private double rooms $50-90, larger private rooms with bath $65-145, open year-round, 725-3443, www.tofinohostel.com.

Bed and breakfasts

There are so many bed and breakfasts in Tofino—this list is just a sampling. Most are open year-round. For more complete and up-to-date listings, contact the Tofino visitor centre at 725-3414, www.tofinobc.org or have a look at www.tofinolodging.worldweb.com. Rates listed are for double occupancy.

African Beach Cabin, 1250 Lynn Rd. a stone's throw from Chesterman Beach, private forested cabin sleeps up to 4 people, full breakfast, $135–175, 725-4465, www.africanbeach.com.

Beach Break Lodge B&B, 1337 Chesterman Beach Rd., suites with private entrance and hot tub, continental breakfast, $200–350, 725-3883, 1-877-727-3883, www.beachbreaklodge.com.

Blue Bear B&B, 327 Tonquin Beach Rd., very short rainforest walk to Tonquin Beach, 10 minute walk to town, full breakfast, $125-185, 725-3860, www.bluebearbandb.com.

BriMar B&B on the Beach, 1375 Thornberg Cres. on Chesterman Beach, great beach views, full breakfast, $120-220, 725-3410, 1-800-714-9373, www.brimarbb.com.

Chesterman Beach B&B, 1345 Chesterman Beach Rd., 1-br cottage and 2-br suite on the beach, from $185-310 ($175-290 without breakfast), 725-3726, www.chestermanbeach.net.

Clayoquot Retreat B&B, 120 Arnet, pet-friendly harbour-view rooms, hot tub, full breakfast, $100-160, 725-3305, www.clayoquotretreat.com.

Emerald Forest, 1326 Pacific Rim Highway, 10-minute walk to Chesterman Beach, 2 private rooms with separate entrance on quiet forested property, $70-100, open year-round, 725-2551, www.emeraldforestretreat.com.

Hummingbird B&B, 640 Mackenzie Beach Rd., rooms with private entrance and bath, wheelchair accessible, continental breakfast, 5-minute walk to beach, $95–150, 725-2740, www.tofinohummingbird.com.

Meares Retreat Waterfront Bed & Breakfast, 140 Arnet, perched on a cliff with sunset ocean views, hot tub, $125–255, 725-4234, www.mearesretreat.com.

Ocean Path, 1298 Lynn Rd. across from Chesterman Beach, rustic cabins $95-225 and greathouse $395 on forested property with yoga studio and onsite spa, leashed dogs welcome, 725-2112, 1-866-725-2112, www.oceanpath.net.

Paddler's Inn, 320 Main, basic but pleasant rooms in the historic original Tofino Hotel, some with harbour view, shared bathroom, continental breakfast, $80–90, 725-4222, www.tofinopaddlersinn. com.

Red Crow Guest House, 1084 Pacific Rim Highway 3 km/1.9 mi from downtown Tofino, large and private property on the inlet, rooms with private entrance and bath on secluded and quiet wilderness property, rowboats and canoes available to guests, full breakfast, $110–195, cottage (no breakfast) $135-235, 725-2275, www.tofinoredcrow.com.

Tofino Swell Lodge, 341 Olsen, a short walk into town and with spectacular harbour views, rooms with private bath, shared kitchen and common area and outdoor hot tub, pet friendly, moorage available, $65-145, open year-round, 725-3274, www.tofinoswell.com.

Cabins and cottages

Crystal Cove Beach Resort, 1165 Cedarwood Place, at the south end of Mackenzie Beach, log cabins and suites on forested site with unique forest-canopy decks and walkways, outdoor hot tubs, cabins $200–400, RV sites also available, open year-round, 725-4213, www.crystalcove.cc.

Duffin Cove Resort, 215 Campbell, unique location right in town yet with wild ocean shoreline and views, cabins, suites and studios $60-365, 725-3448, 1-888-629-2903, www.duffin-cove-resort.com.

Mackenzie Beach Resort, suites and cottages at back of beach, indoor pool and hot tub, gift shop, suites (some with ocean view or kitchenette) $99-199, 1–3-br cottages by beach $129-499, pet friendly, tent and RV sites also available, 725-3439.

Ocean Village Beach Resort at Mackenzie Beach, 1- and 2-br beachfront cottages and duplexes with full kitchens and bathrooms, $135-270, indoor swimming pool and hot tub, coin laundry, open year-round, 725-3755, 1-866-725-3755, www.oceanvillageresort.com.

Tofino Inlet Cottages, 350 Olsen Rd., cute little A-frame cabins with full kitchens sleep 2 to 5 people, with views of the harbour and Meares Island and a short walk to Tofino shops and restaurants, $90-225, also inlet house that sleeps 4, with hot tub, $250-420, 725-3441, www.tofinoinletcottages.com.

Motels

Dolphin Motel, 1190 Pacific Rim Highway a short walk from Chesterman Beach, basic rooms, some with kitchenettes, $60-160, 725-3377, www.dolphinmotel.ca.

Tofino Motel, 542 Campbell, a short walk from shops and restaurants, rooms and 1 suite with kitchenette, all with harbour view, $65–175, 725-2055, www.tofinomotel.com.

Hotels and resorts

Cable Cove Inn, downtown Tofino at 201 Main, small adult-oriented inn, each room with fireplace, private bath and deck with ocean views, some with private hot tubs, $150-340, 725-4236, 1-800-663-6499, www.cablecoveinn.com.

Clayoquot-Orca Lodge, 1254 Pacific Rim Highway, forested property with private rainforest trail to mudflats, a short walk from Chesterman Beach, owners stress that this is a "pets welcome!" resort, some rooms with kitchenettes and Jacuzzi tubs, $70-290, restaurant on-site, open year-round, 725-2323, 1-888-611-1988, www.c-orca.com.

Tofino Food and Wine Festival.

Clayoquot Wilderness Resort (see "Staying out on the water," page 193), 726-8235, 1-888-333-5405, www.wildretreat.com.

House of Himwitsa Lodge, above the Himwitsa Gallery by the First St. Dock, rooms with kitchens, harbour views, some with hot tubs, $175-300, 725-2017, www.himwitsa.com.

The Inn at Tough City, downtown on the waterfront at Main and Second, exquisitely designed and decorated inn overlooking Tofino Harbour, comfy rooms with patios and down duvets on beds $140-230, open for most of the year but usually closed for a few months over winter, 725-2021, www.toughcity.com.

Long Beach Lodge Resort, 1441 Pacific Rim Highway on Cox Bay, 7 km/4.4 mi south of Tofino, magnificent beach view from the comfortable dining room and great-room lounge, forest view and beachfront rooms $169–569, 2-br cottages with kitchen, fireplace and hot tub $279–479, fine restaurant and spectacular ocean-view lounge, open year-round (except for a week or so in early December), 725-2442, 1-877-844-7873, www.longbeachlodgeresort.com.

Middle Beach Lodge, on a secluded beach and forested headland 3 km/1.9 mi from Tofino centre, fine in-house restaurant serves fixed-menu dinners some nights, offers 2 lodges, both with beach access, fitness facility. Family-oriented lodge on the headland with oceanview rooms $120-190 and suites and cabins $140-450; adult-oriented lodge at beach, rooms $110–230. 725-2900, 1-866-725-2900, www.middlebeach.com.

Pacific Sands Beach Resort on Cox Bay, 7 km/4.4 mi south of Tofino, private units with kitchen and fireplace, oceanfront 1- and 2-br suites that sleep up to 4 people $190-620, 2- and 3-br villas $440-730, gift shop and coffee bar on site but no restaurant, 725-3322, 1-800-565-2322, www.pacificsands.com.

Tin Wis Best Western Resort on Mackenzie Beach, 1119 Pacific Rim Highway, owned and operated by Tla-o-qui-aht First Nation, expansive beachfront property with fine restaurant, rooms $130–260, suites with kitchenettes $145-300, executive suites $300-400, all rooms with ocean view, 725-4445, 1-800-661-9995, www.tinwis.com.

Weigh West Marine Resort, 634 Campbell on the edge of town, moorage and fishing charters available, rooms $115-275, suites with kitchenette (some with fireplaces) $145-300, meal and fishing packages available, open year-round, 725-3277, 1-800-665-8922 www.weighwest.com.

Wickaninnish Inn on Chesterman Beach, 4 km/2.5 mi south of Tofino, world-renowned resort that made storm-watching famous, with award-winning spa and restaurant, deluxe rooms $240-500, luxury suites $360–1500, open year-round except for a week in early January, 725-3100, 1-800-333-4604, www.wickinn.com.

WHERE TO EAT
Locals' top choices are marked with ❂.

❂ **Big Daddy's Fish Fry**, Third and Campbell, sit outside in the sun at this great fish and chips stand that serves more than just fish, closed over winter, 725-4415.

❂ **Beaches Grocery**, Ocean Break shops near Chesterman Beach, if you are out at the beach and need a quick bite, pop in for fresh sandwiches, pizzas, spanokopitas and other baked goods, 725-2237.

Blue Heron Restaurant at the Weigh West Marine Resort, 634 Campbell, fine dining on the water with a focus on seafood, open for breakfast, lunch and dinner year-round, appies $8–12, mains $12–30, 725-3277.

❂ **Breaker's Deli**, 430 Campbell, has a small sit-down counter but mainly open for takeout, all-day breakfasts, burritos, gourmet sandwiches, desserts and organic coffee, as well as a selection of salads, sliced meats and other deli items, $5–10, pizzas $15-27, open daily year-round, till late on weekends and in summer, 725-2558.

Café Vincente, on Campbell between Third and Fourth (with internet café), specialty coffees, all-day breakfast, lunch items such as gourmet sandwiches, soups, quiche, chili and salad, $5–12, open daily year-round for breakfast and lunch, 725-2599.

❂ **Calm Waters Dining Room** at the Tin Wis Best Western Resort on Mackenzie Beach, 1119 Pacific Rim Highway, dining with an ocean view focusing on pasta, seafood and meat, appies $5–15, mains $22-40 (great breakfasts $7–13, look for their smoked salmon eggs Benedict), open for breakfast and dinner year-round (may close part of January), 725-4445, www.tinwis.com.

Chuckling Oyster restaurant and lounge at the Clayoquot-Orca Lodge, 1254 Pacific Rim Highway, seafood, chicken and giant burgers, also has separate "Pals and Pets" area where dog owners can eat with their canine friends, mains $12-28, open daily from May to October, 725-2423, www.c-orca.com.

❂ **Common Loaf Bakery**, downtown at First and Neill, and known to locals simply as "the Bakery," open daily til 6pm year-round for baked goods as well as lunch items like pizza, hearty soups and various specials, $3-10, open over summer for dinner, range of curries, 725-3915.

Darwin's Café in the Tofino Botanical Gardens, light meals, sweets, and coffee, open for lunch over the summer months, 725-2247, www.tbgf.org.

❂ **Dockside Pub** at the Weigh West Marine Resort, 634 Campbell, pub-style food with a great ocean view, lunch and dinner $8–16, daily specials and Sunday dinner buffet, 725-3277.

✪ **Green Soul Organics,** Fourth and Campbell, look for light and healthy sandwichs and snacks at the back of the health food shop, open daily year-round, 725-4202.

✪ **Gary's Kitchen**, 308 Neill (behind the Bakery), basic but good small-town Chinese restaurant as well as western cuisine, mains $8–15, open for lunch and dinner year-round except for the Christmas season, 725-3921.

✪ **Jupiter Juicery and Bake Shop**, tucked away downstairs in the yellow building at Fourth and Main but worth looking for, great value fresh sandwiches and other freshly baked lunch items, and fresh-squeezed fruit and veggie juices, $5-10, open daily most of the year (look out for their curry nights some evenings), 725-4226.

Lady Rose, at the time of writing there are plans to convert the historic ship MV *Lady Rose* into a historic 1930s-era floating restaurant. Contact Jamie's Whaling Station for current info: 725-3919, 1-800-667-9913, www.jamies.com.

✪ **Long Beach Lodge Dining Room**, 1441 Pacific Rim Highway on Cox Bay, go for mainstream restaurant dining, focusing on seafoods and local Vancouver Island produce, or enjoy appies and drinks in their stunning ocean-view great room, lunch $8–18, dinner $8–40, open year-round (except for a week or so in early December), 725-2442, 1-877-844-7873, www.longbeachlodgeresort.com.

✪ **The Pointe Restaurant** at the Wickaninnish Inn at Chesterman Beach, 500 Osprey Lane, world-famous restaurant with arresting open-ocean views, awarded for both its cuisine and its wine list, focus on seafood, game and local Vancouver Island produce, appies $15–20, mains $34–40, as well as a great breakfast/brunch menu, open daily year-round except for a week in early January, 725-3106, www.wickinn.com.

Visitors mingle with locals in the Common Loaf Bakery.

✪ **Schooner Restaurant on Second**, downtown at Campbell and Second, a Tofino favourite since

1974, extensive menu specializing in seafood but with many other options, lunches $8–15, appies $12, mains $22–40, open for breakfast, lunch and dinner daily although may close for a short period over winter, 725-3444, www.schoonerrestaurant.ca.

Sea Shanty Restaurant, by the First Street dock with great harbour views, specializing in seafood and pasta, appies $3–10, mains $15–40, with a more casual lunch menu, open daily for lunch and dinner but closed over winter, 725-2902.

Shelter Restaurant, 601 Campbell St., the place to be seen in Tofino, fresh local foods, seafood and grilled meats, lunch $9-14, mains $20–33, open year-round, 725-3353, www.shelterrestaurant.com.

✪ **SoBo**, downtown at First and Neill, Tofino's award-winning restaurant has grown from its original taco truck to a spiffy venue downtown—food that is mostly organic and local and cooked with love: tacos and burritos, seafood, and innovative and exciting mains, lunch $5–12, dinner $15-30, open for most of the year (usually closed for a couple of months over winter), 725-2341, www.sobo.ca.

Spotted Bear Bistro, Fourth and Campbell, Chef Vincent Fraissange offers a small but interesting range of fine cuisine, appies $9-13, mains $24–30, open year-round for dinner as well as Sunday Brunch (closed Mondays in winter), 725-2215, www.spottedbearbistro.com.

✪ **Sweet T's**, at the back of the turquoise building on Main Street at Third, fresh bread, muffins, croissants, specialty cakes and other treats, open Monday through Saturday over summer, Tuesday through Saturday in winter, 725-8911, www.tofinocakes.com.

Tofino Tea Bar, 346 Campbell on Second, range of exotic teas (as well as coffee) and baked goods, open daily except Mondays in winter, closed January, 725-8833, www.tofinoteabar.com.

Tony's Pizza, First Street beside the hardware store, small counter for eat-in, or delivery, pizza $4 slice or $13-25 whole, calzone, donair, caesar salad, open daily year-round, restricted hours in winter, 725-2121.

✪ **Tough City Sushi**, downtown at Main and Second, great sushi as well as other seafood and teriyaki dinners, open for lunch and dinner, mains $8–34, usually closed for a couple of months over winter, 725-2021, www.toughcity.com.

✪ **Tuff Beans** (formerly **The Coffee Pod**), downtown at Fourth and Campbell (with high-speed internet access), open at 7am for specialty coffees, breakfast, baked goods and sandwiches, breakfast and lunch sandwiches $7–10, call for some-time dinner hours, 725-2739.

✪ **Wildside Grill** at Ocean Break shops near Chestermans Beach, a delicious place to grab a tasty meal if you are out near the beach featuring seafood caught by the owner: fish and chips, seafood gumbo, burgers, Mexican and more, $6-12, open daily 9 to 10 in summer, 11 to 7 in winter, may be closed in January, 725-9453, www.wildsidegrill.ca.

Around Tofino

THINGS TO DO

Tofino is located on the tip of a skinny little peninsula. Land-based activities for the south of Tofino are covered in the sections on Long Beach (pages 140–49) and Ucluelet (pages 109–39). If the beaches around Tofino and Long Beach are all fogged in (which has been known to happen in late

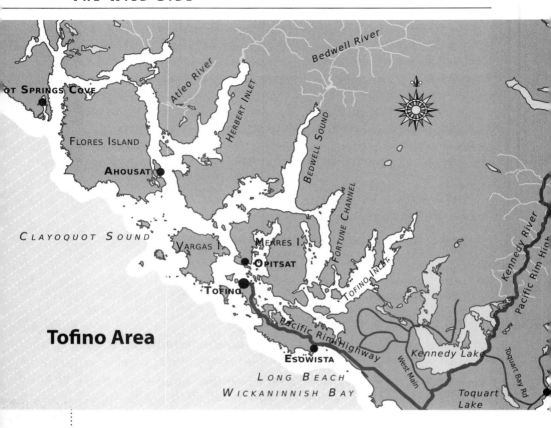

summer), head out toward Kennedy Lake (page 135). Often, the fog just sits right over the shoreline, and you need only to get a few hundred metres inland to escape it.

Looking northward from Tofino, all activities are water-based, from the boat tours and kayak trips offered by companies in Tofino to the more remote places you can stay in Clayoquot Sound.

Provincial parks in Clayoquot Sound— water or float plane accessed only

Most of the parks listed in this section are very remote, undeveloped wilderness areas, and are not accessible by road. All are habitat for wolves, bears and cougars, and in some cases these animals are quite abundant. Human–animal interactions resulting in death or injury have taken place. Campers absolutely must travel respectfully and knowledgeably. If you are unsure, travel with a guide. For more information on BC parks, see page 201. See also "Provincial parks around Kennedy Lake" on page 137, as well as information about Ha'uukmin Tribal Park (page 135) and Meares Island Tribal Park (page 136).

Dawley Passage Provincial Park. This 154 ha (380 ac) park is located at the south end of Fortune Channel to the east of Meares Island. It is accessible by boat or kayak from Tofino (10 km/6.2 mi) or the boat launch at Grice Bay (6 km/3.7 mi). This pretty little passage is swept by strong tidal currents and has abundant wildlife such as seals, porpoises, river otters, bears and eagles. The steep shorelines make it a difficult site to land at, and more appropriate for day use and recreational fishing, kayaking and scuba diving than for camping.

Epper Passage Provincial Park. This 306 ha (756 ac) park consists of two small, steep-sided and rocky islands (Morfee and Dunlap), located between Meares and Vargas Islands, about 7 km/4.4 mi north of Tofino. The shorelines are challenging to land a boat at, even a kayak. The main attraction of this park is the wealth of intertidal life clinging to its rocky shores: sea stars, anemones, urchins and a rare type of purple sea squirt. Marine-life viewing is best for kayakers passing by at low tide, and for scuba divers. Beware of very strong tidal currents and lots of motorboat traffic.

Flores Island Provincial Park. Flores Island is considered the "Jewel of Clayoquot Sound." This is the largest island off Vancouver Island's outer coast, and here pristine rainforested mountain slopes fall to the sea. This undeveloped 7,113 ha (17,576 ac) park covers most of the island's western half, from the mountain peaks to the wave-washed rocky shores. The park is accessible by a rough hiking trail from the village of Ahousat (accessed by

Flores Island's Wild Side Trail follows the beaches from Ahousat village out to wild wave-washed Cow Bay.

water taxi or float plane from Tofino), or by kayak. Some charter boats from Tofino may also drop campers out to the beaches. The beaches on southern Flores Island are a wonderful destination for both hikers and kayakers, and grey whales can sometimes be seen feeding off the island's southern shores. The island's western shore is rocky and exposed to large surf; landing here is not recommended.

The **Ahousaht Wild Side Heritage Trail**, along the southern coast of Flores Island was developed by the Ahousaht First Nation. The km /6.8 mi trail leaves from Ahousat village (accessible by boat or float plane from Tofino, page 153) and follows the sweeping sandy beaches of Flores Island's southern shore, passing through Gibson Marine Provincial Park and Flores Island Provincial Park to Cow Bay. From the west end of Cow Bay a more difficult-to-find path winds through the rainforest, climbing to the summit of Mt. Flores. This part of the trail is in very poor condition, crossed by numerous fallen logs, so hikers should not count on being able to make it all the way up until some major repairs are done here. For those who have more time to spare, an extra few nights out here will certainly not go to waste, between the many beaches and tide pools to explore and the abundant wildlife on and around the island, including bears, wolves, cougars and grey whales. Wildlife encounters are very common here, and it is extremely important that campers keep clean camps, cook below the high-tide line and securely cache all food high up trees. Keep small children close to you at all times.

Ahousat has an administrative office for trail information and maps; check in before you depart. BC Parks does not at present charge camping fees here, but the Ahousaht First Nation charges a $20 fee to access the Wild Side Trail and requires that hikers check in with them both on the way in and the way out for safety reasons. Contact the Ahousaht Band Office, 670-9563, for current information. Camping is permitted on the beaches, but fires are discouraged. There are no facilities other than one pit toilet at Cow Bay.

Gibson Marine Provincial Park. This small park (140 ha/346 ac) is just east of Flores Island Provincial Park, and is centred on a natural warm spring located at the head of Matilda Inlet, near Ahousat. An old trail leaves from the beach at Whitesand Cove for the warm spring (which, although warmer than the ocean, is actually not very warm, and is contained by a cement soaking pool). The Wild Side Trail also passes through this park, between Ahousat village and the beaches to the west. BC Parks charges no park-use fee, but the Ahousaht First Nation charges a fee to access the trail. Camping is permitted on the beaches, but fires are discouraged. There are no facilities other than one pit toilet at Whitesand Cove.

Hesquiat Lake Provincial Park. This tiny and difficult-to-access park (62 ha/153 ac) is located on the east side of Hesquiat Lake, 60 km/37 mi northwest of Tofino. Access is by float plane from Tofino or Gold River. Theoretically it is also accessible by boat, but the short river section connecting the lake to Hesquiat Harbour is often blocked by logs. There are no facilities here and camping is not permitted.

Hesquiat Peninsula Provincial Park. This large and remote park (7,899 ha/19,518 ac) consists of the outer exposed coast that lies between Nootka and Clayoquot Sounds. It is accessible by float plane from Gold River or

Tofino, or by charter water taxi from Tofino (page 153). The Hesquiat Peninsula is a world-class surf spot when a south swell is running. Hiking the outer coast here is a beautiful but tough route, only for experienced wilderness travellers. There are no trails; hikers follow the outer coast along beaches, exposed rock ledges and slippery, seaweed-covered rock shelves, and make their ways over forested headlands. Old Hesquiat Village is populated by only one family, who may or may not be there when you pass through, and Cougar Annie's Garden is not open to the general public (see page 195). Since this stretch of coast is very rocky and exposed to open surf, kayaking is not recommended. Bears and wolves are common throughout the Hesquiat region. Camping is permitted—no fees and no facilities.

Maquinna Marine Provincial Park (Hot Springs Cove). This popular park (2,667 ha/6,615 ac) covers the southern part of the Openit Peninsula. It is about 40 km/25 mi north of Tofino, and accessible by scheduled water taxis, whale-watching tours and float planes. The main attraction here is the hot spring, which bubbles out of the ground and cascades over a waterfall then through a series of natural rock pools into the ocean. Access to the spring is via a 2 km/1.2 mi boardwalk trail through old-growth rainforest. The day-use fee for the park is $3; there are composting toilets at both ends of the trail. Camping is not permitted, but there is a private campground adjacent to the park, and lodge-style accommodation nearby (page 197).

Strathcona Provincial Park. Strathcona is BC's oldest park, formed in 1911, and at 246,000 ha/607,879 ac is the largest park on Vancouver Island. This is a land of ice-crowned rocky peaks, fragile alpine meadows, and tiny mountain lakes. Road access is from the east coast of Vancouver Island; from Tofino, getting into the park is possible but tough (float plane or boat only). For more information on hiking in Strathcona (including trail maps), visit www.env.gov. bc.ca/bcparks/explore/parkpgs/strathco. html.

Most of Strathcona Provincial Park's wilderness hiking trails start in the forested valleys and take you high above the treeline.

Strathcona Provincial Park: Megin-Talbot Addition. The 27,390 ha/67,682 ac Megin River and Talbot Creek areas were added to Strathcona Park in 1995, a result of protests against plans to log the

Megin Valley. These valleys make up the largest undisturbed watershed on Vancouver Island. The Megin River mouth, 40 km/25 mi north of Tofino, is accessible by boat. The lake can be accessed in summer either by paddling and dragging a canoe or kayak up the river—a lovely scenic voyage for hard-core adventurers—or by float plane. There is no trail along the river; although hiking into the lake from the river mouth is possible, it would be a very tough trip. This is an area rich in wildlife, and especially frequented by bears. The river has runs of salmon, steelhead and trout, and there are trout in the lake as well. Fishing is generally permitted, but you should check on the current regulations when you visit.

Sulphur Passage Provincial Park. This little park (2,299 ha/5,680 ac, most of it over water) covers a picturesque narrow passage, the site of the 1988 protests that resulted in the preservation of the Megin River Valley. Access to Sulphur Passage is by boat only, about 35 km/21.8 mi north of Tofino, and it is a popular passage for kayakers who want to take the longer scenic route on their way to Hot Springs Cove. Although camping is permitted here (no facilities, no fees), in reality it is very hard to land a kayak on the steep, rocky shores, and the flatter creek mouths tend to flood out on the night's high tide.

Sydney Inlet Provincial Park. Although this lovely fjord is protected, the Sydney River Valley, one of the few remaining undisturbed river valleys on Vancouver Island, is not. This 2,774 ha/6,855 ac undeveloped park covers the steep, forested shores of the fjord. It can be accessed by boat or float plane from Tofino. The river hosts several salmon populations, and the estuary at the head of the fjord is frequented by bears and other wildlife. Camping is permitted here but difficult; the shores of the inlet are difficult to land at, and Sydney River bears have a reputation for being ornery and aggressive.

Tranquil Creek Provincial Park. This small (299 ha/747 ac) and remote park is hard to get to, other than by float plane from Tofino. The park encompasses forested slopes and alpine meadows around Paradise Lake, the headwaters of Tranquil Creek. There are no trails, but it is possible to navigate up to the alpine meadows above the lake. Camping is permitted— no fees and no facilities—but fires are discouraged.

Vargas Island Provincial Park. This large park (5,788 ha/14,302 ac) covers much of the western half of Vargas Island, just a few kilometres west of Tofino. The main features of this park are the extensive coastal bog ecosystem that covers most of the interior of the island, and the sweeping wave-washed beaches of Ahous Bay. Grey whales are often seen feeding in the bay over the summer months. The park can be accessed by boat from Tofino—either by boating to the Vargas Island Inn on the east side of the island and hiking the 3 km/1.9 mi old telegraph trail across, or by arranging a boat drop-off at Ahous. Kayaking to Ahous Bay is possible for paddlers with experience in open-ocean conditions and surf landings; at times the swell here can come

up, making landing or launching challenging or impossible. Camping is permitted on the beaches, and some pit toilets have been installed. Fires are permitted but discouraged. Wolves have a reputation for being aggressive here; cache your food well and do not encourage interactions. Parks officials have begun to talk of charging a camping fee, so check with them before you head out.

Above left: The thermal waters pass through a series of natural rock pools and into the sea.

Staying out on the water

Tofino was settled by water, and to best appreciate its history you should try to stay out on the water yourself if at all possible. There are places to stay both close to town, as well as in the more remote areas like Ahousat village on Flores Island and Hot Springs Cove. Although you can see the Tla-o-qui-aht village of Opitsat across the water from the Tofino docks, there are no facilities for tourists here; you should not go to Opitsat unless invited by someone who lives there.

Above right: The boardwalk takes you through ancient old-growth rainforest.

Vargas Island Inn, on lovely and wild Vargas Island 5 km/3.1 mi from Tofino, with rooms in a rustic Tudor-style lodge built from timber hewn on the property, as well as private cabins and dorm rooms. Some meals or fresh seafood may be provided if arranged in advance, but in general you should arrive self-contained with your groceries; there are well-equipped kitchens there, as well as a beach sauna with an outdoor shower. A beautiful but muddy 5 km/3.1 mi trail takes you across the island to the sweeping sands of wave-washed Ahous Bay, a summer feeding area for grey whales. $40–60 per person (boat transport extra), open year-round, 725-3309. **Tofino Sea Kayaking Company** also offers guided 3-day kayak trips to the inn over the summer months, 725-4222, 1-800-863-4664, www.tofino-kayaking.com.

Clayoquot Wilderness Resort, all-inclusive luxury resort in central Clayoquot Sound, behind Meares Island, includes a floating lodge at Quait Bay and an "outpost" with luxury tents at the mouth of the Bedwell River. Various packages may include airfare from Vancouver as well as meals, alcohol, guided activities such as kayaking, fishing or horseback riding and spa treatments, $1200-1800 per person per day, open May to September, 725-8235, 1-888-333-5405, www.wildretreat.com.

AHOUSAT, FLORES ISLAND

The village of Ahousat is the largest Native village on Vancouver Island. There is not much to do in the village itself unless you want to just hang out and get to know some locals (which is always interesting), but it is a great base from which to hike the **Wild Side Heritage Trail** (page 190).

You can get to Ahousat by water taxi on the **Ahousaht Pride** (or "Sea Bus"), which makes two scheduled runs daily from the First Street dock, 670-9563, as well as by float plane from Tofino. The village is divided by an inlet which separates the main residential part in the east from the general store and fuel dock in the west; you can access the Wild Side Trail from either side, but to walk from one side to the other is a roundabout two-hour route.

The **Ahousaht General Store** (on the west side of the bay) has a range of **groceries** and produce, as well as gas, diesel and stove oil, and is open daily year-round. Their **Favourite Restaurant** is open for the summer, serving

Ahousat village, accessible only by boat or float plane, is the largest Native village on Vancouver Island.

burgers, sandwiches, fish and chips as well as a daily special, $5–15, 670-9575. **Cathy's Place**, over on the east side by the hydro dock, serves similar fare as well as steak dinners, $6–20, and is open for lunch and dinner year-round except for Sundays, 670-2332.

Where to stay

The **Favourite Motel**, on the west side, is open year-round, double rooms with private bath $50, with kitchenettes $75, 670-9575, hughags@telus.net. **Vera's Guest House**, on the east side, provides "home away from home" rooms in a rustic and comfortable private home, with shared bathrooms, living room and kitchen facilities, $85 per person includes 3 home-cooked meals, open year-round, 670-9511.

HOT SPRINGS COVE

Hot Springs Cove is one of the world's natural wonders: geothermally heated waters pour out from a steaming vent in the rainforest, and trickle down over a hot waterfall and through a series of natural rock pools to the sea. The springs are located about 45 km/28 mi north of Tofino. There are no roads here; access is only by boat or float plane.

The long and narrow cove is flanked on the east side by the Openit Peninsula, most of which is taken up by **Maquinna Marine Provincial Park** (entrance fee $3). A 2 km/1.2 mi boardwalked trail starting at the government dock here winds through ancient rainforest with some spectacular giant cedar trees, taking you to the springs. On the west side of the cove is the Hesquiaht village of Hot Springs Cove, home to about 90 people.

You can get to Hot Springs from Tofino on the daily Hesquiaht water taxi the **Matlahaw**, 670-1100, or by float plane. Both **Atleo Air**, 725-2205, and **Tofino Air**, 725-4454, provide charter service to Hot Springs, and **Tofino Air** also provides daily scheduled flights at $80 per seat one-way. Several of the Tofino-based whale-watching companies (page 171) will provide one-way transport to and from Hot Springs if there is room on their scheduled tours; try **Ocean Outfitters** or **The Whale Centre** (see page 173).

There is no store in the village, so you should arrive in Hot Springs with all your food needs taken care of. There is one small home-run **restaurant, Mr. B's,** often serving seafood caught at the front door, open 9 to 9 daily year-round, 670-1133.

Where to stay

There is a **campground** operated by the Hesquiaht band beside the government dock, at the beginning of the boardwalk trail to the springs, tent sites $20, 670-1133.

The **Hot Springs Cove Lodge**, in Hot Springs village, has basic waterfront rooms with kitchenettes

Cougar Annie's home is still standing (barely) on her old homestead at the back of Hesquiat Harbour.

$85, and they will boat you across to the dock so you can walk to the springs. Open year-round, may close for short periods over winter, 670-1133..

The *InnChanter*, a historic 98' freighter renovated and converted into a floating B&B anchored near the government dock, has dinghies available for guest use. Anchored near the government dock, this luxurious vessel is the perfect base for late-night or early-morning dips in the springs, one of the most amazing experiences this coast has to offer. $135 per person includes a great dinner and breakfast, open May to October, 670-1149, www.innchanter.com.

COUGAR ANNIE'S GARDEN

Cougar Annie is one of the West Coast's legendary figures. Born Ada Annie Rae-Arthur, she moved with her husband Willie and their three young children to a remote part of Vancouver Island's coast: Boat Basin, at the back of Hesquiat Harbour, halfway between Clayoquot and Nootka Sounds. Annie and Willie had a 64 hectare/160acre homestead of beautiful south-facing slopes with an expansive view out the harbour entrance. Over the years Annie carved a garden from the tangled rainforest, and grew fruits and vegetables for the family while operating a mail-order business selling flower bulbs across the country.

Annie became known as "Cougar Annie" for the 70 cougars she is reputed to have shot over the years in order to protect her little farm. Her tough pioneer life is chronicled in Margaret Horsfield's award-winning book *Cougar Annie's Garden*. Cougar Annie, who rarely left her beloved homestead, was finally moved into a nursing home in 1983 at the age of 96. Her old friend Peter Buckland, a long-time prospector in the area, purchased the property from her. Through his self-taught technique of "chainsaw gardening" Peter has managed to stave off the rainforest that was swallowing the garden and restore it to much of its original splendour.

The property is now owned and maintained by the Boat Basin Foundation. The mandate of the Foundation is to preserve the gardens for future generations and to promote interest and education in natural history. They have created a Temperate Rainforest Field Studies Centre which welcomes groups that are interested in learning more about the natural history and heritage of the area.

There are no regularly scheduled tours of the gardens. Individuals or groups who are interested in a visit should contact the Foundation for more information, www.boatbasin.org.

The InnChanter's beautifully finished interior can make you forget that you are living on a boat.

Resources

TOURISM INFORMATION

Port Alberni Visitor Centre, located on the Alberni Highway on the east edge of town, open daily year-round but with restricted hours over winter, 724-6535, www.avcoc.com.

Bamfield tourism information is available at the **Centennial Park Campground office**, open daily over summer and closed for the rest of the year, 728-3006 (not answered over winter) or check out www.bamfieldchamber.com.

Tofino Visitor Centre, located on the highway 7 km/4.4 mi outside of Tofino, open daily over summer and a few days a week for the rest of the year, 725-3414, www.tourismtofino.com.

Ucluelet Visitor Information Centre is located at the bottom of Main Street by the dock, and is open daily in summer, weekdays only for the rest of the year, 726-4641, www.uclueletinfo.com.

Pacific Rim Visitor Centre, located at the Tofino–Ucluelet junction, open daily year-round, 726-4600, www.pacificrimvisitor.ca.

Other helpful websites

www.vancouverisland.com This privately run commercial website provides perhaps the most complete and comprehensive information on the internet for this region; you can look up information under many different headings, such as town name, general subject or recreational activity.

www.coastalbc.com A site oriented toward the surfing/windsurfing community, but contains lots of great information and links about other outdoor activities and accommodation.

www.nuuchahnulth.org The website of the Nuu-chah-nulth Tribal Council, the administrative body of the Native people whose traditional territory includes the Pacific Rim region, with links to the websites of various Nuu-chah-nulth tribes.

www.portalbernitourism.ca A very comprehensive website with business listings, as well as background info about history, culture, and wildlife, covering Port Alberni, Bamfield, Ucluelet and Tofino.

www.albernivalleytourism.com A site with lots of info about the Port Alberni region, a good resource for finding out about current events, as well as business listings including detailed acccommodation listings.

www.longbeachmaps.com More than just maps, this site also provides current information on things to do in the Tofino–Ucluelet area, including a calendar of events, and an up-to-date sampling of accommodation rates.

www.tofinotime.com The website that accompanies the popular (and free) Tofino Time Magazine provides lots of information about current events, entertaining and informative articles by local writers and a listing of local businesses.

www.my-tofino.com A small commercial website with accommodation and tour company listings for Tofino and Ucluelet.

www.gotofino.com A commercial website that lists businesses in Tofino, with some listings for Ucluelet—includes accommodation listings with prices.

WEATHER FORECASTS

The most current and accurate weather information is the marine forecast, updated four times daily. This forecast tells what weather systems are moving in, and focuses on information of interest to mariners, such as wind speed and direction. You can get it along most areas of the coast on the **marine VHF weather channels**, or by phoning 726-3415 (a recorded message, listen for the area "Vancouver Island South"), or from www.weatheroffice.ec.gc.ca (select "Marine Weather," "Pacific Coast," and then "West Coast Vancouver Island South").

For the **five-day forecast**, with more information about sun and rain, check out www.weatheroffice.ec.gc.ca, select "British Columbia," and then "Tofino" from the drop-down menu.

Do you want to actually see what the weather is doing? Have a look at the **webcams**:

Port Alberni Summit Highwaycam: http://images.drivebc.ca/bchighwaycam/pub/html/www/102.html

Bamfield, www.bms.bc.ca/computing/webcam/

Ucluelet: www.amphitritelighthouse.com

Long Beach Lodge on Cox Bay, Tofino, www.westcoastaquatic.ca/webcam.htm

BOOKS

The adventure guidebook *The Wild Coast*, Vol. 1 by John Kimantas (Whitecap, 2005) is an invaluable reference, complete with colour maps and detailed route information, for adventurers who want to plan their own hiking, kayaking or canoeing expedition on Vancouver Island's west coast.

Guidebooks

Backlund, Gary, and Grey, Paul, 2003. *Kayaking Vancouver Island: Great Trips from Port Hardy to Victoria*, Harbour, Madeira Park, 295 p.

Harbo, Rick M., 2003. *Pacific Reef and Shore: A Photo Guide to Northwest Marine Life*. Harbour, Madeira Park, 80 p.

Leadem, Tim, 2005. *Hiking the West Coast of Vancouver Island*, Greystone, Vancouver, 224 p.

Marleau, J.F., 2006. *Kayaking the Broken Group Islands*. Pacific Rim Informative Adventures, Ucluelet, 160 p.

McConnaughey, Bayard H., and Evelyn M. McConnaughey, 1985. *Pacific Coast*. Alfred A. Knopf, New York, 633 p.

Pojar, Jim, and MacKinnon, Andy, 1994. *Plants of Coastal British Columbia, including Washington, Oregon and Alaska*. Lone Pine, Vancouver, 527 p.

Sam, Stanley Sr., 1997. *Ahousaht Wild Side Heritage Trail Guidebook*. Western Canada Wilderness Committee, Vancouver, 92 p.

Sept, J. Duane, 1999. *The Beachcomber's Guide to Seashore Life in the Pacific Northwest*. Harbour, Madeira Park, 240 p.

Snowden, Mary Ann, 2005. *Sea Kayak Barkley and Clayoquot Sounds*, Rocky Mountain, Calgary, 190 p.

Other local interest

Horsfield, Margaret, 1999. *Cougar Annie's Garden*. Salal, Nanaimo, 259 p.

Horsfield, Margaret, 2008. *Voices from the Sound*. Salal, Nanaimo, 366 p.

Pitt-Brooke, David, 2004. *Chasing Clayoquot*. Raincoast, Vancouver, 287 p.

Streetly, J., 2000. *Paddling Through Time*. Raincoast, Vancouver, 153 p.

Windh, Jacqueline, 2004. *The Wild Edge*. Harbour, Madeira Park, 168 p.

IMPORTANT MAPS AND CHARTS

Government topographic maps

Topographic maps are available over the entire Pacific Rim area at scales of 1:250,000 and 1:50,000. All are available as paper maps, and a number of them are also available on Tyvek, a weatherproof high-density polyethylene. For an index or to order maps, contact www.fedpubs.com/mpchrt/maps/british_columbia.htm.

Other maps

Backroad Mapbook Road & Recreational Atlas, Vancouver Island. Mussio Ventures 2005, 128 pages of maps showing all the logging roads, with lots of detailed information about recreation sites, fishing spots and campsites. 604-438-3474, www.backroadmapbooks.com.

South and Central Vancouver Island Recreational Map, 1:295,000 with 1:50,000 detail of Port Alberni–Nahmint Lake area, Davenport Maps Ltd., www.davenportmaps.com.

Tofino–Ucluelet–Pacific Rim Area Backroad Map, 1:75,000, shows logging roads and hiking trails, Pacific Rim Informative Adventures Ltd., for sale at tourist information centres, www.priaoutback.com.

West Coast Trail Map, 1:50,000, International Travel Maps, 604-879-3621, www.itmb.com.

Nautical charts

For index maps and order information see www.fedpubs.com/charts.htm.

Charts presently available are:

3602 Approaches to Juan de Fuca Strait (Vancouver Island coast from Nitinat Lake through Bamfield to Ucluelet), 1:150,000

3603 Ucluelet Inlet to Nootka Sound (Vancouver Island coast from Ucluelet through Tofino and Hesquiat to Nootka Island), 1:150,000

3646 Barkley Sound details (Bamfield Inlet, Ucluelet Inlet, Uchucklesit Inlet, Fatty Basin, scales 1:7500 to 1:18,000)

3668 Alberni Inlet (entrance to Useless Inlet, Port Alberni, Robbers Passage), 1:40,000

3670 Broken Group, 1:20,000

3671 Barkley Sound including the Broken Group and Deer Group Islands, 1:40,000

3673 SE Clayoquot Sound, Tofino Inlet to Millar Channel, 1:40,000

3674 NW Clayoquot Sound, Millar Channel to Estevan Point, 1:40,000

3685 Tofino, 1:20,000

PROVINCIAL PARKS

There are many provincial parks in the areas around Port Alberni, Nitinat and Clayoquot Sound. Some are large, developed parks with campgrounds and facilities, and others are remote patches of wilderness, accessible only by boat or air or by some serious backcountry hiking. For general park information and regulations, as well as more detailed information on individual parks, look up http://www.env.gov.bc.ca/bcparks/.

Strathcona Provincial Park and many of the parks around Port Alberni have campgrounds for both RVs and tent sites. BC Parks do not have electrical hookups. Although most parks do keep a few spots available on a first-come, first-served basis, reservations are recommended. The more remote parks around Nitinat and Clayoquot Sound do not have commercial campgrounds, although backcountry tent-camping is permitted within most of them. If you are visiting the backcountry, please make sure you are informed about local wildlife concerns (page 55) and camping etiquette (page 43).

You may book your campsite up to three months in advance by calling 604-689-9025 or 1-800-689-9025, or online at www.discovercamping.ca, April 1 to September 15. Campsites range from $9–22 per night. Maximum group size is 8 people (maximum 4 adults). For larger groups, make reservations through www.bcparks.ca. Backcountry camping is generally free, although in Carmanah and Strathcona there is a fee of $5 per night. Most parks also charge between $3 and $5 for day-use parking.

OUTDOORS EQUIPMENT RENTALS

You can rent camping equipment, such as tents and stoves, from:

The Ark Resort, Great Central Lake near Port Alberni, 723-2657, www.arkresort.com.

Broken Island Adventures, Bamfield, 728-3500, 1-888-728-6200, www.brokenislandadventures.com.

Storm Light Outfitters, 390 Main St., Tofino, (including VHF radios) 725-3342.

West Coast Trail Bus, which serves both trailheads of the West Coast Trail May 1 to September 30, 477-8700, 1-888-999-2288, www.trailbus.com.

Annual Events

March	• Whalefest (Tofino/Long Beach/Ucluelet) • Winter-spring Fishing Derby (Bamfield)
April	• Shorebird Festival (Tofino)
May	• George Fraser Day and Heritage Fair (Ucluelet) • Clayoquot Days garden festival (Tofino)
June	• Tofino Food and Wine Festival (Tofino) • Edge to Edge Marathon (Tofino/Ucluelet) • Aboriginal Day events (Tofino/Long Beach)
July	• Folk Fest (Port Alberni) • Pacific Rim Summer Festival (Tofino/Long Beach/Ucluelet) • Music by the Sea (Bamfield) • Forest Fest (Port Alberni) • Ukee Days fair and loggers' sports (Ucluelet)
August	• Thunder in the Valley drag races (Port Alberni) • Fall Fair (Bamfield) • Lantern Festival (Tofino)
September	• Salmon Festival and Derby (Port Alberni) • Fall Fair (Port Alberni) • Arts in the Garden (Tofino) • Motorcycle Parade (Port Alberni)
October	• Robertson Creek Salmon Hatchery open house (Port Alberni) • Mushroom Festival, October (Bamfield)
November	• Oyster Festival (Tofino) • Return of the Salmon Festival (Ucluelet)
December	• Christmas Craft Fairs (Tofino/Ucluelet)

Acknowledgements

A big thank you to all of the amazing people who live on this wild coast. Some of you are selfless and dedicated protectors of the environment; some of you are kind, generous, community-minded citizens; some of you are my best friends; and some of you are just plain weird—but you all make this place wonderful and unique.

A special thanks to Yvette Kovacs from Port Alberni Visitor's Centre, and Bamfield residents Anne Weiler and Brunhilde Niederacher, who all helped me to compile information; to Carl Wilson from BC Parks, Pete Clarkson from Pacific Rim National Park Reserve, and John Mass from Broken Island Adventures in Bamfield, for reviewing and fact-checking parts of the text; to Barbara Schramm and Caron Olive for providing digital map bases; and to the companies and photographers who kindly provided photos that grace these pages: Katy Thompson, Rutger Geerling, Salmon Eye Charters, Chase & Warren Winery, Island North Film Commission, Jay Mohl from Clayoquot Ventures, and Peter Mieras from Rendezvous Dive Adventures.

Many thanks to the staff at Harbour Publishing for their contributions to the creation, quality and promotion of this book—in particular Anna Comfort, Mary White and Kathy Sinclair for their hard work in production, editing and fact-checking; Roger Handling for his fine design work; and Marisa Alps for her cheery efforts in publicity and promotion.

A final thank you, *kleco kleco,* to my many Nuu-chah-nulth friends, who constantly teach me new ways of looking at this place, and indeed of looking at our whole world.

Index

List of maps

1 2 3 4 5 — 14 13 12 11 10

Harbour Publishing Co. Ltd.
P.O. Box 219, Madeira Park, BC V0N 2H0
www.harbourpublishing.com

Page design by Roger Handling, Terra Firma Digital Arts.
Front cover photographs: Ahous Bay. Inset (left to right): upstairs at the Schooner, Tofino; humpback tail; Tlaook Cultural Adventures dugout canoe; surf lesson with Surf Sister. Back cover photographs: (top) Bamfield rainbow; (bottom) black bear. All photographs by Jacqueline Windh unless noted.
Maps by Barbara Schramm and Roger Handling.

Printed and bound in Canada

Harbour Publishing acknowledges financial support from the Government of Canada through the Book Publishing Industry Development Program and the Canada Council for the Arts, and from the Province of British Columbia through the British Columbia Arts Council and the Book Publisher's Tax Credit through the Ministry of Provincial Revenue.

Canada Council   Conseil des Arts
for the Arts   du Canada

BRITISH COLUMBIA ARTS COUNCIL
Supported by the Province of British Columbia

Library and Archives Canada Cataloguing in Publication

Windh, Jacqueline, 1964–
    The wild side guide to Vancouver Island's Pacific Rim : Long Beach, Tofino, Ucluelet, Port Alberni, Nitinat and Bamfield / by Jacqueline Windh. — Rev. 2nd ed.

Includes index.
ISBN 978-1-55017-485-4

1. Pacific Rim National Park Reserve Region (B.C.)—Guidebooks. I. Title.

FC3844.2.W56 2010   917.11'2   C2010-900458-2